Making Transnational Feminism

Making Transnational Feminism takes the "ant's eye view" of global social movement relationships from the ground. Using ethnography, Thayer takes us inside transnational feminist alliances, viewing them from the local perspective of two women's movements in Northeast Brazil—one in the remote semi-arid interior and the other in Brazil's fourth largest city, Recife. She finds rural women and NGO feminists appropriating and translating global gender discourses, negotiating with each other over political resources, and strategizing to defend their autonomy from distant donors.

In the process, she argues, the Brazilian organizations help to constitute a transnational feminist political space—a "counterpublic," in which movements debate strategies, articulate new identities, and work to develop alternative social practices. Feminist alliances in this space are characterized by a precarious balance between solidarity and self-interest, collaboration and contention. At the turn of the twentieth century, as markets extended their reach into new regions and social sectors, they also threatened to reshape feminist relationships, undermining the very values on which they were founded, and pushing them toward competitive and instrumental behavior. Thayer shows us how feminist movements in Northeast Brazil struggled to sustain their alliances and to defend their endangered counterpublic against the long hand of the "social movement market."

Millie Thayer (2004 Ph.D., University of California, Berkeley) is Assistant Professor of Sociology at the University of Massachusetts where she teaches classes in field research methods, social movements, gender and globalization, and Latin American societies. Her research work is in cross-border feminist relationships, Latin American women's movements, and the social movement/international funding agency nexus. Her articles have appeared in the journals *Ethnography* and *Social Problems* and in books published by University of California Press and Cornell University Press.

Perspectives on Gender
Edited by Myra Marx Ferree
University of Wisconsin, Madison

Making Transnational Feminism

Rural Women, NGO Activists, and Northern Donors in Brazil

Millie Thayer
University of Massachusetts, Amherst

Routledge
Taylor & Francis Group

NEW YORK AND LONDON

First published 2010
by Routledge
270 Madison Ave, New York, NY 10016

Simultaneously published in the UK
by Routledge
2 Park Square, Milton Park, Abingdon, Oxon OX14 4RN

Routledge is an imprint of the Taylor & Francis Group, an informa business

© 2010 Taylor & Francis

Typeset in Minion by EvS Communication Networx, Inc.
Printed and bound in the United States of America on acid-free paper by Edwards Brothers, Inc.

Library of Congress Cataloging in Publication Data
Thayer, Millie.
Making transnational feminism: rural women, NGO activists, and northern donors in Brazil / Millie Thayer.
p. cm. — (Perspectives on gender)
1. Rural women—Brazil, Northeast—Social conditions. 2. Feminism—Brazil, Northeast. I. Title. II. Series.
HQ1542.T49 2009
305.420981'3—dc22
2009012896

ISBN 10: 0-415-96212-9 (hbk)
ISBN 10: 0-415-96213-7 (pbk)
ISBN 10: 0-203-86988-5 (ebk)

ISBN 13: 978-0-415-96212-4 (hbk)
ISBN 13: 978-0-415-96213-1 (pbk)
ISBN 13: 978-0-203-86988-8 (ebk)

For my mother, Caroline Blanton Thayer

CONTENTS

SERIES FOREWORD

This Perspectives on Gender series began a little over 20 years ago, and from the start was dedicated to the idea that it would present feminist research on gender that spoke to issues of social change and was intersectional (though the term itself had not yet been coined). Some of the earliest books in the series, such as Natalie Sokoloff's *Black and White Women in the Professions* and Patricia Hill Collins' *Black Feminist Thought*, specifically sought to bring the race-gender intersection to the forefront; others, such as Wendy Luttrell's *School-smart and Mother-wise* and Mary Romero's *Maid in America*, dealt with racial and ethnic issues quite directly as well, but were more attuned to how social class shaped gender experience. The early and enduring commitment of this series is to highlight the specificity and dynamism that characterize the social relations of gender. Margaret Nelson's study of white rural working class women struggling to get by with a little help from their friends, *The Social Economy of Single Motherhood*, is just as important in doing so as the studies that make racial/ethnic women their subjects.

No less importantly, books in this series took up issues of how women worked, as women, on and for social change. These studies of social movements around women's health (Verta Taylor's *Rock-a-by Baby*), violence against women (Patricia Yancey Martin's *Rape Work*) and poverty (Nancy Naples' *Grassroots Warriors*) also raised issues of class and race, of course. Other social movement studies selected for this series spoke most directly to the processes of developing a feminist identity and commitment (Sue Tolleson Rinehart's *Gender Consciousness and Politics*, Angela Miles' *Integrative Feminisms: Building Global Visions*, Cheryl Hercus's *Stepping Out of Line*), but did so with a strong focus on the intersections of gender with national location and historical position, two types of diversity that are also crucially important for understanding the complexity of gender as a social relation.

These two concerns that have characterized the series over the past two decades now come together in Millie Thayer's study of gender mobilization in Northeast Brazil, one of the poorest parts of that country. By contrasting the understandings of feminism and the strategies for social change adopted by rural labor union women, on the one hand, and a women's health collective in the city, on the other, Thayer brings the class dimension of women's social change work to the forefront. One must be hesitant about over-generalizing, but some of the class dynamics that she reveals in Brazil seem more familiar than not to me, based on my research, reading and observations in Europe and the US. Moreover, Thayer focuses on two specific groups that as local social movements are also participants in wider transnational processes, one tied to socialist labor organizing and the other to feminist health education. Thus she is able to show how globalization matters for social movements, as the transnational connections of money and ideas alike shape these gender projects.

As Thayer puts it, her book explores how Joan Scott came to Brazil, or at least how the seemingly esoteric ideas of this noted feminist historian became part of the organizing discourse and practices of women peasants, workers and health care professionals in these local Brazilian backwaters. Because even the most remote locales and impoverished activists are not working in isolation from the push and pull of markets, Thayer offers a critique of how the resources and the framing ideas that travel across borders also carry with them distorting demands for fitting into the global economy. Women who are trying to change the gender relations that shape their home and work lives in one place are inevitably part of a process that is much larger than these sites alone reveal, and one that they do not control. As a study of how feminism travels and changes everything, Thayer's research is simply superb.

Although its focus on class-gender intersections and social movements for women's empowerment make this book a perfect fit to the long-standing priorities of this series, Thayer's approach is also a harbinger of the series' increasing focus on the global dimension of gender relations and social change. Although the earlier studies of feminism by Angela Miles (a Canadian) and Cheryl Hercus (an Australian) also took a non-US-centered perspective on movements for gendered social change, neither made the transnational aspect of actual movement organizing work as central as Thayer does. I believe that this attention to globalization as a process is neither merely a matter of one idiosyncratic book nor only an expression of my own increased work on international feminism, but reflects the actual development of feminist work, as testified eloquently also by another recent book in this series, Christine Bose and Minjeong Kim's *Global Gender Research*.

Both the Bose and Kim reader and Thayer's multi-sited research monograph point in a direction that Perspectives on Gender will be following in future years. The idea that gender is not only locally specific but relationally connected in regard to class, race, sexuality, age, nation and time period has become more familiar, but as Thayer shows, there is also a need to highlight these gender relationships as changing in and through global political and economic transformation. Whether this is the fuller expression of liberal modernity, as some world policy scholars argue, or a post-modern collapse of unified collective subjects, as Thayer's work might suggest, a scholarship interested in really understanding intersectional gender arrangements and movements to change them will have to take a more dynamic, historical and global view. By taking up the questions raised by the interrelationships of social movements across borders and doing more comparisons among the gender relations movements target for change, feminist scholarship will be following where feminist activism has led, as Thayer has done in this case. The insights she has won from her cases offer more general conclusions as well: that money and ideas both matter and need to be tracked across time and space; that gender politics is also (always) about more than gender alone; that social change is hard work but it does happen, and it does matter for ordinary people's lives.

I look forward to seeing more such studies that make intersectional comparison, international change and the communities that struggle for gender justice their core concerns. I hope that readers will stretch their own attention to encompass parts of the world that they have not before encountered, and find both the familiar and the strange that they encounter there to be helpful in making sense of the transnational tensions in which their lives are also entangled.

Myra Marx Ferree
Series Editor

PREFACE

Through ethnography, *Making Transnational Feminism* provides a window on global social and political processes as they play out on the ground. New theoretical insights emerge out of the encounter between previous scholarship and participant observation of feminist struggles in Northeast Brazil. It is, I hope, an approach that makes the subject matter accessible to and engaging for a wide variety of audiences across academic disciplines and fields of interest. The book addresses issues of concern to students and scholars of gender, social movements, Latin America, globalization and transnationalism, and qualitative methodologies. In these pages, I trace the emergence of Brazilian women's movements in the face of hostile forces, their struggles with processes of professionalization, and their painstaking efforts to construct alliances with one another across both class and national borders.

Chapter 1 includes a theoretical framework, a discussion of methodology, and an introduction to the empirical context of my fieldwork; Chapter 2 then provides a historical perspective on transnational feminist movements in Latin America from the 19th to the late 20th century.

In the four ethnographic chapters that follow, the book explores three dimensions of feminist organizing. In terms of cultural politics, I show how discourses shift as movements engage with transnational and local meanings (Chapter 3); on the level of institutional relations, I analyze the kinds of leverage organizations exert in negotiations with one another (Chapters 4 and 5); in the economic arena, I describe their struggles to hold their own in relations with international donor agencies (Chapter 6). Through these different kinds of relationships, movements like the ones I studied stitch together a heterogeneous transnational feminist "counterpublic" which, I find, increasingly confronts the growing power of market-oriented discourses and practices (Chapter 7). The book concludes with an appendix that probes the links between researcher and field, methodology and substantive conclusions.

All authors hope that their work is read in its entirety and, like most books, this one is written so that the parts build on one another to the conclusion. However, for classroom purposes, teachers may choose to focus on certain chapters whose content best complements their course plan. Those most interested in the ethnographic material might skip the historical account, going directly from Chapter 1 to Chapter 3; those most concerned with rural movements could focus their attention on Chapters 4 and 5; those teaching about processes of "NGOization" and international funding would find the latter half of Chapter 2 and Chapters 3, 6, and 7 particularly useful; and those whose primary subject is methodology could assign Chapter 1 along with several of the ethnographic chapters, the conclusion, and the Appendix.

Whether read by colleagues or used as a teaching tool, my hope is that the book will both bring to life the struggles of Brazilian feminists and extend our understandings of transnational social movements and the contemporary challenges that they face.

ACKNOWLEDGMENTS

The road to this book has been a long and winding one, which I could not have traveled without the many people who have accompanied me along the way. My first thanks go to my research subjects—the members of SOS Corpo and the Rural Women Workers' Movement, as well as my interviewees among the Pernambucan feminist community and its allies. I am deeply indebted to them for their willingness to share their time and wisdom, their lives and struggles. They have taught me much about constructing and sustaining transnational feminist relationships. I only hope that what I have written here conveys to some small degree their extraordinary vision and dedication to the transformation of unjust social relations and the preservation of the counterpublic.

In Berkeley, where it all began, I owe heartfelt thanks to Michael Burawoy, my dissertation advisor, whose sense of humor, keen critical faculties, and uncanny ability to see through a thicket of data to a nascent theoretical claim, were crucial in helping me define the project. I won't soon forget his urgings to be bold, to address the big questions, or his passion for the intellectual enterprise. I hope that I can someday pass these on to my students as he has to me.

I am grateful too to the other members of my committee. Sonia Alvarez provided enthusiastic support and insight based on her long experience with Latin American feminisms. Raka Ray gave me careful feedback on chapter drafts, and commiserated on the challenges of participant observation. Caren Kaplan's work played an important role from the beginning in my thinking about transnational feminisms. And Peter Evans' consistent optimism and faith in the value of my project and my ability to see it through kept me going even when neither of these things were entirely obvious to me. With Michael, they all provided important role models as public intellectuals engaged with the issues that all of us care most about.

At Berkeley I found a wonderful community of graduate students who sustained one another in myriad ways. Cecilia Santos generously shared her friends, family, and contacts in Brazil and we spent many hours talking about our respective projects. The group that began as Michael Burawoy's dissertation group and ultimately became the co-authors of *Global Ethnography*—Joe Blum, Sheba George, Zsuzsa Gille, Teresa Gowan, Lynne Haney, Maren Klawiter, Steve Lopez, Seán Ó Riain and Michael—helped me frame my project in the nexus of global and local. As we wrestled with our projects, Teresa Gowan became my comrade and guardian angel, teaching me more about friendship—and sociology—than I can say. Her insight and unflinching honesty made my work far better than it would have been. In the years at Berkeley, discussions with or readings by Leah Carroll, Jenny Chun, Bill Hayes, Linus Huang, Patrisia Macías, Leslie Salzinger, Amy Schalet, Rachel Sherman, Susana Wappenstein, and Michelle Williams also left their imprint on these pages. I received warm and consistent encouragement as well from faculty members Arlene Kaplan Daniels, Laura Enriquez, and Gillian Hart.

Early on I also benefited from the insights of others who read or listened to pieces of this project and took time to share their thoughts. These include: in Brazil, Vanete Almeida, Maria Betânia Ávila, Mary Garcia Castro, Claudia de Lima Costa, Hulda Stadtler, Maria Amélia de Almeida Teles, and the members of the Family and Gender Group of the Masters Program in Anthropology, Universidade Federal de Pernambuco; in California, the members of the Hemispheric Dialogues Working Group on Feminist Theories in the Latin/a Americas (the "Translocas"); and, in Ithaca, the participants in the Rethinking Feminisms in the Americas conference. I am also grateful for the comments on an early version of Chapter 3 from the anonymous reviewers—whoever they may be—at the University of California Press, and for the guidance of the editors of *Ethnography* on an article that pushed my argument toward its current incarnation.

As the project has made its way from dissertation to book, I have been lucky to find supportive colleagues at the University of Massachusetts who have given precious time to do careful readings of my work. I am especially thankful to Sonia Alvarez, now a UMass colleague, and to Robert Zussman, who have read the manuscript in its entirety. Dan Clawson, Barbara Cruikshank, Naomi Gerstel, Millian Kang, and Joya Misra, at UMass, and Leslie Salzinger, Rachel Sherman, Jeff Rubin, and Francesca Miller from elsewhere, have read sections and given much appreciated feedback at crucial moments. Millian and I kept each other company as we wrote throughout the last several years, and she gave me much support, feedback, and sound advice. Teresa Gowan's wise editorial eye has continued to help shape the manuscript through many incarnations, in our writers' retreats from France to New England, where Rachel Sherman joined us for one buggy but productive session. In the final stages, I have benefited enormously from the hard work and insights of the Series Editor, Myra Marx Ferree, my Routledge editor, Steve Rutter, and the anonymous reviewers, whose provocative comments pushed me to extend my thinking in new directions.

The ways I conceive of my work has continued to be shaped through countless conversations with colleagues and friends. At the UMass Center for Latin American, Caribbean and Latino Studies, I found a lively community of researchers, including director Sonia Alvarez and sociology colleague Agustín Lao-Montes, as well as Kiran Asher, Gianpaolo Baiocchi, Jeff Rubin, and the other members of the international Consortium on *Social Movements and Twenty-First Century Cultural-Political Transformations*, which the Center coordinates. My understanding of Brazil has been enhanced by exchanges with numerous *brasilianistas*, including Carmen Diana Deere, Marguerite Harrison, and Malcolm McNee—all of whom welcomed me warmly to the Pioneer Valley. James Greene, Maria Cecilia Santos, Sarah Sarzynski, and the members of the Five College Afro-Luso-Brazilian Faculty Seminar have also generously shared their knowledge of the country. Don Tomaskovic-Devey and my other colleagues in Sociology helped "discipline" me—to the extent that was possible—and provided useful insights in our many conversations. I also want to thank Arlene Avakian, Ann Ferguson, Julie Hemment, Janice Irvine, and Jackie Urla, all of whom form part of the invisible network at UMass that has helped stimulate me intellectually and sustain me personally in this journey. Five College Women's Studies Research Center fellow Suzanne Swingel brought much welcomed fresh perspectives during her sojourn here. And, finally, I am grateful to my graduate students for their provocative questions and the ways they continue to teach me new ways to think about my work.

Then there are those who facilitate the research and writing process. My work was supported in part by the Andrew W. Mellon Foundation, the University of California, Berkeley, Vice Chancellor's Research Fund, and by a University of California, Berkeley, Humanities Graduate Research Grant. My transcribers, Tiana Arruda, Regina Camargo, Cida Fernandez, and Ana Nery dos Santos did invaluable work, as did translator Clarissa Becker. In the final push to finish the manuscript I was grateful to have the indispensable logistical assistance of Stephanie Boucher, who wrestled with the references for countless hours, Karen Mason who did meticulous proofreading, Irene Boeckmann who produced diagrams in the blink of an eye, and Michael Fazio who created just the right maps. Jennifer Kotting, who conveyed the concept of the book so beautifully in her cover design, deserves a special mention, as does the MMTR-NE who graciously allowed me to use the photo. Thanks to them all for their labor—and their good humor. I cannot fail to mention, as well, the staff members of the Sociology Department—Juliet Carvajal, Sandy Hunsicker, Maureen Warner, and Wendy Wilde, and of the Center for Latin American, Caribbean and Latino Studies—Gloria Bernabé Ramos and Ramón Ruiz, who contributed indirectly to this project by smoothing the bumps in the road on innumerable occasions.

No one could complete a project like this without friends and family to remind her that there is more to life than sociology. Heartfelt thanks to all the friends who walked this path with me during these too many years. They are legion, though I can only mention a few. My thanks go to: Bill Bigelow, Norm Diamond, Julie Light, and Rich Stahler-Sholk for friendship and political insight; Maxine Downs for conversations about work and life; Linda Shapiro for helping keep me sane; Teresa de Barros Correia and family, Hulda Stadtler, Regine Bandler and Ana Bosch, Dinalva Tavares, and Amelinha Teles and family for taking me in; the *Mujeres Desesperadas,* the *Mafia Nica,* and the *Brujas,* for helping me survive my transnational journeys; and Bruni Dávila, Susan Holland, Joan Kruckewitt, Jenny Ladd, Sherry Novick, Bob Roden, and Natalie Roden, for being there when I needed them as I worked on the many stages of this project.

My family deserves enormous thanks for their love and willingness to take up the slack while I worked on this project. During these years, my sister, Helen Chapell, and niece Mildred, shouldered far more than their share of our collective burdens, as I pored over interview transcripts and wrote chapter drafts. George and Liane, Caroline, Richard and Sara cheered me on from near and far, letting me know they believed in me, no matter how crazy the whole thing seemed. I am grateful for all of their support.

I thank my parents, Caroline Blanton Thayer and Sherman Rand Thayer, for encouraging me to follow my star and giving me the steadiness to do so, even when it was not the one they would have chosen. I owe my love of learning and interest in the transnational to my mother, whose heart and mind were always open to the world.

Finally, Rosa Oviedo is the one who kept my feet on the ground and the lightness in my heart. Throughout the process, she put up with my prolonged withdrawals into writing and did all she could to give me the space and time to work. She also made important contributions to my research, accompanying me to Brazil, where her warmth, spirit, and love of music created connections with people that I never could have made alone. Her astute perceptions as well as her uncompromising humanity had a profound influence on my thinking about what I saw. She has my love and deepest thanks.

1

INTRODUCTION

Re-Reading Globalization from Northeast Brazil

In the global imaginary, the vast semi-arid reaches of the Northeast Brazilian *sertão*, or "backlands," have long been synonymous with poverty,
backwardness, and remote desolation. It is a region that people have
traditionally left behind, fleeing from cyclical droughts, which leave fields
parched and animal carcasses strewn across barren hills. The colonial era
remains deeply imprinted on both economic and gender relations there:
On the one hand, precarious subsistence farms and cattle-raising *latifun-
dia* remain linked in semi-feudal relations; on the other, a patriarchal family structure renders women's back-breaking labor invisible, while strictly
controlling both their sexuality and their mobility. It is the figure of the
rural woman, confined within the household and subordinated to male
authority throughout her life, that seems best to capture the image of the
sertão as a place apparently located somewhere back in time, untouched
by the reach of an increasingly globalized civilization.[1]

Yet, despite its seeming isolation and supposed stagnation, there are
signs that the *sertão*—and the women who live there—are, in fact, deeply
embedded in global flows. In 1995, in the early stages of fieldwork, I
found myself at a workshop organized by a rural women's movement in
the remote town of Serra Talhada, named after the rocky outcroppings
carved out of the landscape that loom nearby. The women had invited
some male colleagues from the agricultural unions in the area to join
them in studying and discussing an unfamiliar concept: gender relations.
As a pitiless afternoon sun seared the tile roof of the borrowed union
hall, some thirty-odd participants sat at rickety student desks, clustered

in small groups around the meeting room. The walls were covered with butcher paper, filled with lists of terms describing rural men—"vain," "hard-working," "jealous," "affectionate"—and women—"courageous," "pretty," "many children," "suffering." Some entries, like "calloused hands" and "like to dance" appeared in both columns.

Having learned through their discussions that gender was a socially constructed power relation between men and women, the participants moved on to consider how it shaped local institutions: the Church, community associations, family agriculture, and rural workers' unions. It was a perspective I was familiar with from reading Princeton feminist historian Joan Scott's work. What was not familiar was seeing her post-structuralist theoretical discussion brought to life in this context, so far from the halls of Northern feminist academe.

It was evident that despite the remoteness of the setting and the poverty of the participants, this women's movement was linked to discourses with roots half a world away. Even in the far reaches of the *sertão*, the local had no fixed boundaries. At the same time, this was not a case of overbearing global cultural forces penetrating a helpless and backward social sector. In the discussion I observed, participants with their own political histories and context engaged the unfamiliar discourse and made it their own. Given their precarious standing as members of an agricultural peasant class in the late twentieth century, the rural women conceived of "gender" in a particular way. At a time when most feminists in the global North were privileging gender over class, this group was linking the two.[2] Women of the *sertão* used gender to strengthen a class-based movement by rebuilding ties with their male comrades on the basis of equality. They were appropriating a transnational resource and reconstructing it to help them meet their own local political challenges.

But how did Joan Scott travel from Princeton to the *sertão?* Who were the agents and what were the peculiar mechanisms of discursive travel and transformation? And in what kinds of transnational political and economic relationships were these social actors implicated?[3] Did their alliances mirror or challenge the movements of global capital and dominant political and cultural forces? My research followed this trail, exploring the nature of global connections among women's movements and the means by which these links were created and sustained across vast social, as well as geographic, divides.

THEORIZING TRANSNATIONAL CONNECTIONS

Much of the literature on globalization in the late 1980s and early 1990s conveyed an exhilarating but ultimately hopeless view of it as a set of

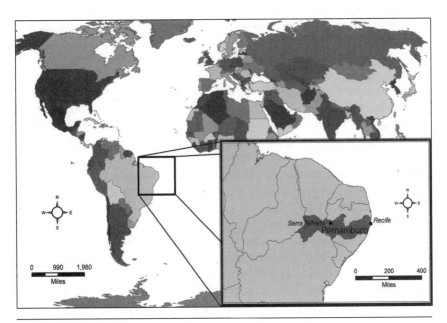

Figure 1.1 Northeast Brazil in Global Perspective

inexorable forces beyond the control of ordinary human beings. In this dominant genre, flows of capital and technology swept the globe, incorporating the lucky few, while condemning vast regions and populations to "structural irrelevance." Extrapolating from their economic analysis, those who wrote from this perspective reached the conclusion that the local had also ceased to matter in a political and cultural sense. As Castells' "space of flows" came to dominate the "space of places," meaning evaporated from the local—individual places became increasingly isolated from one another and vulnerable to overwhelming outside forces.[4]

In this scenario, some, like Bauman, saw geographically mobile elites holding the reins of the global system, while others viewed power as more diffuse. Harvey cited the unfolding dynamic of an accelerating capitalism as the causal force, while Castells located control in "the nonhuman capitalist logic of an electronically operated, random processing of information," to which even powerful economic interests were subject.[5] However they conceived of the locus of global power, theorists in this tradition shared the view that inhabitants of the local were spatially confined, lacking in community, and unable to construct their own meanings or articulate their own alternative visions. What resistance there was, they claimed, took the form of a reactionary fundamentalism based on territorial and primal ascribed identities.[6]

Feminists and other scholars have since challenged this pessimistic portrayal, arguing that capitalist globalization is not a *fait accompli*, but rather a discourse—a "rape script" of the inevitable penetration of helpless regions and social sectors, in the words of Gibson-Graham.[7] The discourse of global power, they argue, masks a heterogeneous set of processes, ridden with contradictions and vulnerabilities. Though capital seeks to extend its reach and universalize its logic, to do so it must come down to earth, engaging with the particularities of social relations at a local level. While globalizing forces do reshape these relationships, Tsing observes that they too are transformed by the "friction" of the encounter.[8] Rather than a *deus ex machina*, feminist critics argue that globalization is a god with feet of clay.

The perspective of pioneering globalization theorists like Bauman, Castells, and Harvey was profoundly rooted in the particular experience of class and class-based movements. Empirical studies have repeatedly shown the ways in which workers have lost ground in the face of the transnationalization of capital, economic restructuring, and the imposed "flexibility" of labor.[9] Though unions have long had international ties, and there have been increasing efforts in recent decades to create cross-border solidarities, these have often been nationally circumscribed and undermined by the entanglement of workers' movements with the state. In the case of class-based movements, gloom may have some purchase in the empirical world.[10]

The effects of globalization on gender relations, however, are much more ambiguous. The flourishing local space of yesteryear, so fondly remembered by globalization theorists, was too often a suffocating enclosure for women in patriarchal families. Though many have seen their class position deteriorate, global flows have not always had the same negative effect on their experiences of gender.[11] Nor does the despairing view reflect the kind of globally connected feminism I found even in a "structurally irrelevant" region like the *sertão*.[12] Rather than turning inward or being confined in the local, women's movements have developed sophisticated and extensive transnational networks over the last several decades. They represent the other face of globalization—the emancipatory possibilities created by new inter-local connections.[13]

While the perspective once dominant depicted global flows occurring of their own volition and at their own rhythm, feminist researchers have shown how the purposeful activity of social actors—whether Filipina migrant domestic workers, Barbadian "higglers," Dominican sex workers, or Mexican immigrants to global cities—underpins the global economy.[14] In a similar vein, my study finds social movement actors purposefully constituting transnational political relationships.[15] The feminists described in this book appropriate and transform discourses, exchange political currencies of legitimacy and authenticity, and negotiate the requirements of international development funding. In the process, their movements transform meanings and material resources as they facilitate their displacement to new contexts.

The recent literature on transnational social movements takes account of these developments among feminists, as well as among indigenous, environmental, peace, human rights, queer, and global justice movements. By chronicling these proliferating forms of activism, social movement scholars have made an indispensable contribution to understanding the forms of agency that have emerged alongside new kinds of domination.[16] They explore the ways social movements have responded to global economic restructuring and to a shifting "transnational opportunity structure" with innovative forms of cross-border collaboration.[17] Networks, coalitions, transnational social movement organizations, regional and global gatherings, international advocacy campaigns, and Internet-based activism all push politics beyond the confines of the state and form the basis for new kinds of collective identity. At the same time, these authors make the convincing claim that politics has not entirely lost its grounding in the nation-state. There are continuities between domestic and international activism, and the constraints and possibilities of each shape the other.[18]

However useful, the literature on transnational social movements has limitations for grasping the cultural dimension of cross-border politics. For the most part, its objects of analysis are particular formalized structures—whether they are organizations, such as People's Global Action; campaigns, such as the Global Campaign for Women's Human Rights; events, such as the World Social Forum; or venues, such as the United Nations. From this perspective, movements appear as pre-constituted. The focus is on how already existing entities respond to opportunities and obstacles in a globalizing context, rather than on the processes by which movements come into being and sustain alliances.[19] The origins and outcomes of particular strategies adopted by collective actors receive much of the scholarly attention. Culture, from this perspective, is viewed primarily as a resource to be used instrumentally for political ends, rather than as fluid sets of meanings that tacitly shape movement practices and discourses.[20] Connections like the invisible discursive trajectories that link feminist scholars in Princeton to rural women in the Northeast Brazilian backlands lie outside the scope of this literature.

Then, too, the organizational bias of the literature often leads to an emphasis on social movement entities and campaigns based in or dominated by the global North. Given the disproportionate share of resources and institutional power in the countries of Europe and North America, it is not surprising that most of the formalized transnational organizations have their roots there. Because of this and also because of the location of many scholars in the global North, these groups draw more analytical scrutiny. But such a focus misses the ways South-North dynamics are experienced by movements in much of Asia, Africa, and Latin America.[21]

This book takes the perspective of feminist movements in the global South and specifically in Latin America, locating them in a larger web of political and cultural relationships. It explores the multiple forms of collaboration and connection—both inside and outside formal structures—that link them to one another and to movements in the global North. Geographer Doreen Massey's conception of place provides a useful starting point for theorizing transnational social movements in this broader framework. She views globalization as intensifying links between internally differentiated local sites, rather than as simply the growing power of anonymous "global" forces to penetrate and dominate a defenseless local community. The identity of a particular place—or node—in this web consists of its shifting configuration of links to other near and distant locales. The local "matters," therefore, not simply as a passive and static counterpoint to the global, but as the primary site where globalization is constituted, as well as where its effects are played out.[22]

This perspective helps us to rethink social movements, not as bounded entities, but as relational constructs, nodes in a larger web of connections. I argue that, like local places, oppositional social movements, and the organizations that give them concrete expression, come to be through their relationships—with members and allies, as well as with dominant institutions. Their politics—goals, strategies, structures—are defined through their engagement with others; there is no essence that exists outside these connections. Social movements do not *have* relationships; they *are* relationships: a set of always shifting interactions with a variety of allies and interlocutors, whether individuals, organizations, discourses, or other social structures.

As this study will show, social movement connections are the source of their greatest power and deepest vulnerabilities. The "goods" that flow through these linkages, and sometimes remake them in unexpected ways, are both material and intangible. Social movement relationships are vectors for discursive travel, as well as the transfer of resources.[23] Organizations do not simply absorb all of the discourses that pass their way; they make choices about which new meanings to incorporate and how to reinterpret them. However, their choices are increasingly constrained as the reach of the global market extends into new social spaces.

THE ANT'S EYE

Beginning in the 1980s, feminist theorists, including scholars from the global South, launched a trenchant critique of the "discursive colonialism" that has characterized contacts between Western feminism and women in Asia, Africa, and Latin America.[24] At the same time, they underlined the urgency of creating new kinds of transnational alliances to confront the growing threats to the well-being of women and communities around the world, and some have theorized new kinds of relationships that valorize, rather than erase, difference.[25] But, in fact, we know little about empirical efforts to construct these kinds of alliances across borders. Drawing on the insights of ethnography, in this book I examine the multiple connections that stretch across the transnational feminist public, holding it together against the centrifugal forces of differing social locations, interests, identities, and access to resources.

This study takes the ant's eye view of global flows, analyzing not only how globalization is experienced but, more importantly, how it is constituted on the ground in a part of the world often perceived as a forgotten backwater of the global economy. My research began with two organizations in the Northeast Brazilian state of Pernambuco: the rural women's movement in Serra Talhada and an urban feminist nongovernmental organization (NGO) in Recife, the state's largest city, and the fourth largest in the country. Rather than treating these organizations as separate "case studies," the study moved outward to examine the web of connections in which they are located. In this book, I analyze the relations both between the two organizations and between each organization and its feminist allies in the United States and Europe.

The organizations described here inhabit a transnational feminist space—or "counterpublic"—in which scattered and differently situated local movements both collaborate and struggle with one another over flows of discursive and material resources.[26] In the process, movements in Brazil and elsewhere construct collective identities, articulate critiques, and debate strategies to challenge prevailing norms and institutions. In theory, public spheres can be conceived as either idealized arenas of democratic deliberation and mutual sustenance, or as sites of competitive and self-interested maneuvering. At the turn of the twentieth century, the feminist counterpublic traced in this book lay between these two poles. It was a hybrid space in which participants were linked *both* by relations of power *and* by bonds of solidarity.[27]

This study of transnational connections among social movements joins feminist and other critics in offering an antidote to the dominant strain of the literature on globalization. While acknowledging the devastating effects of the extension of global capital and neoliberal political regimes around the world, like the transnational social movement literature, it calls attention to the simultaneous emergence of a more encouraging trend: the construction of networks among movements with diverse visions of social transformation. The process of globalization may accelerate some forms of domination, but it also facilitates the linking and empowering of once-disconnected oppositional forces.

At the same time, transnational social movements not only reflect, but are also active and explicit participants in, processes of globalization, engaging with and producing cross-border cultural, political, and economic flows. While movements like those described in this book sometimes resist foreign influences, they also often appropriate and transform discourses from afar, draw economic resources across borders, and carry on explicit political negotiations in a transnational context. In this way, movements become a vehicle through which globalization is both constituted and contested.

FEMINISMS IN BRAZIL

As a country located in the economic semi-periphery and engaged in a process of neoliberal democratization, Brazil at the dawn of the twenty-first century offered an ideal vantage point to conduct a study of the heterogeneous arena of transnational feminisms.[28] On the one hand, its revitalized civil society embraced a diversity of women's movements around a wide variety of issues and constituencies. On the other, Brazil's intermediate status in the world economy allowed some of these movements to cross geographic borders, while the country's continuing internal inequalities forced them to cross social divisions as well.

The history of Brazilian women's movements, like that of transnational feminisms more broadly, is a story of relations between differently situated groups of women. Movements among middle- and upper-class women took different forms than those among working-class and Afro-Brazilian women. Because the intersections between the two groups were laden with power reflecting race, class, and other markers of inequality, their relationships were not always harmonious. But their mutual engagement transformed each group and created a constellation of movements that was both unique to Brazil and had commonalities with those of many other Latin American countries.[29]

Feminism in Brazil among middle- and upper-class white Brazilian women dates back to the first half of the nineteenth century with the agitation around education for women. It continued, later in the century, through female-led movements for the abolition of slavery and the appearance of the first women's newspapers, and became more explicit in struggles for the vote in the early twentieth century. Meanwhile, Afro-Brazilian and working-class women engaged in their own struggles against slavery and for the eight-hour day, decent wages, and better working conditions in urban factories. Women participated in unions and socialist movements, and played an important role in the opposition to fascism during the years leading up to World War II.[30]

Contemporary Brazilian women's movements emerged in the shadows of dictatorship. In 1964, a coup brought a military regime to power, initiating a period of censorship and political repression, as well as state-led economic development. In the first few months, more than 50,000 suspected subversives were rounded up and imprisoned, tortured, and, in some cases, murdered or "disappeared." Purges were carried out in government agencies, universities, labor unions, and the judiciary. More than a thousand unions suffered government intervention; over two hundred were closed down. The press was censored, civil rights suspended, and opposition parties banned.[31]

The opposition to the dictatorship included an array of forces, from liberation theologists and Christian base communities in the poor neighborhoods of the urban periphery, to labor unions, left-wing parties, student activists, and a small guerrilla movement. While repression forced most forms of protest underground, ironically, the authoritarian regime helped to mobilize both urban working-class and middle- and upper-class women around distinctive forms of gender-based politics.[32]

The regime's development policies favored industry over agriculture, uprooting rural populations and drawing them to the industries in the Southeastern part of the country. Working-class families moved into the vast new marginal neighborhoods that sprang up around cities like Rio de Janeiro and São Paulo. Though some found jobs in the factories that churned out consumer goods for the middle and upper classes, government wage controls quickly eroded working-class livelihoods. Residents of the urban periphery struggled to survive and to cope in the face of the regime's neglect of basic infrastructure and public services for the poor.

Many working-class women had entered the workforce and, like men, suffered sharp declines in their purchasing power.[33] But whether they worked outside the home or not, the women in these neighborhoods experienced economic hardships in particular ways. Gendered expectations of mothers held them responsible for their families' well-being, a charge that was becoming increasingly difficult to fulfill. As basic expenses outran family budgets, as children fell ill from poor sanitation or tainted water, and as health services failed to materialize, these women politicized their survival strategies. In the early 1970s, they began to organize movements against the high cost of living, and demanded clean water and working sewer systems, day care centers, and health clinics. Motherhood also motivated some to challenge the regime more directly, forming commissions to demand amnesty for sons and daughters imprisoned by the regime, as well as an end to political violence and disappearances. These different *movimentos de mulheres* often grew out of mothers' clubs or housewives' associations sponsored by the Catholic Church, one of the few organizations whose activities were tolerated by the National Security State.[34]

The economic development model embraced by the dictatorship affected elite women very differently than it did their working-class counterparts. The expansion of higher education offered new opportunities, and middle- and upper-class women flocked to take advantage of them. But the lack of access for women to higher-status occupations left many university graduates un- or underemployed and acutely aware of the discriminatory practices that continued to exclude them. In the late 1960s and early 1970s, a few intellectuals, academics, and journalists began to research and write critically about women's issues.[35] At the same time, younger women joined radical student movements, clandestine political parties, or the armed struggle.[36]

For nearly a decade, economic prosperity based on massive industrialization, foreign investment, and draconian controls on workers' wages and rights to organize won the quiescence of the middle classes. In the early 1970s, however, the "Economic Miracle" began to fade and dissent spread. In hopes of shoring up the regime's legitimacy, military rulers began to loosen their grip. A gradual political opening—the *abertura*—was soon pushed wider by a burgeoning civil society.[37] It was a kind of democratization from above, a transition unusual among dictatorial regimes in Latin America at the time. The dichotomous political field of state and opposition splintered, and new political subjects with a diversity of identities began to emerge. The hegemony of class discourses in the opposition eroded, as movements around race, gender, and sexuality challenged social, as well as political, authoritarianism.[38]

In 1975, the U.N.'s proclamation of International Women's Year—and the Mexico City conference that accompanied it—legitimated gender-based concerns, offering new opportunities to both women's and feminist movements in Brazil. Stimulated by these developments, citywide public gatherings to identify and discuss women's issues were held for the first time in Rio de Janeiro and São Paulo in 1975 and 1976. In the aftermath, a few small consciousness-raising groups emerged in the major cities of the Southeast, women's centers were founded, and the first post-coup women's newspapers appeared.[39] During this period, International Women's Day celebrations planned by broad coalitions became an annual event in a number of cities, including Recife, as they did in many countries.

A few feminists, including the academics and intellectuals mentioned earlier, began to take on issues, such as violence against women and reproductive rights, which had until then taken a back seat to demands for economic rights. In 1979, an amnesty law was passed and a wave of political exiles returned to Brazil, among them women who had been exposed to the feminist movements then flourishing in Europe. Their presence contributed to the growing strength of Brazilian feminism.

As feminists increasingly claimed political autonomy from mixed-gender organizations, they came into conflict with the parties and movements of the male-dominated left. Both the mainstream media and left leaders had long portrayed feminism as a foreign "import," irrelevant to the lives of the majority of Brazilians. Worse yet, many of the regime's opponents saw it as an ideology that would divide women and men at a moment when unity was sorely needed. They argued that the "general" struggles around class and against authoritarianism had to take precedence over the "specific" concerns of women.[40]

But the left was facing its own internal gender crisis. Many female militants were no longer as receptive to the arguments against feminism as they might once have been. Facing a gap between egalitarian political rhetoric and the realities of their own discriminatory treatment by male comrades, many of these young middle- and upper-class women had begun to question party gender doctrine. Increasing numbers began to leave male-dominated political organizations. Their search for ways to combine their newfound gender awareness with commitments to fight the injustices of class took them to the marginal *bairros* around the major cities. There, they joined the struggles of working-class women, seeking to raise critical consciousness about gender.

Initially, their brand of feminism was heavily influenced by the Marxist categories with which they, as former party militants, were most familiar. They promoted women's economic interests and participation in the labor force, but kept gender-specific grievances off the agenda and largely out of the public sphere.[41] While issues such as sexuality, reproduction, and the family were increasingly being raised in middle- and upper-class feminist circles, they were seen as too controversial for the *bairros*. Instead, together with women from the urban periphery, as well as union and progressive church activists, these young feminists helped create citywide movements to protest the high cost of living and demand free day care for working mothers, and they collaborated with other struggles around issues linked to women's conventional gender identities.[42]

Class-based women's movements multiplied in the late 1970s as domestic workers, union members, and residents of the urban periphery took advantage of the political opening to expand their mobilizations.

In these early years, most members of the *movimentos de mulheres* did not identify with feminism, and sought to distance themselves from its elitist image. However, as elsewhere in Latin America, the experiences of working-class women in movements to defend their rights as wives and mothers took them out of the home, gave them new skills and a sense of empowerment, and led many to question unequal gender arrangements in families and other institutions. As a result, they became more vocal about their subordination as women, sometimes voicing the kinds of radical stands that middle-class feminists had hesitated to take for fear of alienating these same women.[43]

Over time, the cross-class encounter between women produced what was known in Latin America as "popular feminism"—working-class movements that fought women's subordination with their own brand of class-based feminist politics.[44] In the process, it also transformed middle- and upper-class Brazilian feminism. What might have remained a small, elite-based, and internally focused movement instead was linked to a broad array of other struggles for social justice. At the same time, new organizations of black women, single mothers, lesbians, rural women, female professionals, union members, and others proliferated. By the 1990s, feminism had become feminisms, as the field of Brazilian gender-based movements expanded and diversified.[45]

Yet, even with the growing diversity of constituencies organized around questions of gender, some issues were more easily integrated into feminist agendas than others. In particular, though class was ubiquitous in feminist discourse, race was a glaring absence, except in the few organizations made up of black women. On the one hand, Brazil's racial stratification meant that the ranks of middle- and upper-class feminists were predominantly white and most were not attuned to the powerful effects of racism in the society. On the other, the prevailing ideology of "racial democracy," trumpeted by the Brazilian state, also contributed to erasing racial categories from the field of politics.[46] The power of this ideology is illustrated by the fact that most working-class women, many of whom were phenotypically Afro-Brazilian, did not identify as black or seek to incorporate race into their gender-based struggles.[47]

The late 1980s and 1990s brought challenges to the tenuous cross-class feminist relationships forged in the waning days of the dictatorship. Democratization meant the opening of political institutions to at least some previously excluded social actors. While working-class women remained largely on the outside, feminist movements were among those to gain *entrée* into new spaces of power. In the early 1980s, when opposition parties were legalized, some feminists entered these previously all-male arenas. As the decade wore on, women's health activists were increasingly drawn into collaboration with the Ministry of Health. By 1985, feminists had also made inroads into the criminal justice system, as women in São Paulo successfully fought for a female-run police station to which women could bring their complaints.[48] That same year, in response to pressure from opposition party activists, the *Conselho Nacional dos Direitos da Mulher* (CNDM [National Council for Women's Rights]) was established, giving feminists a new channel for influencing the state.[49]

Simultaneously, flows of international funding toward Brazil accelerated, seeking to strengthen—and to shape—this newly unleashed civil society. These resources, and the new opportunities to enter the political institutions, combined to accelerate the professionalization of some women's organizations, particularly those that had been founded by middle- and upper-class feminists. The NGOs that emerged became active participants in the growing web of global women's networks, while other, less formalized or well-funded, organizations remained for a time on the sidelines. Brazilian gender-based movements became increasingly diverse not only in relation to constituencies and issues, but also in organizational structure and access to power and resources.

The new terrain of the latter two decades of the twentieth century favored those with economic and cultural capital: Middle- and upper-class feminists found it easier to enter the state and international funding circuits than did their rural and urban working-class counterparts. Their victories had positive effects on the lives of Brazilian women, but they also generated new challenges for sustaining cross-class alliances.

TRANSNATIONAL FEMINIST GEOMETRIES

Globalization has intensified the articulations among women, making more transparent what Massey calls the "power geometry of time-space compression"—the differential positioning of social groups vis-à-vis global flows.[50] Once, inequalities between women in different social and geographic locations appeared as remote and static facts, mediated through national political institutions and class structures. But the increasing density of transnational connections—from jet travel and the Internet to increasingly overlapping feminist discourses—has transformed social movement arenas by drawing diverse movements together.

When I arrived in Northeast Brazil in the mid-1990s, I found local women's movements with links to a wide variety of collective actors across the globe. Many organizations had relations with counterparts in Asia, Africa, and Latin America. But the asymmetries of power among feminists paralleled global economic inequities and were more starkly visible in their connections to movements in the early industrialized countries where economic resources were more plentiful. Interested in the challenges to sustaining democratic transnational feminist relations, I chose to focus my research along the North-South axis.

From this perspective, I identified four types of feminist actors—two in the North and two in the South—whose relationships played the most significant role in facilitating transnational connections during the period I was studying.[51] In the United States and Europe, second-wave feminist theorist/activists, located both in and outside of the academy, and sympathetic program officers within development agencies represented the most important points of transnational contact. In Brazil, the participants in North-South flows of discourses and resources could be roughly grouped into two categories: NGOs and grassroots membership organizations. My study looks at the connections among these four actors from the perspective of two Northeast Brazilian women's organizations that each represent one of the ideal types.

In the United States and Europe, late twentieth-century feminisms, for historical reasons, developed a broad base and political influence a decade or more before they did so in the global South. With their middle- and upper-class constituency, and access to institutions, both liberal and radical strains of feminism in the North were able to express their politics materially through publishing, conferences, development policies, scholarships, and the like, projecting particular versions of feminism around the world. What came to be thought of as "global feminism" was, in fact, specific local configurations of gender politics rooted in the United States and Europe and endowed with sufficient resources to travel.[52] In this context, *activists in the industrialized countries*, first in independent movements and later in the academy, generated feminist discourses and practices that found their way to Northeast Brazil, beginning in the late 1970s. The radical feminist politics of the early women's health movement and, ten years later, academic discourses of gender were appropriated by the organizations studied here, which gave them new meanings.

In the global North, *international development agencies* mushroomed in size and numbers in the 1980s and 1990s. They channeled a growing share of state and private foreign aid from the United States and Europe to NGOs and, to a lesser extent, to grassroots movements in the global South.[53] The quantities disbursed to women's movements in Brazil, while small in relation to overall foreign aid, were nonetheless an indispensable condition of survival for many of them, given the lack of local philanthropy and scarcity of state funds. Along with funding came ways of conceptualizing feminism that grew out of U.S. and European movements and became part of the discursive terrain on which Brazilian women defined their politics. The unequal distribution of these economic and conceptual resources among women's movements aggravated previously existing hierarchies among them, granting visibility and power to some, while marginalizing others.[54]

Among the relatively empowered were Brazilian *feminist NGOs*.[55] In the 1980s, with democratization, the expanded availability of international aid, and a state that looked increasingly to the private sector to fulfill social needs, these institutions proliferated, as did NGOs in general.[56] As we saw earlier, the middle- and upper-class women who formed these organizations saw themselves as part of a larger cross-class feminist movement. Unlike staff in charitable or service-oriented NGOs, they believed they were building a movement that would better their own lives, as well as those of the poor and working-class women who were their primary constituency. This characteristic meant that inequalities between elite and poor women were tempered—though not erased—by efforts to construct relations of mutual solidarity.[57]

Initially, many of these feminists, like their counterparts in the global North, gave their organization an informal, anti-hierarchical structure consistent with the values and goals of the larger movement. But this did not last long. Alvarez describes the decision to form nongovernmental organizations as a "strategic choice" for Brazilian feminists.[58] Democratization created a political opening where, for the first time, there was hope that their proposals could become policies. During the 1980s, their increasing success in advocating changes within the state and offering services outside it led to further demands for their gender expertise, increased dependence on international funding, and growing institutionalization and professionalization.

Alvarez argues that these feminist NGOs had what she calls a "hybrid identity" that combines ethical and political considerations with institutional and instrumental ones. At the turn of the century, the broader context of growing market hegemony created increasing pressures in the latter direction. Critics claimed that some NGOs were becoming more accountable to funders than to their intended beneficiaries, and were imposing "institutional imperatives" that undercut goals of social transformation.[59] Others pointed out that, despite the best of intentions, professionalization had the effect of exacerbating inequalities among different kinds of women's organizations. In her study of São Paulo feminist organizations, Lebon concludes:

> [A]s professionalized activists gain more access to information on gender issues, more time to dedicate to movement activities, more resources to do so, as well as more visibility in society, than non-professionalized activists, they also hold more power in the movement.[60]

Grassroots women's organizations represented the collective actor with, apparently, least power in the transnational feminist arena. As we have seen, these organizations, many of them sponsored by the Catholic Church, proliferated during the 1970s and 1980s in the marginal urban neighborhoods that encircled major Brazilian cities like Recife, as well as in some parts of the rural interior. Initially organized by women to defend the well-being of their families and communities, the self-confidence generated by their organizing, the opposition of men in their communities, and the direct or indirect contact with feminist discourses reshaped their awareness of the gender dimensions of their struggles. These organizations functioned, for the most part, on volunteer effort. To the degree that they received outside support, the amounts were small, and dedicated to specific projects, rather than institutional funding. Activists with somewhat more education or resources often played an important role as advisors to these movements but, given the lack of spoils for the taking, this was almost always a labor of love.[61]

These four actors, then, constituted distinctive sites within a larger feminist political space. On the one hand, they shared partially overlapping identities and interests as activists committed to transforming gender relations. In this spirit, they made common cause in struggles against different forms of women's subordination; shared skills, knowledge, and pedagogies; and channeled funds and political opportunities to one another.

On the other hand, differential access to resources among them created power relations that paralleled those produced by the globalization of capital. Though women's movements in the global periphery have generated their own unique discourses and practices, Northern feminists, both in and outside of development agencies, were most often the source of the discursive and material resources that flowed across borders; in turn, professionalized urban feminist institutions in the global South most often served as interpreters and transmitters of these resources to grassroots organizations of working-class women. In this way, global inequalities ensured that cultural and political flows traveled primarily between movement nodes from North to South, and from upper- and middle-class to working-class organizations, in a hierarchical chain of interdependence.

These configurations of power ensured greater mobility to discourses from the global North and supported them with material resources. However, this study finds that traveling feminist theories and practices were not, in fact, simply exported by the powerful and incorporated uncritically by weak and vulnerable local movements. The gender politics being constructed in Northeast Brazil represented the outcome of a complex process of contestation, appropriation, and negotiation in a transnational social sphere. In this process, despite their position of economic disadvantage, Northeast Brazilian women asserted their relative autonomy by drawing on resources of their own, based on the very local-ness whose demise is bemoaned by globalization theorists.

It is their carefully defended autonomy that allows relations of solidarity among women's movements to survive. Without the recognition of difference and the capacity to define their own collective identities, there would be no basis for constructing egalitarian alliances. As global forces draw feminists into affiliations increasingly shaped by expansive forces, such as the market and neoliberal ideologies, their targets and organizing contexts may converge. At the same time, however, the erosion of independence and the commodification of relationships leave their mutual solidarities at increasing risk.

My understanding of these dynamics emerged from my research with two Brazilian feminist organizations in the state of Pernambuco: a nongovernmental feminist women's health organization called *SOS Corpo* (SOS Body) and a grassroots membership organization, the *Movimento de Mulheres Trabalhadoras Rurais* (MMTR [Rural Women Workers' Movement]). Dorothy Smith argues, following Hegel, that "relations of ruling" are better understood from the perspective of those with least access to power.[62] While no organization in my study was without some form of leverage, each of the two that I studied entered transnational circuits at a material disadvantage in relation to feminist actors in Europe and the United States. By studying the "geometries of power" within the feminist counterpublic as they were experienced in Northeast Brazil, I hoped to gain insight that perhaps would not have been available from the vantage point of the global North.

WOMEN'S ORGANIZING IN PERNAMBUCO

As a "semi-peripheral" nation-state, Brazil had one foot in the global networks of the industrialized world, and one foot among the poor and excluded.[63] The ambiguity of its status was also reflected in the dramatic internal differences between its elites and its marginalized populations: In 1999, the richest 10 percent of the population earned fifty-three times as much monthly income as the poorest 10 percent. That same year, 35 percent of Brazil's population lived below the poverty line.[64] Its location at the intersection of wealth and poverty, integration and exclusion, offered ample opportunity to observe the relations among differently situated women's movements, within as well as outside the country.

Pernambuco, the state where I conducted my research, lies in the Northeast—the least developed and most impoverished region of Brazil.[65] Pernambuco stretches inland from the fertile coast, through a transitional zone, to the dusty semi-arid interior. In the 1960s and 1970s, state-led economic development made itself felt here, as elsewhere in the country, stimulating urbanization and migration from rural areas to Recife, the state capital on the coast, as well as to the industrial Southeast and to the agricultural frontier in the Amazon region. Historically, the economy of the coastal *zona da mata* had been dominated by sugar plantations; as the demands of the global economy shifted, the agricultural economy was eclipsed by light industry and, increasingly, information technology and the production of knowledge in universities and nongovernmental organizations in Recife. Women of the middle and upper classes who had benefited from opportunities in the expanding public educational system found a niche in these new economic spaces. These women became the social base of incipient feminism in the city and, in particular, of one of the organizations I studied—the women's health NGO, SOS Corpo.

Meanwhile, hundreds of miles to the west, the small farmers who had long populated the social landscape of the *sertão* were among the casualties of Brazil's economic opening. The establishment of Mercosul—a regional trade agreement among Argentina, Brazil, Paraguay, and Uruguay, founded in 1991—and the trade liberalization that accompanied it, increased competition for the farmers of the region, at a time when policymakers favored export agriculture over subsistence or small-scale farming. As prices stagnated or dropped and agricultural credit and other subsidies dried up, many found themselves forced to sell out to the highest bidder. By the 1990s, many *sertanejan* families subsisted, not on agriculture, but on government handouts or meager municipal salaries. Rural women bore the brunt of the crisis—either left behind by men who abandoned home in search of work, or managing a family economy in increasingly impossible circumstances. These women formed the second organization included here, the MMTR , based in the Pernambucan *sertão*.[66]

This book examines transnational political relationships from the perspective of these two women's organizations, chosen because they were situated at opposite ends of a continuum of relations with global flows: SOS Corpo, an urban middle-class feminist NGO in Brazil's fourth largest city, well-known both nationally and internationally for its work on women's health; and the MMTR, an organization of women small producers from the impoverished semi-arid *sertão* region, with origins in the rural trade union movement and limited connections outside Brazil. While the urban NGO had found a niche of sorts in the New World Order, the rural women's movement struggled from a position of exclusion from it.

Through a series of trips to Brazil between 1995 and 2005, including ten months in 1998, I studied SOS Corpo, the MMTR, and their allies at home

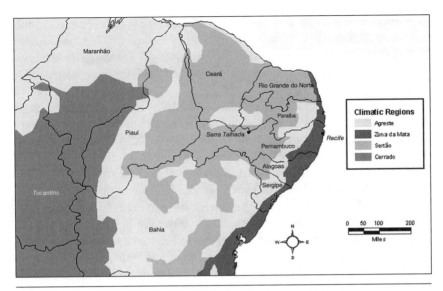

Figure 1.2 Northeast Climatic Regions. Source: The Brazilian Cacti Project, http://www.brcactaceae.org/ecosystems.html

and abroad. Using a variety of qualitative methods described later in this chapter, I traced the links between each of my collective subjects and what is often thought of as "global feminism," but what are, in fact, particular local feminist sites based in the United States and Europe. In the process, to my surprise, I discovered that global flows passed through and *between* the two movement sites I had chosen to study, as well as *across* national boundaries. The relations between the two Brazilian organizations were as significant for understanding the transnationalization of feminism as were their respective connections outside of the country.

The urban SOS Corpo, as we shall see, was more thoroughly integrated with flows of material and discursive resources from women's movements around the world, while the rural MMTR, at least in the 1990s, relied on the mediation of SOS and other Brazilian feminist "brokers" to tap into such flows. Both organizations faced fundamental inequalities, whether between North and South or between classes within Brazil. This context, as we will see, posed fundamental challenges to their transnational feminist alliances.[67]

RESEARCHING TRANSNATIONAL SPACE

I did not begin with the intention of studying the internal workings of a transnational social movement space, but rather with a more bounded project—the comparative study of two organizations—for which there was ample methodological precedent. However, as my research and the effects of globalization on my field of inquiry led me toward the broader public in which SOS and the MMTR were located, I struggled with how to accommodate my methodology to the study of changing transnational relationships.

I adopted an approach that relied on ethnography scattered across multiple sites, and incorporated the use of in-depth interviews and archival research to supplement my observations and provide a historical dimension to the study. As a student of Michael Burawoy at Berkeley, I had been trained in the extended case method, a form of participant observation that requires four moves: from observer to participant; from one temporal moment and geographic location to others; from micro experience to the macro forces in which it is embedded; and from observed empirical practices to theories reconstructed to make sense of them.[68] In the mid to late 1990s, Burawoy and a group of graduate students, including myself, adapted this approach to study global processes through local ethnographic case studies.[69]

Entering the "field" for me meant, first, moving from my position as Northern feminist academic observer to that of participant in the universe(s) of Brazilian rural women's organizations and professionalized urban feminists. Second, my fieldwork led me to move from Berkeley to the coastal cities and rural backlands of Northeast Brazil, as well as other sites where Brazilian feminists gathered. It took place through multiple sojourns over the span of a decade. Third, the inquiry stretched outward from daily feminist practices to the larger material and discursive forces with which they engaged, whether theories like that of Joan Scott, global investment patterns, or the international aid policies of Northern donor agencies. Finally, I followed a zigzag course from theories of globalization, public spheres, and political agency to the ethnographic field and back again, seeking surprises—ways that what I was seeing might challenge conventional wisdom and push the insights of pre-existing scholarship in uncharted directions. I emerged with new understandings of globalization, of the transnational feminist political space, and of the threats confronted by counterpublics at the turn of the twentieth century.

The character of my fieldwork varied with the sites and time periods I was studying. Because of their different structures, social compositions, and trajectories, SOS Corpo and the MMTR offered distinctive points of access (and closure) to a feminist ethnographer from the global North. Their histories stretched from the late 1970s to the present and required research that was, at some moments, rooted in the ethnographic here and now, at others, in the memories of participants probed through interviews, and, at yet others, in the study of artifacts, documents, and newspaper accounts. These multiple modes of research provided different kinds of data, which are woven together in my narrative.

SOS Corpo, Recife

In the 1990s, SOS Corpo's offices were located in what was once a private home on a shady side street on the edge of Recife's hot and busy downtown. A wall blocked the sounds of traffic and hid the building from curious passersby. Those who came through the open gate and up to the house were buzzed into the building by a receptionist at a desk in the front hall. Visitors waited on the covered porch, just inside the door. Off the porch and off the hallway that led from the front door toward the back of the house were a series of small offices, furnished simply and shared by SOS coordinators, program staff, and administrative workers. A small alcove to one side housed an often cranky photocopy machine; across from it, a doorway led to a small kitchen. At the back of the house, an open porch, jokingly referred to as "the swimming pool" because of the bright tiles which covered the floor and walls, served as a meeting room. It was used not only by SOS staff members, but also by visiting researchers and by the Pernambucan Women's Forum, a coalition of local feminist groups that met regularly to plan events and campaigns. Beyond this space was a sunny backyard ringed by several small outbuildings—another office, a video library, and a documentation center, which held materials on women's health, sexuality, feminism, and other topics.

In my imaginings of this feminist workplace, I had expected to find staff members eating lunch together or socializing around the proverbial water cooler, but there was little time for relaxation. Phones rang incessantly and a steady stream of visitors came through the gate. For the most part, office doors were closed, and people were hard at work, doing research, producing materials on health issues, and preparing workshops or presentations. Over and above the already overwhelming demands of the NGO's programmatic work, there were endless grants to be written, budgets to be formulated, interim reports to be produced, and annual evaluations to be provided to the institution's multiple funding sources. Deadlines for all of these things were a constant source of stress. In addition to what the staff did at the office, they spent significant periods of time out of the office, flying to every corner of Brazil, and often abroad, where they held workshops and training sessions, consulted with state agencies and NGOs, attended feminist meetings and international conferences, and met with development agency and government representatives. Their itineraries and work schedules were dizzying.

In this context, private lives were jealously guarded. Though some staff members saw one another outside the office, by the 1990s, this was not as common as it had once been. In addition to the constraints of time and stress, geographic factors conspired against stronger social ties. The staff lived scattered around the Recife metropolitan area, whose massive traffic jams and ubiquitous street crime made travel from one neighborhood to another time-consuming and sometimes dangerous. Family responsibilities also kept many close to home, tending to aging parents or small children.

This was the scenario that I entered in the mid-1990s. I asked for, and was granted, permission to study the organization, its history, and its location in global networks. I sought means of participating in SOS's projects and was assigned the task of translating grant applications and, later, creating abstracts in Portuguese of the English language materials in the documentation center. I also attended workshops, presentations, and training sessions, organizational planning sessions, meetings with other NGOs, and feminist gatherings. In between, I conducted interviews with nearly all of the current staff members, as well as some of those who had moved on, and pored over SOS's publications and historical records. On occasion, I spent time with individuals in our off hours—at the beach, local bars, movie theaters, and *festas*—but these kinds of connections were uneven and limited by the forces described above. For this reason and because of the structure of work at the NGO, my observational data on SOS has a relatively formal, rather than an immediate and personal, feel. On the other hand, the organization's extensive documentation and its institutional culture provided many markers for memory, offering invaluable historical resources for my research.

MMTR, Serra Talhada

Because its membership was scattered across the countryside, the MMTR did not have a fixed site. Instead, the life of the organization stretched across a field of encounters in isolated rural homes, union halls, agricultural schools, urban conference centers, country churches, and the Northeast regional office, located in the town of Serra Talhada. Much of the "business" of the organization was conducted as well on long bus rides to regional or statewide workshops, over meals, or in late-night conversations at the end of a long day of meetings.

With this in mind, I organized my ethnographic research around days-long organizational encounters, moments when the members or their chosen representatives gathered for business meetings, educational workshops, or political and cultural events. On these occasions, I also interviewed MMTR participants, elected leaders, and their advisors—unpaid activists with more education and experience in union organizing, progressive church-based activism, or NGO work. I began with a focus on the local organization in the central *sertão*, but soon followed members to statewide and Northeast regional meetings and events, and traced the organization's varied relations with rural unions, urban feminists, local governments, state politicians, NGOs, funding agencies, and the Catholic Church.

The gatherings that I attended brought together anywhere from fifteen to several hundred women, who had often traveled long distances to attend. Smaller meetings of leaders from around the region were held in the Northeast regional office in Serra Talhada, where we camped out on the floor; larger *encontros* were held in schools or union training centers where we slept in dorm rooms filled with cots, covered by sturdy cotton blankets against the evening chill.

Lacking phones or other modes of communication across the long distances, most members had little or no contact between meetings. Their periodic encounters were marked by high spirits. As women arrived, they greeted one another joyously, exchanging news from home and tales of the trip. The nature of the gatherings themselves helped deepen these relationships. Even business meetings would always begin with rousing songs written by women in the movement and familiar to all. This would often be followed by a *dinamica*, an activity designed to break the ice and reconnect the group. Participants would dance together, massage one another's feet, or share a cherished dream. In educational workshops like the one on gender, leaders relied on small group discussions, role-playing, the use of artwork, and other popular education techniques learned in their years as progressive Catholic activists. It was an environment that made it easy to form relationships with my subjects and to participate in activities meaningful to them.

In between meetings, I made a number of other trips to the *sertão* from Recife, staying with one of the organization's founders in a *povoado*—a small community—near Serra Talhada. I attended local rural women's meetings, interviewed male union members who had been involved in (or resisted) the MMTR at different points, and read through the organization's archives. I also made my way over rutted roads to the homesteads of some of the key figures in the MMTR's history, some of whom, because of ill health, were no longer able to participate. These interviews gave me a sense not only of the early years of the movement, but also of the extreme hardships these women faced in their day-to-day lives.

The very nature of the MMTR made possible certain kinds of insight. As a grassroots membership organization, its activities were directed toward outreach to and engagement with its constituency. In discussions of women's health and sexuality, family relationships, and the future of small farming, the personal and the political were very much intertwined. I had many opportunities to hear and see how the women of the MMTR experienced gender and class relations and how they constructed their own forms of what I would call feminism—though many of them, perhaps, would name it differently.

My sporadic, but intense, contacts with the rural organization in a wide diversity of settings produced a somewhat different kind of data than I was able to gather at the urban NGO. My fieldnotes and interview transcripts were full of vivid descriptions and personal stories, as well as anecdotes that illustrated the MMTR's discourse and political strategies. On the other hand, reconstructing organizational history was sometimes difficult. My interviewees, perhaps unused to marking the passage of time in the ways that I was looking for or with a different sense of what was important, sometimes could not recall the sequence of events, who was present, or what they had said. The archives produced declarations and minutes from early meetings, but these were usually short on specifics, merely recording decisions or outcomes rather than offering descriptions of political processes. Unlike my understanding of SOS, I had a sketchier sense of MMTR history, but a richer set of data about the movement's political practices and the lives of its members.

Locating the Transnational

From my vantage point with each of these organizations, I looked outward, trying to see what their relations with "the global" might be. Clearly, their constituencies were suffering from a variety of economic assaults related to globalization: cuts in state subsidies, shifts in global investment patterns, monetary dislocations, and the inauguration of "free" trade on an unequal playing field, to name a few. But I soon became aware that each organization had other kinds of transnational relations as well. At SOS, a slow, but steady, stream of international visitors came through the door offering services or seeking the NGO's expertise in organizing around women's health. Faxes, emails, and newsletters from abroad poured in and phones rang with requests for information, invitations to conferences, and proposals for international collaborations. The flows went in the other direction as well. SOS members participated in global networks, traveled to feminist meetings outside Brazil, and sought funding from agencies based in Europe and North America. The organization was, I discovered, embedded in a dense web of transnational relations. Their very language and the issues that they took on reflected these ties. Discourses of "gender," as well as the view of women's bodies as a locus of empowerment, were linked to feminist conversations across many countries at the end of the twentieth century.

At first glance, the MMTR had appeared to be cut off from these global circuits of feminist discourse and practice, isolated in a remote rural hinterland. But my sojourns in the *sertão* soon taught me otherwise. The discussions of "gender" described at the beginning of this chapter made evident one kind of transnational connection—the travels of feminist theories from one part of the world to another. But there were other signs as well: the money acquired from a European funding agency through the efforts of an Italian friend of the movement, the video filmed by a young North American volunteer a few years earlier, contacts made with rural women in neighboring countries at a Latin American feminist conference held in 1985, visits from a German supporter based in Recife, and the presence of two representatives of the MMTR's Northeast umbrella organization at the 1995 U.N. Conference on Women in Beijing, to name a few. The rural women's organization too was a participant in transnational political relationships that linked it to feminist movements around the world. Some of these connections involved direct contacts, while others occurred through urban Brazilian intermediaries, like SOS Corpo, with more access to communications technology and the resources to travel. These NGOs served as brokers of a sort, appropriating and reinterpreting feminist discourses from afar and redistributing them within Brazil, where they were again reinterpreted and transformed by working-class movements like the MMTR. SOS and other NGOs also helped less well-connected women's organizations make contacts and expand their influence beyond Brazil.

Observing these processes, I worked outward from the day-to-day practices of each of the organizations I had chosen to study, seeking the threads that linked them across borders to what I came to understand as a larger feminist political space. At the same time, in the tradition of the extended case method, I looked for the anomalies in my fieldwork, the ways that the activism and networks of these organizations challenged conventional academic wisdom. My conclusions, summarized below, build on and extend theories about globalization, social movements, and public spheres.

SOLIDARITY, POWER, AND THE FEMINIST COUNTERPUBLIC

This book illustrates how global processes are constituted by links among social actors based in particular local sites. Globalization is not the set of overwhelming and anonymous forces so often depicted in popular accounts and scholarly literature. Rather, globalization "happens" in geographically specific locations, and the players who enact it—whether rural women or development agency staff—represent particular sets of interests and identities. By analyzing global processes through the lens of the local, this book makes visible the tensions, contradictions, and forms of active resistance that form an integral part of global connections.

In tandem with the spread of capital and neoliberal politics, social movements have also extended across borders. Transnational social movements are best understood not only as structured institutions that engage in formalized campaigns, coalitions, and events, but also as cultural actors who practice less visible forms of cultural politics as they create collective identities and stitch together alliances.[70]

In this study I argue that social movements, like globalization itself, are constituted by relationships—among constituencies, allies, immediate targets, and larger institutions, such as states and markets.[71] Linkages occur at multiple scales, from the local to the transnational. The point at which these multiple connections intersect is the collective identity of a given movement, whether individual organization, local alliance, discursive community, or transnational network. Among the relations most important for the survival of a social movement are the ties it maintains with those whose identities and interests overlap, at least partially, with its own. In the case presented here, the formal and informal alliances among feminist and women's movements played a key role in sustaining and defining the organizations and individuals that I studied. The fabric of their connections is the subject of this book.

The diverse and geographically scattered feminists described here together form what is known as a "counterpublic"—an oppositional space in which networks, organizations, and individuals who share certain values or identities engage with one another around a core theme.[72] Though here I focus on gender relations as the common thread of concern, there are multiple intersecting counterpublics, which challenge dominant discourses and practices in areas such as race or class, ethnicity or immigration status, sexuality or global inequalities.[73] Their members articulate collective identities, debate discourses and strategies, and construct alternative forms of social relations with one another. These forms of activist culture serve both as a means of and as preparation for engaging with dominant public spheres.[74]

Counterpublics are broader, more internally heterogeneous, and less coherent than the term "social movement" usually implies. Their boundaries are defined, not by fully shared strategic visions, but by the choices of social actors to engage with one another in some form, however partial or tentative. Though they may construct solidarities, counterpublics are traversed by the same social fissures that divide the larger society.[75] Like the feminists I studied, participants may share subaltern status on one axis of oppression, such as gender, but have varying relations to privilege on others, such as race, class, or national origin.[76]

This study highlights yet another layer of internal fractures that challenge the integrity of the feminist counterpublic—those embedded in contemporary forms of globalization. Whereas until relatively recently publics were confined within national frontiers, in the last few decades, social space has transnationalized in tandem with the global extension of capitalist markets.[77] The Brazilian women in this book now define their gender politics in relations with differently situated counterparts scattered from neighboring communities to faraway countries, as feminist discursive space has spilled across not only social divisions, but also national borders.[78] Once distant facts of inequality have now become sets of directly experienced power relations between allies. U.S.-based gender theorists and rural women from the *sertão*, middle-class Brazilian activists and feminist funding agency representatives now engage with one another within the same political space.

Most literature on counterpublics emphasizes their discursive or textual nature.[79] I argue that the material and discursive dimensions of counterpublics cannot be separated. The feminist alliances described in this study revolved around meanings, as well as around tangible resources; they demanded from participants their active engagement, as well as their cognitive attention. In the process, discursive and material assets intertwined and constituted one another as forms of power. Rural women leveraged discourses of local authenticity to win funds from international aid agencies that would further their cause; in turn, Northern dollars came embedded in market-oriented meanings that restructured movement practices in unanticipated ways.

Given the differences and inequalities among participants, relations within counterpublics are often tense and conflictive. This study finds repeated instances of the defense of narrow institutional interests and the exercise of power among supposed allies. International donors identified with feminism imposed their agendas on Brazilian feminist grantees through timelines and evaluation criteria; working-class women's organizations accused professionalized women's NGOs of building their reputations at the expense of the poor; and women within the agricultural union hierarchy defended their institutional authority from the claims of independent rural women's organizations.

However, though the operations of power and interests certainly explain some aspects of the relations within the feminist counterpublic, they do not tell the whole story. Social movement alliances may often be contentious, but they are not simply reducible to competitive fields within which individuals or institutions pursue their own advancement at one another's expense. In this book, the Brazilian NGO, SOS Corpo, and its feminist donors made common cause around advocacy of funding for women's empowerment in the global South; members of the rural women's organization, the MMTR, collaborated with professionalized urban feminists to produce knowledge about the sexual and reproductive experiences of women in the countryside; and the MMTR worked alongside agricultural unions to develop ecologically and economically sustainable farming practices. Though counterpublics are defined in part by the power relations among members, they are fundamentally hybrid spaces where collaboration and collective action, as well as conflict and self-interested maneuvering, take place.[80]

In fact, the distribution of power and resources within a public does not always follow predictable patterns. While more economically advantaged feminisms often establish discursive parameters, and control flows of resources, their hegemonies are only partial and relatively short-lived. Power within counterpublics is destabilized by the way political spaces organized around distinctive issues and identities intersect with one another. The women in my study, like most people, straddled multiple counterpublics, including those organized around class, regional identity, gender, and anti-imperialism. Access to a variety of discourses gave them alternate sources of political capital and provided tools to critique power relations in other counterpublics. Rural women, for example, drew on discourses of class to negotiate with middle-class feminists; in turn, professionalized activists critiqued the stance of development agency staff, using the language of the Marxist left, a counterpublic in which they also participated. The outcome of these dynamics was a feminist counterpublic characterized by constant negotiations, shifting hegemonies, and fragile unities.

The transnational feminist public, like other counterpublics, plays a fundamental role in the articulation of oppositional perspectives, even as it is riven with internal contradictions. It provides a space partially sheltered from the corrosive effects of dominant discourse, in which alternative cultures and values can be nurtured and new identities can be constructed. Publics are internally heterogeneous; the differences that constitute them, as Calhoun observes, are one part of their reason to exist.[81] Diversity among participants may sometimes produce internal dissonance, but it may also lead to constructive debates and creative synergies for marginalized constituencies. Inequalities between members suggest a greater hurdle, yet this study also finds that, within counterpublics, issues of representation can be disputed and accountabilities can be demanded by less apparently powerful participants. It is a space, in short, where the internal democracy so crucial to social movement alliances can be struggled for, if not always won.

But there are clouds on the horizon. The kind of hybrid social arena I am describing, in which collective action coexists with self-interest, and hegemonies are tenuous and shifting, is a historical phenomenon, not a timeless category. While globalization produces intersections among previously disparate publics, multiplying possible identities and forms of politics, it also facilitates the mobility of economic capital. Counterpublics that aspire to fostering democratic solidarities persist, but the power of the global market to restructure the relations among feminist movements puts them increasingly at risk.[82]

CULTURAL FLOWS, POLITICAL CONNECTIONS, ECONOMIC TIES

Chapter 2 moves from theory to history, tracing the emergence of a transnational feminist counterpublic from the perspective of Latin America. I begin with the first stirrings of feminist activism in the region in the nineteenth century, arguing that Latin American feminisms were both internally diverse and dissimilar in important ways from the movements that developed in the global North. The chapter then traces cross-border connections, from early international contacts among feminists, through Pan American activism in the first half of the twentieth century, to the transnational feminist collaborations of the 1970s and beyond. The story illustrates the painstaking and uneven process of constructing relationships among feminists; it also provides a historical perspective to the challenges to sustaining solidarities across difference and inequality.

The argument of the book is then developed in four ethnographic chapters, which take us inside the counterpublic to see how this oppositional space is actually constituted, what sustains it, and what risks it is facing in the contemporary period. I focus on the *relations* among different members of the transnational feminist public, rather than on individual organizations per se. Each substantive chapter trains an eye on the links among a different set of actors, and each foregrounds a distinctive kind of connection—cultural, political, or economic (see Figure 1.3). Though each of these connections could exist between any pairing of feminist sites, in fact, each dominates and is more visible in the context of the relationship between a particular set of social movement actors. I discuss them in roughly chronological order, beginning with discursive connections between Northern feminists and SOS Corpo in the late 1970s to mid-1980s. This is then followed by two chapters on the relations of negotiation and exchange of political resources between the MMTR and its two principle allies: agricultural unions in the 1980s (Chapter 4), and urban feminists and rural unions in the mid-1980s to late 1990s (Chapter 5). The final ethnographic chapter examines flows of aid and commodifying practices between both Brazilian organizations and development agencies in the United States and Europe from the late 1980s to the late 1990s.[83]

The moves from primarily cultural, through mainly political, to predominantly economic relations represent a movement through time as feminist movements developed. The shifts in substance also reflect progressively greater obstacles for the less advantaged actors as they sought simultaneously to construct solidarities and negotiate the power relations among feminists and with other allies. While Northern discourses were relatively easy to reinterpret in a Brazilian context, hierarchical political relationships, consummated through institutions, proved a greater challenge, and asserting autonomy in the face of economic dependence was the most difficult task of all.

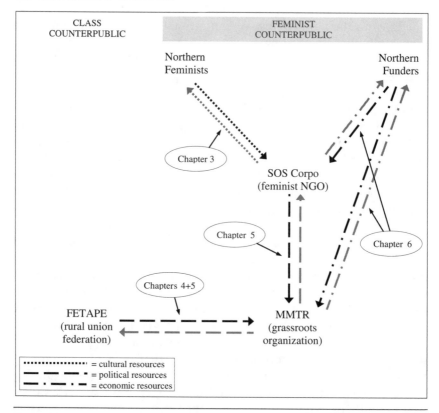

Figure 1.3 Relations in and beyond the Transnational Feminist Counterpublic

In Chapter 3, the cultural connections among members of the feminist counterpublic are the point of departure. The chapter examines the relationship between feminists based in the United States and Europe and SOS Corpo, as a professionalized Brazilian feminist institution, and exposes the ways power was embedded and disrupted in discursive flows from North to South. Second-wave feminist discourses slipped—or, rather, were pulled—across borders long before material resources, more entwined in institutional relationships, had a chance to follow.[84] While feminists in Pernambuco had their own histories of gender-based politics, the discursive terms were set—at least initially—by Northern movements privileged by their greater access to material resources and somewhat earlier organizational experiences with late-twentieth-century activism.

The encounter was contested; Northeast Brazilian feminists did not simply incorporate conceptions imported from the United States and Europe, but rather waged a cultural struggle to establish their own parallel but distinctive feminist identities. Members of SOS Corpo selectively appropriated activist discourses and academic theories from their allies in the global North, translating and reconstructing them through their practices, as the NGO engaged with discourses, constituencies, and institutions local to Brazil.

Discourses cannot travel on their own volition; they require translators to help them cross borders and set down roots in new places. Through the process of translation, SOS Corpo both defended its local political autonomy and forged transnational discursive connections. At the same time, I find, discourses did not move as easily from South to North as they did in reverse, a reflection of enduring global disparities.

In Chapters 4 and 5, we move from cultural connections to the political relationships among social movement organizations, where power within the counterpublic takes on a more institutional form and inequalities pose greater challenges to feminist alliances. The chapters take the MMTR as their focus, and compare its two most important political relationships: in Chapter 4, with the federation of rural unions in the Northeast interior and, in Chapter 5, with professionalized feminism in the form of SOS Corpo, as well as with the unions at a later historical moment. Each relationship linked the MMTR to a distinctive counterpublic: While the one was a local liaison founded on class commonalities, the other was an alliance around gender solidarity which had transnational dimensions.

Chapter 4 takes us into the vast semi-arid *sertão*, introducing both the rural women's movement and the agricultural unions from which it originated. Throughout the 1980s, the MMTR drew on a series of resources, both tangible and symbolic, to critique gender inequalities and negotiate for its autonomy with the male-dominated unions. The women's movement encountered increasing resistance as its own influence spread, clashing with the gendered prejudices of union leaders and threatening a longstanding "welfarist" model of unionism linked closely to the state. The power of social movement resources, I argue, is context specific, depending on the political relationships in which they are deployed. In this early historical moment, and in the context of the MMTR's local class-based alliance, the resources available to the organization had only limited effect.

The story, told in Chapter 5, of the rural movement's links to professionalized urban feminists is quite different. If, in relationship to the unions, rural women were devalued partners in a class struggle, in their relations with SOS Corpo they were prized allies in a gendered revolution. The legitimacy attached to their large rural constituency had both political and instrumental value to the urban feminist organization. For women in NGOs, access to this grassroots base of support was indispensable, both to their feminist aspirations and to relations with the funding agencies that guaranteed their organizational survival. The MMTR's more direct and outspoken negotiating stance with SOS reflected the power that these symbolic resources gave them in relationships with feminists in Recife and beyond. In the 1990s, as the unions too entered global circuits, where discourses of gender and funding circulated in tandem, the MMTR's female constituency gained both political and exchange value for the union. The balance of power in the relationship began to shift and the MMTR's challenges to male comrades shifted from covert to confrontational.

Taken together, the two chapters show how distinctive counterpublics offer movements located at their intersections discursive tools for critique and negotiation with their different allies. They also illuminate the effects of globalization on social movement relationships. As movement alliances stretch across borders, locally rooted forms of leverage are endowed with new symbolic value.

Chapter 6, the last substantive chapter, highlights the connection between feminist staff members in U.S. and European funding agencies, on the one hand, and each of the Northeast Brazilian women's organizations that I studied, on the other. The two organizations represent distinctive paths taken by many Latin American feminist organizations and women's movements. The chapter foregrounds the relationship of SOS Corpo to development agencies and to the flows of funds that these agencies facilitated, using the MMTR's experience as a comparative case.

SOS's access to international aid developed in counterpoint with its growing engagement with the state. By the 1990s, the organization had been transformed from penniless collective to professionalized NGO and had begun to shift its strategy from working with local grassroots organizations to lobbying national and international policy-makers. The MMTR, on the other hand, like many other working-class organizations, struggled to get the attention of faraway agencies and received only sporadic international donations. The rural movement retained a structure based largely on members' volunteer efforts and an identity as grassroots social movement rather than professionalized institution.

As feminists in Northeast Brazil entered international funding circuits and took on new discourses and practices, the chapter argues, they were increasingly drawn into what I call a "social movement market." Their allies in development agencies in the North faced growing pressure to justify their outlays to advocacy projects in the global South; they passed the pressure on to grantees in the form of intensified demands for immediate quantifiable results and locally generated income. As a consequence, the more well-funded feminists in countries like Brazil became brokers of transnational resources and purveyors of feminist goods and services to working-class clients. The creation of these kinds of market relations within the feminist counterpublic threatened to undermine the very solidarities that gave it meaning. In response, both organizations in this study used their local power to contest the hegemony of the development industry and to defend their autonomy vis-à-vis their feminist supporters within it. In doing so, they emphasized their mutual collaborations and resisted the pull toward commodified social movement relationships.

The four central chapters trace the relationships in the transnational feminist public across time from the early 1980s to the end of the century (see Table 1.1). They follow the displacement of these relations from primarily (but never only) cultural, to political, to economic terrain, as well as from local, to national, to global space—and back again to the local. As some women's movements in Northeast Brazil became increasingly

Table 1.1 Conceptual Overview of Chapters

	Chapter 3	**Chapters 4 & 5**	**Chapter 6**
Time Period	Early 1980s	1980s–1990s	Late 1980s–1990s
Nature of Resources	Cultural	Political	Economic
Primary Space of Feminist NGO Engagement	Local	National	Global
Level of NGO Professionalization	Low	Medium	High
Tendency in Feminist Relationships	Collaboration	Negotiation/ Exchange	Commodification

entangled with the state and international funding circuits, their structures grew more formalized. In the process, relationships within the feminist public that had begun with a more purely collaborative spirit shifted subtly to an emphasis on processes of negotiation and exchange, and became ever more endangered by the commodifying pressures of the market.[85] In the face of these compelling forces, the women's movements in this study engaged in valiant efforts to sustain their political autonomy and preserve the principled feminist alliances they had so painstakingly constructed.

The three kinds of dynamic connections described here work together to constitute a transnational feminist public characterized by both relations of mutual solidarity and tensions around the growing inequalities within it. In the final chapter, I argue that the counterpublic is a historical phenomenon that is increasingly at risk, endangered by the extension of neoliberal capitalism into wider arenas of social life. The incursions of discourses and practices of the market into transnational feminist relationships over the past few decades threaten to upset the delicate balance between power and solidarity that has so far prevailed in this hybrid political space, turning political alliances into commodified exchanges. But markets are more vulnerable than they may sometimes appear, and they are facing new kinds of challenges from the outside as well as from within. In short, the demise of the counterpublic is not a foregone conclusion. Its future, I argue, depends on the political struggles of feminists, North and South, to defend it as a site for democratic debate and the articulation of egalitarian forms of social relations.

2

UNEASY ALLIES

The Making of a Transnational Feminist Counterpublic

I hope that at least *Mujeres de América* may help to form a new concept of "patria" that is progress; "patria" that is peace; "patria" that is unity.... We are working with faith, with love for the time where we will be one great country, a "patria" without frontiers.

(*Mujeres de América*, Argentina, July–August, 1933)[1]

We were received in the United States, not as if we were representatives of unimportant countries as happens at the international congresses of the Old World, but with a frank cordiality and with the same consideration that has marked the relations of women of the Americas since the days of our pioneering foremothers.

(Bertha Lutz, Federação Brasileira pelo Progresso Feminino, Rio de Janeiro, 1926)[2]

I, in the United States, see and know what you don't know and don't see.... The North American women have won all their rights and are now allies of the domineering politics of their men. They have not purified politics.... One thing are the *yanquis* and we are another.

(Elena Arizmendi, Liga Internacional de Mujeres Ibéricas e Hispanoamericanas, writing from New York, 1930)[3]

Women's movements were among the earliest social movements to construct international alliances and they have created and sustained extensive cross-border networks for more than a century. The dreams of unity and the mixed experiences of collaboration, expressed by the Latin American feminists of an earlier generation quoted above, speak to some of the many contradictions involved in the process of constructing connections across national, linguistic, cultural, class, ethnic, racial, economic, and other kinds of boundaries.

From their beginnings in the nineteenth century, national feminist counterpublics in Latin America were linked with one another, first through discursive and personal connections and, somewhat later, through organizational ties. These early contacts involved the crossing of borders, but not the transcendence of national differences in any significant way. Though there were mutual influences and small groups of activists took on common strategic projects, most feminist movements were firmly rooted in local cultures and political systems, and their international gatherings were sporadic and limited in their reach. It was not until the late twentieth century that feminist relations stretched to include more distant allies and took on a more transnational character, as economies and polities became increasingly implicated with one another and communication and travel became more widely accessible. Simultaneously, the forces of militarism, fundamentalism, environmental destruction, and market relations reshaped the experiences of a wide variety of women in overlapping, though not identical, ways.

This chapter traces the development of one segment of the transnational feminist counterpublic, viewed from the perspective of Latin America. I begin with the origins of Latin American feminisms and their incipient international connections within the region in the late nineteenth century, then follow their early encounters with feminists from the global North and the gradual and uneven transnationalization of the feminist political space across the twentieth century.

EARLY LATIN AMERICAN FEMINISMS
AND THE INTERNATIONAL ARENA

There is a popular misconception that Latin American feminisms have, historically, simply followed the example of more "advanced" movements in the global North. In fact, while movements in the region had their origins in a similar period and drew on some of the same discursive influences as those in the industrialized North, they blazed their own set of independent trails. As time went on, there were increasing opportunities for exchange with their counterparts to the North, but influences were multidirectional and Latin American feminisms were far from pale and arrested imitations of those in the United States and Europe.

In the nineteenth century, the republican ideals of the French Revolution were appropriated both by Creole patriots struggling for independence from colonial status and by women aspiring to inclusion in the national project. In 1824, a petition to the government of Zacatecas in Mexico asked that the title of "citizen" be extended to women, some of whom had also fought for independence.[4] By the 1840s, articles advocating education for women were appearing in the press with frequency in many countries; thirty years later, feminist periodicals throughout the region took up the cause of educational and legal reform. Rather than viewing themselves as backward on gender issues, Latin American feminists of the time saw themselves as setting an example for their European counterparts. In an 1873 issue of *O Sexo Feminino*, commemorating Brazil's independence day, Motta Diniz wrote, "It will be seen that America will give the cry of independence for women, showing the Old World what it means to be civilized, that women are as apt for education as young men."[5]

The class base and ideologies of women's rights movements in Latin America were diverse. In the cities of the Southern Cone countries, where secular and reformist influences were particularly strong, the advent of organized activism was linked to the emerging middle classes. In Argentina, Uruguay, Chile, and Brazil, schoolteachers, many of them graduates of newly established teacher training schools, formed the core of feminist movements, which also included a small group of other professionals and some factory workers.[6] Though bourgeois liberal feminism was the dominant model in this part of Latin America, in some countries, such as Argentina and Uruguay, socialist and anarchist women also organized strong feminist movements. In countries with more polarized class structures, such as Mexico and Cuba, feminism was linked to class-based revolutionary movements.[7]

In spite of the differences within the region, there were also commonalities that set Latin American feminists apart from their counterparts in the United States and Europe. Feminists in the North were mainly concerned with political rights but, for most Latin American activists, social and economic issues were the primary concerns until the 1920s. Suffrage for men as well as women was severely restricted, and there was no history of reform through the ballot box. Given the dominance of the Catholic Church in the region, many potential supporters on the left feared that enfranchised women would fall under the sway of conservative clerics and that their votes would only further entrench dominant patterns of inequality. Evidence to the contrary was slow to shake this paternalistic stance.[8]

Rather than fighting for suffrage, most Latin American feminists turned their energies to issues such as education for women, legal protections within marriage, the right to divorce, and equal pay. Socialists advocated for protectionist legislation to ensure that women workers would not face the same grueling conditions on the job as did men. "Maternalist" feminists, meanwhile, insisted on women's particular responsibilities for family welfare and demanded state support for working-class mothers as a means to their empowerment.[9]

The early international connections among feminisms in different Latin American countries, precursors of a regional counterpublic, took a variety of forms. Individual feminists made personal contact with one another through visits and correspondence, seeking advice and moral support and often acting as "godmothers" to one another's organizations.[10] More formalized links were initiated at a series of Latin American Scientific Congresses held in the Southern Cone countries between 1898 and 1908. Educated men and women came together in these meetings to discuss social problems, and feminists lobbied to include issues, such as child welfare and nutrition, that traditionally fell under feminine purview.[11]

The cohort of professional women who met at these male-dominated conferences played a part in organizing the first Latin American feminist gathering—the *Congreso Feminino Internacional* (International Feminist Congress)—in Buenos Aires in 1910.[12] Over two hundred participants from diverse class backgrounds and ideological orientations debated issues from the legal rights of married women to the prevention of infanticide, and passed a series of proposals from socialist representatives.[13] While some Congress resolutions enjoyed widespread backing, the demand for special protections for women workers went down to defeat in favor of an "equal rights" position.[14] The controversies over strategy and goals at this congress foreshadowed the kinds of discursive struggle and collaboration that would resurface toward the end of the century in transnational feminist gatherings.

Feminist "Missionaries" from the North

The move to create links between feminisms in different parts of the world came from multiple directions. As Latin American women reached across borders, so too did those located in the early industrializing countries. The difference was that feminisms in Europe and the United States were located at a different set of coordinates within the global political economy, had greater access to resources, and were propelled by a colonial discourse that imbued their internationalism with a sense of paternalism that ranged from the overtly imperious to the more subtly superior.

In the nineteenth century, North American and European women were active in international campaigns, such as those led by the antislavery and temperance movements, and feminists also agitated for the abolition of prostitution, Chinese footbinding, and the trafficking of European women to the colonies, among other issues.[15] Beginning in the late nineteenth century, they formed a series of international organizations with head-quarters in the United States and Europe to promote women's rights and social reform around the world.[16] At the turn of the century, European and North American feminists set out with missionary zeal to organize the rest of the world, and affiliates sprung up in their wake.[17]

The protagonists of these early organizing efforts were inspired by a "spirit" of internationalism.[18] But from early on, the divisions of class, nation, and empire were deeply embedded in feminists' discourses and practices. The international organizations described above were domi-nated by members from the more economically powerful countries of the global North, while their largely middle- and upper-class leadership reflected the class hierarchies within those societies. The economic and social resources to which these women had access were, in fact, an im-portant factor fueling their international connections, making possible their speaking tours, visits, and international conferences.[19]

Women in less privileged locations in the global North were also building international constituencies, though they faced greater hostility and had less economic backing. The International Council of Women of the Darker Races, founded in 1920 by members of the National Association of Colored Women's Clubs in the United States, and col-leagues from a few other countries, aimed to investigate and improve the status of women in Haiti, India, and African nations, among other places.[20] In Europe, members of the German Social Democratic Party, the largest socialist party of the day, organized a Socialist Women's In-ternational whose founding conference attracted representatives from fifteen countries.[21]

Inequality among women was deeply embedded in the structures of international political and economic relations, and the discursive uni-verses in which activists moved. In spite of their formal political exclusion in their nations of origin, most feminists from the global North were active participants in the colonial project. Burton argues, for example, that British suffragists demonstrated their own fitness for citizenship through their defense of race and nation and through a sense of superior-ity to "native" culture, shared with British men.[22] Even the International Council of Women of the Darker Races took a compromised approach, praising the French government for its policy against discrimination while choosing to disregard colonial exploitation of the very women in whom they hoped to inspire racial pride.[23] In her research on first- wave international feminist organizing, Rupp revises Wallerstein:

From the perspective of the women in charge, Western and Northern Europe and the United States represented the core, Southern and Eastern Europe a semiperiphery, and Latin America, the Middle East, Asia and Africa the periphery of a feminist world system.[24]

Though significant shifts occurred, the consequences of this formative stance reverberated in feminist relationships over the next century.

Pan American Women's Organizing

The first women's organization to cross the divide between Latin and North America, bringing together members from both regions, was born out of their common exclusion from a Pan American Scientific Congress held in 1916. A keynote speaker at the founding meeting of the Pan American Union of Women stressed the commonalities between North and South and called for hemispheric cooperation: "We, the women of North and South America, which possess similar conceptions of individual rights and constitutional government, possess a common duty to mankind which we must not ignore."[25]

The Pan American feminist movement used its meetings to draw attention to women's issues, including suffrage, and to call for peaceful solutions to conflict as the world grew closer to a second world war. Its lobbying efforts followed the Latin American precedent of bringing feminist issues to the early Scientific Congresses. In like manner, the Pan American movement pressed the Inter-American Conferences of American States to incorporate the rights of women in their mandate. In 1928, the Inter-American Commission of Women (IACW), the first governmental organization in the world dedicated to the rights of women, was founded as a result of their demands.[26]

Through the IACW, the movement set its sights on the broader international arena, in a move that would be echoed in the transnational feminist organizing around the United Nations, beginning in the 1970s. Early Pan American feminists lobbied the League of Nations to address women's issues, such as the rights of married women to choose their own nationalities, regardless of those of their husbands. Later, at the founding of the United Nations in 1945, a delegation that included Brazilian Bertha Lutz and other IACW members from the Dominican Republic and Mexico successfully insisted that the U.N. Charter commit the organization to addressing gender inequities, by including the phrase "the equal rights of men and women."[27]

North-South relations within the Pan American movement reflected a mixture of tensions and goodwill that foreshadowed patterns in late-twentieth-century feminist relationships. Some Latin American leaders, like Lutz, found welcome at Pan American women's gatherings and developed close working relations with a number of their North American counterparts.

U.S. feminists varied in their relations with Latin American women. Some prominent North American leaders were explicitly ethnocentric. Carrie Chapman Catt, first president of the International Women's Suffrage Association and leader of the Pan American Women's Association, expressed this stance in her reflections on a visit to Uruguay and Argentina:

> The climate and the inherited racial inadequacies make the people languorous and willing to put things off until tomorrow. They eat too much.... The waste of food is shocking. In after dinner coffee cups people drink from 3 to 5 lumps of sugar.... Sweets are plentiful and desserts are very sweet. The women are therefore fat and probably less easy to move.[28]

Others, like Mary Wilhelmine Williams, a historian who dedicated her life to promoting inter-American understanding, argued that the "backwardness" of the region was based on historical and geographic factors, rather than innate racial or cultural inadequacies.[29] Nonetheless, she shared with other Northern feminists a belief in the superiority of U.S. institutions.

Disregarding the rich history of activism in the region, most North American feminists saw themselves as leading the women of the South into the feminist struggle. Many also aimed to promote the kind of Pan Americanism that they hoped would bind the hemisphere together and act as a counterweight to the growing nationalism and anti-imperialism in the region in the 1920s and 1930s.[30]

Latin American women increasingly asserted their autonomy vis-à-vis their counterparts in the global North. Alliances began to erode in 1920 when women in the United States won the vote. Their victory affirmed the conviction of U.S. feminists that theirs was a higher form of civilization and it undermined the shared interests that had masked North-South inequalities in the hemisphere. As their political systems had undergone reform, Latin American women had incorporated demands for suffrage into their platforms, but now found their Northern allies distracted by other priorities. The persistence of U.S. intervention in the region, with the support of many female voters, was further evidence, for Latin American feminists, that gender bonds could be trumped by national chauvinism.[31]

While a number of Latin Americans continued to work within the Pan American women's movement, others opposed the overbearing influence of feminists from Western Europe and the United States. In the early 1920s, together with allies from the Iberian Peninsula, some liberal feminists formed the *Liga Internacional de Mujeres Ibéricas e Hispanoamericanas* (International League of Iberian and Hispanic-American Women), an organization that served as a nationalist alternative to the U.S.-dominated IACW into the 1930s.[32]

Historians have described U.S. feminist movements as being "in abeyance" from the 1920s into the 1960s, and it is widely assumed that women's organizing around the globe falls into the same framework of "waves" used to describe North American movements.[33] Historians of Latin American feminisms, however, argue that the movements in the region do not conform to identical patterns of periodization.[34] While U.S. movements lost steam after the suffrage victory in 1920, in many countries in Latin America, the struggle for the vote, as well as for marriage and employment rights, continued through the 1950s.[35] Their influence grew in this period as conventional political parties began to view women as an important constituency and increasingly sought to recruit them to their ranks. Whereas World War II drew U.S. feminists away from women's issues, in Latin America the movements were not subsumed in the war effort to the same degree. Even as the Cold War was launched in the late 1940s, delegates from women's clubs throughout the hemisphere gathered at the *Primer Congreso Inter-Americano de Mujeres* (First Inter-American Women's Congress) in Guatemala City, where they spoke out against militarism and the diversion of resources from development and human services to weapons of war, as well as insisting that women's voices be heard at international fora.[36]

By the late 1950s, according to Miller, glaring socioeconomic inequalities and the drift toward dictatorship in the region posed dramatic challenges to the liberal reformism that had underpinned prevailing models of feminism in Latin America. Male-dominated revolutionary movements took center stage, beginning with the overthrow of Batista in Cuba in 1959. In the face of these forces, the vitality of feminist organizing waned briefly before re-emerging in new forms in the early 1970s.[37]

The historical record shows that Latin American feminisms, while resurfacing slightly after the North's "second wave," were not, in fact, derivative of U.S. and European models. They had their own rhythms, concerns, strategies, and array of discursive influences, only one of which was the feminism developing to the North. These elements varied from one national context to the next, producing a diversity of movements which, nevertheless, shared the commonalities of colonial history and marginality in the global economy. The links formed within the region ranged from discursive exchanges to personal connections, and from strategic debates to institutional affiliations and coordinated campaigns. Though they may not have recognized it, the U.S.-based international organizing efforts of the twentieth century relied on and extended already long-established relationships among Latin American feminists, as well as borrowing from their tactical repertoire.

In the early cross-border alliances within and beyond Latin America we can already see the kinds of differences and solidarities, tensions and negotiations that characterize transnational organizing in the late twentieth and early twenty-first centuries. As in the more recent period, some feminists targeted international institutions, while others prioritized organizing at home. Some institutionalized their connections, while others preferred more informal relations. Some had access to abundant material resources, while others did not. Some worked through or with social movements around class or other issues, while others saw gender as their primary arena of struggle.

In their first century, feminisms developed largely, if not entirely, within national borders, despite the aspirations of some to create a "*patria* without frontiers." Over time, the increasing efforts to create long-distance alliances would produce a new transnational phenomenon.

FROM INTERNATIONAL TO TRANSNATIONAL FEMINISMS

In the late twentieth century, feminist cross-border connections intensified, creating a dense web of affiliations through which discourses and practices were debated and strategies were constructed. What had been a series of national counterpublics, linked by the border crossing of a relatively small group, now increasingly overlapped to create a transnational political space, which embraced a broad range of social actors. Certainly, the process was uneven across classes, countries, and continents, and states continued to play a key role as interlocutors for feminist movements. But, more and more, feminists engaged around similar issues or even specific campaigns, and certain common discourses began to emerge across widely scattered locales. For some, a feminist culture that transcended national boundaries was in the making, an extension, perhaps, of the earlier experience of those who participated in the Pan American women's movement.

The thickening alliances among feminists were facilitated by a series of interrelated factors. First, the fact that "scattered" global economic and political hegemonies were ever more linked with one another meant that movements in different places increasingly confronted similar or related social practices or institutions.[38] Though they took distinctive forms in different places, global production systems, neoliberal policies, militarized societies, and religious fundamentalisms posed dangers for women that often demanded coordinated responses. The greater ease and lower cost of travel and communications, in turn, helped facilitate their coalitions. Whereas the precursors of late-twentieth-century feminists had had to rely on letters and infrequent conferences, it was now possible to hold regular international meetings and to maintain ongoing electronic contact with distant allies.

Finally, the United Nations played a key role in the promotion of transnational linkages among feminists in the latter part of the twentieth century. In part due to the advocacy of development activists in international institutions, in part to demands from feminist movements outside them, the United Nations declared 1975 to 1985 the International Women's Decade.[39] The next ten years were punctuated by international conferences on women—1975, Mexico; 1980, Copenhagen; 1985, Nairobi—and followed, ten years later, by the Fourth World Women's Conference in Beijing.[40] These events provided a powerful stimulus for feminist organizing around the world, with the conference in Mexico having a particularly important impact in Latin America.[41]

Not only did the official intergovernmental meetings—after intense lobbying—produce documents on women's issues that helped legitimize their demands back home, but they attracted thousands of members of nongovernmental and grassroots organizations from all over the world to parallel gatherings. These unofficial events—part movement conference, part celebration—formed the basis for ongoing networks among feminists around the world. As the networks extended and intersected, a transnational counterpublic began to germinate.

The character of relations among participants in this newly created space varied over time, from a contentious field in the late 1970s to a hybrid formation of collaboration and conflict from the mid-1980s to the beginning of the twenty-first century. The first two U.N. women's conferences, in 1975 and 1980, were dominated by tensions between North and South. Feminists from the industrialized countries insisted on the primacy of the kind of struggles for political and legal equality between men and women that they had been waging in Europe and North America. Their counterparts from Asia, Africa, and Latin America, on the other hand, demanded attention to the devastating economic and social conditions—such as poverty, debt, and dependency—that characterized their regions, and they rejected the imposition of narrow models of feminism that did not reflect what they saw as more pressing concerns.[42]

By 1985, in Nairobi, though differences were still apparent, the animosities among feminists had begun to ease.[43] Despite continued Northern dominance of the NGO gathering, women from the South, who by then composed 60 percent of the attendees, played a more significant role than they had in previous conferences.[44] The accelerating spread of global capital and the rise of the "New Policy Agenda," with its prescription of so-called "free trade," shrinking state budgets, and belt-tightening for the world's poor, had made inequality in the 1980s ever more glaring.[45] A variety of religious fundamentalisms were also on the rise, and women, North and South, faced assaults on hard-won rights.

In the United States, critiques by women of color had de-centered once dominant liberal feminism and opened space for multiple forms of gender-based politics.[46] At the same time, in the South, women activists' encounters with sexist post-colonial states and political parties had led to more interest in questions of gender equality in the political realm. While global economic developments often made class divisions within countries and regions more salient, new networks forged at earlier U.N. conferences had begun to link feminists in different parts of the world and fostered solidarities around particular issues, interests, and identities.[47]

By the early 1990s, feminist professionalization was in full swing, giving new impetus to transnationalizing processes and facilitating a shift in strategy whose outlines were already evident in Nairobi. Donor-supported NGOs, particularly those based near the centers of global power in Western Europe and the United States, now had the resources and expertise necessary to carry out sustained coordination and lobbying activities. Feminists in these NGOs increasingly took an "insider" approach to global politics, working to influence international platforms through official channels.[48] With the help of the growing number of feminists in policymaking roles both North and South, they targeted a series of U.N. conferences on topics including the environment, human rights, population, and social development.[49] The culminating event was the Fourth World Women's Conference in Beijing in 1995.

In the process of lobbying official delegations, these activists developed new organizing strategies and gained further experience with often arcane bureaucracies. Their discursive victories established issues until then considered private matters—such as violence against women, maternal mortality, and sexual and reproductive rights—as urgent public concerns at an international level. Interpretive struggles around conference resolutions shifted language in ways that articulated new understandings. The meaning of violence against women, for example, was broadened to include not only rape and domestic abuse, but also violence caused by structural adjustment, poverty, environmental degradation, political repression, and armed conflict. Women's rights were defined as universal human rights, rather than as a set of particularistic entitlements.[50] By legitimizing topics that had been taboo and setting new standards for gender justice, conference resolutions gave powerful ammunition to feminists in countries where change had been difficult to achieve through local government channels.

There was also some evidence of a discursive impact on international institutions. The United Nations Development Program, for example, began to include new indices of "gender empowerment" and "gender development" in its annual Human Development Report, which ranked the progress of individual countries. Meanwhile, the World Bank incorporated gender considerations in its lending programs, and established an External Gender Consultative Group, made up of prominent feminists. At least on paper, gender was being "mainstreamed" by development institutions.

But there was discord within the counterpublic about participation in these official spaces and the significance of the victories won. Involvement in the U.N. process required a huge investment of time and energy and some feared that it was draining local initiatives of leadership and resources while producing ambiguous results. Though feminists had succeeded in shifting international norms, there was frustration at the slow pace of their translation into policies, and concern that much of it was no more than window dressing. The local impact of feminists' focus on the international policy arena was, in fact, mixed: In some countries and historical moments it generated new forms of mobilization, while in others it divided local activists and depleted their movements.[51]

One of the thorniest issues was the discursive price being paid for engaging on the institutional terrain of policy reform. What did it mean to have international institutions adopt the language of gender? Were feminists really contributing to reshaping official paradigms? Or were their discourses simply being absorbed within dominant frameworks that sapped them of their radical critique and potential for transforming gender relations and other forms of injustice?

Feminists involved in the policy arena argued that they could co-opt powerful discourses to their own advantage. They believed that only by tapping into already recognized frameworks, such as development, human rights, or population control, was it possible to shift policy-makers' conceptions of issues and achieve real change. Critics, most working outside institutional arenas, insisted that this strategy forced women's concerns into the dominant frame of Western individualism, and directed struggles onto the domesticating terrain of international diplomacy. Activist energies, they felt, would be less compromised and better spent mobilizing grassroots pressure on states and international institutions from below.[52]

Some activists in the international policy world heard these critiques. They acknowledged that, by invoking human rights in the context of the United Nations, feminists were tangling with a "discursive field of power relations," but insisted that they had little choice but to enter it. As scholar-activist Rosalind Petchesky put it, this set of discourses is "simply the rhetorical structure 'given to us' in the present historical conditions for asserting counter-hegemonic statements of justice." As for the structure of the United Nations itself, she asserted, "We need democratic, accountable institutions of global governance in the face of globalization and enfeebled, complicit national governments. In this respect, the U.N. system *is all we have.*" She argued that feminists should work both inside and outside its walls.[53]

The debates about whether and how to engage with multilateral organizations were linked to others about inequalities within the counterpublic. Some celebrated the new expertise and visibility of professionalized feminists, but there was concern in other quarters about increasing polarization. Feminist agendas, critics claimed, were increasingly set by a small group of relatively privileged women, while those lacking the necessary resources, cultural capital, or political inclination to operate within international institutions were excluded from strategic decision-making. How to bridge the gulf between the two was the subject of much anguished discussion on both sides.[54]

As these debates around politics and class inequalities raged, antagonisms along North-South lines among participants in the NGO forum were waning, and by the time of the Beijing Conference in 1995, were much less apparent than they had once been.[55] In part, this was an outcome of two decades of networking and political discussions across hemispheres. In part, it reflected the very phenomenon of professionalization that was provoking so much soul-searching within movements worldwide. The growing cadre of well-trained full-time NGO feminists from the South had strategic visions that often aligned more closely with those of their Northern counterparts than with those of working-class women in their own countries.

This phenomenon was, to a large extent, the product of earlier feminist struggles. The incorporation of feminist discourses by states and other dominant institutions created a demand for gender expertise to monitor government and intergovernmental programs and drew feminists into positions of power. At the same time, international donors hoping to prepare civil society for its new role as partner in democracy began to fund what Alvarez calls the "NGOization" of feminist movements.[56] Once all-volunteer shoestring operations, feminist organizations across Latin America, like SOS Corpo in Brazil, began restructuring, hiring staff, and redirecting their strategies toward the state and multilateral organizations. Though NGOs varied tremendously in terms of their structures, access to resources, and relationships to conventional forms of politics, the trend toward professionalization in the South was unmistakable.

As activism in the global North declined, challenged by public complacency and an increasingly powerful conservative movement, feminisms elsewhere in the world were flourishing. Though the panorama was patchy, the increasing activism of "femocrats" and professionalized NGO staff, along with the explosion of local working-class activism in response to neoliberal policies and economic crisis, had created vibrant and diverse feminist movements in many regions of the South and particularly in Latin America.[57] These developments facilitated the beginnings of a sea change. While feminists in Europe and the United States continued to control significant resources, by the 1990s the political leadership had begun to pass to the South.[58]

Ironically, as the South gained international influence, the political space at the United Nations that had been appropriated by feminists was becoming more hostile to their critiques. Beijing marked a high point of mobilization for the forces of fundamentalism—Christian, as well as Islamic—and feminists spent their energies at the conference defending past gains and making heroic efforts to advocate for relatively small semantic changes in platform language.[59] Though the unofficial parallel meeting at Huairou, like those at previous gatherings, fostered important transnational connections and exchanges, the aftermath of the event saw intensified questioning of the efficacy of work centered on U.N. conferences. The General Coordinator of Development Alternatives with Women for a New Era (DAWN), one of the earliest feminist networks to be based outside the global North and an important participant in transnational feminist policy advocacy, wrote in 2001:

> The current global environment is not at all conducive to advancing gains for women through a new round of inter-governmental negotiations. In DAWN's assessment, the risks of seeing gains… seriously eroded, or, worse, reversed are simply too high.[60]

In the wake of 9/11, the effervescent moment of transnational feminist organizing in the highly structured sphere of international organizations had apparently passed.

TRANSNATIONALISM BEYOND THE "GLOBAL WOMEN'S LOBBY"

But the feminist counterpublic had always been broader than the advocacy that revolved around U.N. conferences. Transnational connections also encompassed multiple instances of informal collaboration, unofficial gatherings, and discursive connection. As the political landscape of the early twenty-first century made the "insider" approach to international policy a less viable strategy than it might have been in preceding decades, the significance of these less formal linkages became more evident. In difficult political times, the web of relationships beyond institutional venues continued to provide a means for feminists to construct provisional alliances. They also drew in a broader range of participants, including those who had been on the margins of international feminist diplomacy.

As noted above, the encounters in the U.N. arena had facilitated the formation of myriad transnational networks, focused around identities, issues, or world regions. Black women and lesbians, health activists and human rights advocates, Latin American and South Asian women were among the many who maintained ongoing cross-border relationships. Though some of their energies were devoted to conventional forms of lobbying aimed at international institutions, these networks also served as a means to share information, coordinate strategies, or offer other kinds of mutual support.[61] They took a wide range of institutional shapes, from formal organizations with strong central coordination to loose linkages among autonomous entities or individuals. Most of those that dated from the late 1970s and early 1980s had a leadership dominated by the global North, but in later years increasing numbers were founded by women in the South and reflected their concerns.[62]

Returning to Northeast Brazil, we can see that networks were often also stimulated by developments independent of U.N.-related gatherings. The transnational connections in which SOS Corpo and the rural Pernambucan women's movement were embedded illustrate the importance of initiatives that began as informal connections between organizations and individuals and led to the construction of cross-border relationships that functioned largely outside the realm of intergovernmental diplomacy.

In the 1970s, revelations about forced sterilizations carried out by population programs in Bangladesh, India, and Colombia, as well as the dumping of unsafe birth control devices in the Third World by international family planning agencies, spurred women's health movements to reach out to one another.[63] Groups like the Boston Women's Health Book Collective in the North and SOS Corpo in the South collected and shared data on abuses and alternatives, and slowly built relationships with one another. In 1977 in Rome, feminists held their first International Women and Health Meeting, designed as a forum to discuss health matters consistently neglected by government officials and the population establishment. Participation in these triennial conferences, like that in policy advocacy and networks, was initially dominated by the global North, but became more diverse over time.[64]

In 1985, rural women workers from Northeast Brazil made contact with other rural women at a Latin American feminist gathering held in Southeast Brazil. They sustained ad hoc communications and, five years later, at another such meeting in Argentina, representatives from a number of countries founded a Latin American and Caribbean network.[65] When two members of the MMTR's Northeast regional umbrella organization attended their first U.N. conference in Beijing in 1995, their network had already been in existence for five years. The next year, they held their first international meeting of rural women workers, in Northeast Brazil.[66]

By the early 1980s, because of their long history, the politicizing experiences of anti-dictatorial organizing and democratization, and the early availability of international funding, feminisms in Latin America were among the most diverse and had some of the densest transnational relationships of any region in the world. These connections were nurtured, challenged, and sustained in part by biannual Latin American and Caribbean feminist *Encuentros* (Encounters), initiated in 1981.[67] As Alvarez et al. put it, these events were—and continue to be—"productive transborder sites that not only reflect but also reshape local, national, and regional movement discourses and practices."[68]

In many ways, these participatory events, organized in rotation by committees led by host country representatives, reflected the dynamics of the larger transnational feminist public in microcosm. The *Encuentros* brought together Latin American and Caribbean feminists from across the spectrum of ideologies, strategic approaches, and organizational structures, as well as, increasingly, from diverse class, ethnic, and racial backgrounds, sexual orientations, and generations. At the *Encuentros*, activists engaged in dialogues across their differences, articulating new feminist identities, and struggling over strategic questions.

The debates at these events over the last quarter century revolved around the themes of autonomy, difference, and inequality that have been central to feminist struggles elsewhere as well.[69] The question of autonomy in relation to the Latin American left roiled the waters in the 1980s, dividing those loyal to opposition political parties from those who viewed them as bastions of male supremacy. The issue of feminist independence would reappear in new form in the 1990s, in resistance to participation in the politics of dominant institutions and in challenges to the power of international funding agencies to shape feminist agendas.

Despite the aspirations to inclusiveness at the regional gatherings, diversity among participants came slowly. The *Encuentro* that MMTR members attended in 1985, as well as others throughout the 1980s, was the scene of acrimonious disputes over issues of class. Longtime feminists, known as "*históricas*," resisted the influx of working-class women with organizing experience, but little knowledge of feminism. Some feared that the newcomers were being manipulated by left-wing political parties interested in colonizing feminist constituencies; others argued that if no feminist credentials were required, the event would lose its character as a site for much needed discussions of theory and strategy. Activists from the *barrios*, on the other hand, insisted that "We are all feminists!" and that the *Encuentros* should be an accessible space where they could contribute, as well as expand their understandings.[70]

In the 1990s, even as the development of popular feminism mitigated some of the old divisions, new fissures appeared. Black and indigenous women questioned the lack of attention to their concerns; participants from the Anglo- and Francophone Caribbean expressed frustrations with the domination of Spanish-speaking Latin America; and lesbians struggled for visibility and acceptance.

As in feminist circles beyond Latin America, issues of difference went hand in hand with questions of power and inequality. Conflicts about the professionalization of feminism and the priority being placed on international policy advocacy over local organizing surfaced in the *Encuentros*. The issues first emerged in 1993 in contention over participation in the Beijing conference, as well as over whether to accept funding from the United States Agency for International Development (USAID) for the preparatory process leading up to it. In the end, most attendees favored advocacy efforts around the U.N. event, but in 1996 controversy erupted again in clashes between the self-identified "*autónomas*" and those they labeled "*institucionalizadas.*" The "autonomous" grouping accused those who had founded NGOs or accepted positions in state or international bureaucracies of selling out to "patriarchy and neoliberal capitalism" and of profiting at the expense of the movement.[71] The "institutionalized" defended themselves and pleaded for mediation, while a third group, calling itself "*ni las unas, ni las otras*" (neither one, nor the other) criticized the polarized stances of both parties.

These frictions eased at later *Encuentros*, as the "*autónomas*" splintered into factions and their institutionalized counterparts began to re-evaluate their strategies. In the new millennium, Latin American feminists struggled to conjugate their distinctive approaches, acknowledging the need for heterogeneous strategies to address power in its varied forms. Meanwhile, new voices clamored for political space. In 2005, a younger generation chafed at the rigidity of the older movement leadership, indigenous women denounced white feminist paternalism, and transgendered people clamored for inclusion. Their claims were articulated and negotiated within a regional feminist counterpublic. Like its broader transnational counterpart, this public was not always harmonious. But it offered an arena in which battles could be waged and conflicts at least partially adjudicated. It was also a productive space, in which new discourses were generated and refined, and collaborations fostered.

The transnational feminist counterpublic, as an arena constituted by political relationships, is more intangible, more multifarious than the Latin American feminist *Encuentros*. But it shares with them the indispensable function of providing shelter within which widely divergent movements and organizations, networks and individuals can construct and negotiate their politics, develop and debate new critiques of gendered power, and convene dialogues across differences. Historically, this has occurred in a wide variety of venues and moments, from the early exchange of letters among feminists throughout Latin America, to the hierarchical structures of Pan American feminisms, from the bureaucratic maze of U.N. committees and conferences, to the multiple networks spun off from parallel gatherings.

Since its inception, the transnational feminist counterpublic has been a hybrid space, one where discourses and practices, the cultural and the material intersect and clash with or accommodate one another. It is also hybrid in the sense that it holds both solidarities and the manipulations of power within its embrace. It is a terrain fraught with dangers that imperil the delicate balance between the two. The following chapters will give a glimpse into the inner workings of the contemporary feminist counterpublic and how it is constructed, threatened, and defended. In Chapter 3, the story begins with the transnational travels of feminist discourses between differently situated movements.

3

TRANSLATING FEMINISMS

From Embodied Women to Gendered Citizenship

In 1980, a small group of pioneering feminists in the city of Recife, in the Northeast corner of Brazil, gathered in one another's living rooms, with the most common tool of the gynecological trade in hand: the speculum. The participants were intent on learning about their own bodies and taking charge of their medical care by conducting self-examinations. As they struggled to master the awkward instrument and to survey the hidden wonders of their anatomies, they pieced together bits of data that they had gleaned. Their new knowledge represented a "great discovery" for these young middle- and upper-class women, according to one participant, and they were eager to share it with women in poor neighborhoods who had little access to such information and faced wretched health conditions.[1] The group founded an organization, giving it the name "*SOS Corpo: Grupo de Saúde da Mulher*" (SOS Body: Women's Health Group) to reflect their concern with women's bodies, and began doing outreach to women in the working-class *bairros* that had formed around the periphery of the city.

The approach to women's health initially taken by the members of SOS Corpo bore a strong resemblance to those of feminist movements in Europe and North America at the time.[2] In the United States, the Boston Women's Health Book Collective (BWHBC), founded in 1969 in the heyday of the women's liberation movement, was one of the earliest advocates of women's empowerment through knowledge of their own bodies.[3] "The information [about women's anatomy and physiology] is a weapon without which we cannot begin the collective struggle for control over our own bodies and lives," the group wrote in its book, *Our Bodies, Our Selves (OBOS)*, first published in 1970.[4]

The health manual sought to demystify medicine by equipping women with the tools to make informed choices about their medical care. At a time when knowledge about the female body was still seen as the province of male medical experts, topics such as sexuality, contraception, pregnancy, and childbirth, as well as women's feelings about them, were discussed openly in accessible language. The Collective made the revolutionary claim that women themselves were the best source of knowledge about their own bodies. Placing women at the center of their strategy for change, the BWHBC advocated for individual self-empowerment linked to a collective process in which personal problems would be transformed into political issues.

It was not long before this discourse on women's bodies began to travel. In the latter half of the 1970s, Collective members began to take a leadership role in the incipient international women's health movement and to make contact with the many organizations that were beginning to emerge around the world. Early on, the book was snapped up by commercial publishers, aware of its burgeoning audience. By 1976, *Our Bodies, Ourselves* had made the U.S. best-seller list, and, by 1980, when SOS was founded, it had been adapted and translated by local women's groups from English into eleven other languages and had sold more than two million copies. The book was read and its influence felt on every continent.[5]

In the process, discursive connections were forged among movements at different sites within the transnational feminist counterpublic. But this was not a simple story of "cultural diffusion," an innovation promoted by hegemonic experts being slowly and passively incorporated by less advantaged or creative "adopters," as if it were hybrid corn.[6] Northern feminist discourses were not so much meekly accepted as actively appropriated; the meanings they conveyed were less quietly absorbed than boldly—and "faithlessly"—translated.[7] In the case of *Our Bodies, Ourselves*, activists around the world resignified feminist discourses developed in Boston for use in their own diverse locations.[8]

In the mid to late 1970s, feminists in Recife seized on the message that knowledge and control of the body were central to the project of women's liberation. A number of the women who founded SOS Corpo had read *Our Bodies, Ourselves* and others had participated in the feminist self-help movement as exiles in France. In the early 1980s, discourses of "women's bodies," apparently similar to those of women's health movements in the North, predominated within SOS, and the group practiced gynecological self-exams, shared natural remedies, and discussed the members' own sexuality and relationships much as their peers were doing in Paris and Boston.

By the 1990s, however, a striking shift became evident in the organization's discourses and practices. "Women" had been displaced by "gender relations," and the focal point of SOS's work had shifted outward from "the body" to "citizenship," while still remaining focused on questions of health. Rather than practicing self-help, the organization engaged directly with the state in a quest for bodily rights for all Brazilian women.

Transnational counterpublics are held together and defined by relationships made of different strands. This chapter explores the strand of cultural connections that link feminists in different parts of the world, the discourses that one party borrows from another and re-elaborates in her own context.[9] These discourses represent ways of thinking about politics and understanding issues; they take shape in practices that give them material life. The convergences and divergences in meanings given to them by feminists in distinctive locations tell a story of the political affiliations and cultural contentions between them.

TRAVELING FEMINISMS, POLITICAL TRANSLATIONS

Theories, as Edward Said observed, are products of particular times and places. As they travel from one location to another, they are transformed in a variety of ways.[10] Meanings meet resistance in new contexts, and are forced to shift as they cross or, more accurately, are trafficked across different kinds of borders. In her study of relations between feminist theorizing in the United States and India, John describes theory as a "composite," geological construction whose sedimentations reflect the locations in which it was created or through which it has passed. Relocation and assimilation are not smooth processes, because fundamental assumptions embedded in the theory reflect its itinerary through the fractured transnational feminist counterpublic. Often, in fact, it is not coherent theories, but fragmentary, unstable, and contradictory sets of ideas and practices that travel and are taken up by social movements.

The structural inequalities among the differently situated nodes of discursive travel give some sectors in the global North the power "to render selectively permeable the boundaries of other states and nations."[11] With the benefit of the material and cultural power at their points of origin, conceptions *local* to the richer, early industrialized countries are transformed into *global* forces as they travel to, and become embedded in, the former colonies of the "Third World." But if theories and discourses do more often move from North to South, carried by the power of publishing houses and ample travel budgets, or the cultural cachet of European and American academe, they do not cross borders independent of human effort. Whether they are pushed from one side or pulled from the other, they require an apparatus of dissemination. Many concepts, in fact, don't survive the journey, finding no resonance at their intended destination.[12] Others are actively refused by their targeted populations.[13]

Theories, as well as more fragmentary sets of ideas, need translation to effectively "arrive." Concepts that make sense in one context are likely to be inadequate or unintelligible in another. They are often initially appropriated by brokers with a foot in each of several worlds—members of transnationalized business sectors, academic disciplines, and feminist NGOs, among others. These "cosmopolitans" translate meanings elaborated somewhere else to a local idiom, working to accommodate them to their new environs.[14] Discourses, then, don't just flow of their own volition; they must be actively chosen and require the labor of translators to take root in unfamiliar soil.[15]

While imported concepts may reshape local practices, their translations inevitably shift the meanings they may previously have had. Davis, for example, recounts the divergent transformations that the text of *Our Bodies, Ourselves* went through in the hands of Bulgarian and Latina translators. The former found it too "collectivist" for the newly de-sovietized sensibilities of their readership; the latter found its prescriptions for activism too individualized for a Latin American audience schooled in popular struggles against authoritarian regimes. Each made cultural adaptations of the text that differed significantly from the English-language version, even as the model of women sharing knowledge of their bodies provided inspiration to both.[16]

Tsing urges us to think of the discourses shared among movements as "shaped in continuous processes of translation."[17] There is no real "original" meaning that these translations seek to convey; all expressions of meaning involve borrowings and reinterpretations, even those—like *Our Bodies, Ourselves*—which have been constructed as the bedrock of contemporary feminism.[18] While the discourses of the global North still have greater wherewithal to travel, viewing them as non-original constructions challenges their totalizing cultural power vis-à-vis other forms of feminism.

Translations are not only textual or theoretical material exchanged among academics—they extend to the sharing of political discourses between members of social movements who inhabit different universes of action.[19] This kind of political translation plays an important part in the construction of transnational and translocal relationships; it is part of the web of linkages that holds a counterpublic together. But the process is not without conflict. Like other forms of interpretation, it is embedded in shifting relations of power. On the one hand, global inequalities give the upper hand to discourses from privileged sectors of the counterpublic; on the other, the interpreter herself also exercises a kind of authority, as she chooses or refuses and resignifies conceptions of issues or strategic visions in her own context.[20]

The process is perhaps best conceived as a cultural struggle, a battle to assert local particularities and values in the face of globally hegemonic—though also locally rooted—discourses and their enactments. Though it may imply hostilities among organizations or individuals, this is not necessarily the case.[21] More fundamentally, struggles like these are an expression of the cultural and political autonomy so crucial to the possibility of solidarities that respect differences.

What are the dynamics of translation among social movements? How exactly do political actors make new meanings out of old? And, how are global power relations implicated in their discursive struggles? I argue that political discourses come to life through the practices by which movements enact them.[22] But the practices inspired by a given discourse are not inextricably bound up with it in a seamless package; the two are semi-autonomous with respect to one another, change at different rhythms, and are capable of mutual influence, even as they present an apparently unified facade. It is in the cracks between discourse and practice that social movements wage cultural struggles to resignify meanings and create their own collective identities. Through practices, movements enter into relationships with constituents, with allies, and with dominant institutions. New meanings are shaped in and through these relationships.

There is also a temporal dimension to the process: Social movements appropriate discourses at particular historical moments and points in their own development. In the case described here, one such moment occurred in 1980, around the founding of SOS Corpo, at a time when both the organization itself and the larger Brazilian feminist movement were still relatively young, lacking formal structures and established strategies and tactics. "Women's bodies" initially reached SOS in Recife as a set of European and North American discourses linked to particular kinds of feminist practices. At this juncture, for a brief period, it appeared that Northern feminism gone global had found an echo in Northeast Brazil. But, as Recife women's health activists engaged with the forces around them—the state, international funding agencies, local social movements, and their own constituency of working-class women—their practices developed in different directions from those in the North, and ultimately outgrew the old language.

At a second moment, traveling feminisms once again played a catalyzing role, but this time SOS leaders drew, not on movement discourses, but on academic theory, to at least partially fill the discursive gap left by the obsolescence of "women" and "the body." Theories of "gender relations" had become pervasive in Northern academic feminist circles in the late

1980s and began to circulate as well among Brazilian intellectuals in the universities and nongovernmental organizations. In 1990, SOS Corpo literally translated and launched discussions of post-structuralist U.S. historian Joan Scott's work on gender.[23] By then, SOS had become a professionalized institution and a leader in the Brazilian feminist movement, as well as an active participant in international women's networks. At this historical juncture, the Recife NGO grappled with Northern theoretical conceptions from a position of relative strength and organizational maturity. Rather than simply adopting Scott's approach to gender, SOS members chose to reconstruct her theory and incorporate it into their work on their own terms. Unlike the discourse of women's bodies, they appropriated the theory directly from the academy as text, unencumbered with activist methodologies. This facilitated the process of articulating "gender relations" with SOS's pre-existing organizational practices and relationships.

Like "women" and "the body" before it, activists in Brazil translated the discourse of gender differently than had their counterparts in the United States. The differences were crystallized in the links SOS made between "gender" and another political discourse, that of "citizenship." The historical trajectory of "citizenship" in Brazil was much more rooted in the local context than their conceptions of gender. In the struggle against dictatorship, "*cidadania*" had become a rallying cry. As the process of democratization unfolded, it expressed the desires of the Brazilian opposition for the extension of entitlements far beyond their conventional limits. By coupling "gender" with demands for new kinds of rights, Brazilian feminists politicized what they had initially encountered as academic theory, transforming it into an organizing tool as well as an analytical category.

The discursive moves made by SOS reflected both the appropriation of new language and the remaking of old meanings in the process of fashioning a collective identity. Feminist discourses and the practices associated with them were not locked together in one-to-one correspondence, but rather operated in loose relation to one another. The discourses of women and body "imported" in 1980 brought with them a certain set of practices based in feminist self-help movements in the United States and Europe. However, while the language remained essentially the same over the next decade, in the hands of Brazilian feminists and through their political engagements, the practices quickly began to change. The new forms they took ultimately undermined a language and conception that could no longer make sense of them. After a decade, new discourses, this time with roots in academic theory, were adopted to replace the old.

Through the process of zigzagging from discourse to practice and back to discourse, the feminists of SOS Corpo seized cultural tools from the North and transformed them in vastly different local circumstances. On their own turf a battle, of sorts, was won: The power of hegemonic transnational discourses was disrupted and made to serve new ends—the construction and reconstruction of (relatively) autonomous Brazilian feminist collective identities.[24] But in the North, the story was different. While dramatic changes occurred in the discourse and practice of feminist movements in Northeast Brazil, the same was not true for the women's health movement in Boston, where the language of women and the body persisted nearly three decades after its initial appearance.

EMBODYING WOMEN, 1980–82

> But why this silence? Why does the woman's body remain so un-known, so mysterious, so forbidden for the very owner of this body? Could it be that we never had the curiosity to know ourselves? How is that possible, if knowing oneself is an elementary right of human beings? Could it be that this right has always been denied to us?
> (SOS Corpo, *Corpo de mulher*, 1982, p. 5)

The founders of SOS Corpo were, for the most part, white, well-educated, middle- and upper-class women with links to or sympathies with the left opposition to the dictatorship then in place.[25] The majority had interna-tional connections or experiences: three had lived in Europe as political exiles, one had traveled in the United States and Mexico, and another was from Switzerland. A number of them had read and been influenced by *Our Bodies, Ourselves*, and some had had contact with gynecological self-help movements in France. Most had participated in an earlier femi-nist consciousness-raising group, *Ação Mulher* (Woman's Action) which disbanded in 1980 as members' interests and strategic visions diverged. Those who conceived SOS, like their counterparts in the North, were united by their concern with sexuality and women's health.

Though other women's groups in Brazil had been organizing around political and class-based issues, at the time, SOS was one of a small number of new groups to put the focus on themes of women's health and sexual-ity not traditionally seen by the left as legitimate arenas of contention. In a December 1980 fundraising letter written to a woman in France, its founders stated their goals:

> Knowledge of our bodies, of our sexuality, of possible maladies, of their cure and prevention, in order to diminish the dependence which has tied us to doctors and allopathic medicines; to make this new knowledge known.... [and], in the medium term, to form other groups of the same kind.[26]

Initially, like the Boston collective, they aimed to educate themselves and to help other women develop the knowledge to change doctor-patient relations and enjoy their sexuality to the fullest. Though they had ambitions to transform the institutions that affected women's lives, they were not, at first, oriented toward pressuring the state, which remained under authoritarian rule.

For ten months the group concentrated on conducting self-exams together and experimenting with herbs and other alternative cures. But their links to the left and to a politics of class soon led them to the working-class neighborhoods around Recife, where they hoped to build a cross-class movement focused on women's health. With this in mind, the group produced a booklet, *Corpo de Mulher* (*Woman's Body*)—a Brazilian version of *Our Bodies, Ourselves*, written in accessible language—and began doing outreach in low-income areas where some members had contacts.[27] They presented a theater piece designed to stimulate discussions about women's lives and reproductive issues, offered workshops on sexuality, female anatomy, and the use of herbal treatments, and answered questions on a popular weekly radio call-in program.

SOS founders considered setting up a women's clinic, on the model of the Swiss feminist *Dispensaire des Femmes* (Women's Health Center), but the idea was ultimately rejected as too restrictive in terms of the constituency that they would have the resources to serve. Instead, as a means of extending their contact with women in the *bairros*, and of better understanding the health conditions they faced, SOS members conducted a series of research projects, interviewing women about their experiences with sterilization, abortion, and the public health system. The plan was to use the data to improve their organizing strategies and to disseminate the results in popularized form to their research subjects.

Central to SOS's work in these early years was a discourse of the body, expressed also in the content of their practices. As one founder put it:

> The question of [the slogan] "Our Bodies Belong to Us!" and of the body as a physical reality, as a metaphor, of the body as a symbol... as personal existence, was a very powerful thing which was emerging in the debate.

Empowerment for women, SOS members believed, would come through knowledge of their own bodies. Their first publication urged women to "get to know this body better, and to love it," and both their self-education and their outreach in the poor communities on the periphery of the city reflected this exhortation.[28]

The attention to matters of the body reflected, in large part, the long reach of feminism in the global North. "We drank from that wellspring," said one of Recife's early feminists, referring to the local influence of European and U.S. movements.[29] The transnationalized experiences and connections of many SOS founders had put them into contact with European and North American feminisms. Because of their roots in the left, SOS members had little interest in the liberal feminism that predominated in the United States and that was influential among development workers in the 1970s who became advocates of the "Women in Development" (WID) approach.[30] Instead, they were drawn to radical feminism, whose discourses celebrated women's difference and focused on the body and on reproductive health. These discourses reached SOS members at a time in their lives when sexuality and the bodily experience of reproduction were key personal issues, as they were for young women elsewhere.

But Northern feminism was only one of the institutions with which feminists in Recife were entangled: their relationships to working-class women, other local social movements, the state, and international funding agencies also played a part in the course of the organization's discursive development. SOS members' literal inward turn toward their own bodies came at a time when the state was beginning to open up, and democratization of some sort had begun to seem inevitable, if not yet a reality.[31] Unified opposition to and focus on the state no longer seemed imperative, and women, along with other social actors throughout Brazil, had begun to make claims based on new kinds of collective identities. Self-help for one's own body was a discourse and tactic that befitted this brief moment of transition, when the regime still clung to power, new possibilities for intervention in the state had not yet solidified, and the class-based movements that had dominated the opposition struggled to adjust to the new political conjuncture. Then too, as the dictatorship sputtered to an end, the focus on the body by a political generation which had seen many of its members physically "disappeared" may have also served as a means of reasserting ownership over their corporeal selves and their right to exist in the world.

SOS members navigated a complex field in which women's rights to make decisions about their own fertility were under assault from all sides. As feminists, they rejected both the official pro-natalist position of the Brazilian government in the early 1980s, and the neo-Malthusian alternative, promoted by the Brazilian elite and the international population control establishment.[32] At the time that SOS founders launched their project and structured their practices around a discourse of the body, there was little to suggest that their stance might win the approval of Northern donors. Since the 1950s, development agencies, such as the Ford Foundation, had supported international population control programs that emphasized demographic targets while ignoring women's health and well-being.[33] But the failure of this approach to limit fertility, along with growing pressure from feminist movements culminating at the 1985 U.N. women's conference in Nairobi, led to a shift in strategy.[34] Ford, which funded SOS's first research project in 1982, was one of the first to reframe its population control activities as a reproductive health program, and was soon followed by other agencies.[35] Subsequently, SOS's decision to focus on women's health issues was consistently rewarded with funding, making possible institutional consolidation and expansion, as well as SOS's growing hegemony within the local and national women's movements.

The Marxist-inspired left had long argued that a feminist approach to the body would not resonate with working-class women. Indeed, SOS's plan to teach low-income women to conduct their own gynecological self-exams fell flat, because of what one SOS member called the "cultural abyss" between the middle- and upper-class activists and their constituency. But even though that practice proved unpopular, women in the *bairros* remained hungry for knowledge of their own bodies, and confirmed the sense of SOS's founders that those who claimed that "this business of the body is a middle-class women's thing" were entirely wrong. The enthusiasm and continued demands from the urban periphery reinforced the discursive choices made early on by the group of feminists in Recife.

The same set of political relationships also influenced the appropriation of the discourse of "women" by SOS, as well as by many other Brazilian feminists of the time. According to the 1980 letter mentioned above, the group's proposed research "aims to know the voice of women…to understand how to describe their lived experience…to make known their testimonies….to try to let women speak."[36] Women, in SOS discourse, were both victims of patriarchy and potential carriers of their own liberation through knowledge and self-awareness.

This was a discourse that reflected in part that of *Our Bodies, Ourselves* and other Euro-American feminisms with which SOS founders had had contact but, given the Brazilian political and social context, "women" came to have a particular meaning. For Recife activists, it meant not women in general, but the poor women of the urban periphery and rural interior, and their more well-to-do feminist allies. Rejecting "militancy for me," SOS members saw themselves as sharing the knowledge that privilege had granted them.[37] As one woman explained, unlike what she had seen in the United States, in Brazil the outreach to low-income women

occurred immediately because there were women [in SOS] who came from participating in the movement for direct elections, and for amnesty. So, there was already a concern with the democratization of the country and of information and a clarity that the majority of women lived in conditions of poverty and didn't have access to what we were experiencing.

SOS's discourse reflected the influence of the political ideology dominant in the opposition in other ways as well. "Women" was a category parallel to "working class" in Marxism; both represented groups whose oppression was seen as fundamental to the social structure and who themselves were the potential carriers of transformation. Unlike the discourse of class, however, "women" (and "the body") offered a bridge across the "cultural abyss," as well as across the stark economic differences, that separated SOS founders from the women they sought to reach. Both groups of women had common concerns with, though perhaps distinctive perspectives on, sexuality and reproductive health.

The authoritarian state participated as well, though indirectly, in the construction of the discourse of "women." In the 1970s, middle- and upper-class feminists and residents of marginalized neighborhoods formed cross-class alliances against repression and the high cost of living, as well as other issues. Alvarez argues that their own machismo caused military leaders to conceive of women's organizing as non-political and therefore unthreatening.[38] By tolerating their activism, the state allowed "women" as a category to consolidate itself in public discourse. Within a few years of SOS's founding, international funders too began to offer support for projects framed within this category.

During this first moment, the incipient Recife women's health organization adopted a set of discourses and, along with them, particular practices from movements in Europe and the United States whose early development and location in the Northern centers of power gave their conceptual frameworks global reach. But, in the context of SOS's other political relationships, the ties between these imported discourses and the practices that had accompanied them soon began to unravel.

LOCALIZING PRACTICES, 1983–89

Between 1983 and the end of the decade, though SOS discourse remained centered primarily on women and the body, the organization's practices began to shift as it engaged with a web of local and global interlocutors and expanded its arenas of action. Changes occurred in four areas: themes of organizing, tactics and strategy, constituency, and institutional structure. In each, the new forms of practice ultimately came to outgrow the discourses with which the organization was founded and to pose new kinds of risks and challenges.

In terms of broad themes, over the decade SOS moved from an initial emphasis on sexuality to questions of reproductive health, from pleasure toward self-preservation. One staff member explained:

> [T]he door of entry was sexuality, and from sexuality you passed immediately to health issues or to issues of violence. Given that this NGO works in Brazil, if you put a foot down in the field of health, you have no way to leave because health conditions are really very dramatic.... [S]o we practically stopped working on sexuality... [and] health occupied a greater and greater place.

Working first in the marginal *bairros* and, several years later, in the rural areas as well, brought SOS members into contact with women's urgent health needs and the incapacity or unwillingness of the state to address them. Reproductive health conditions, in particular, were alarming. As economic development and urbanization restructured the labor market and changed values, many women entered the labor force and large families became economically disadvantageous. The state, meanwhile, maintained an official pro-natalist policy until the early 1980s, while allowing private family planning programs to operate without oversight and fostering sales of the pill through its pharmaceutical policy.[39]

The practice of "planned omission" meant that contraceptives were distributed indiscriminately with little or no education or medical supervision. SOS's research found that women were discouraged by the side effects and ineffectiveness of available methods, and increasingly turned to clandestine abortion and sterilization promoted by "philanthropic" physicians. The result was a 50 percent drop in Brazilian fertility rates between 1970 and the late 1990s.[40] The problem was particularly acute in the Northeast; by the mid-1980s 18 to 20 percent of women under twenty-five in the state of Pernambuco had been sterilized, according to an SOS estimate.[41] Conditions such as these and the demands of the women at their seminars and events increasingly led the organization toward basic reproductive health concerns, an arena that was simultaneously becoming the object of interest for international agencies concerned more with lowering birth rates than with the right of women in the Third World to sexual pleasure.

At the same time, the organization made another transition, from an emphasis on practices of self-help and the autonomous development of knowledge in local communities to a growing engagement with the state at a national level. One of the first tentative contacts occurred in 1984, in the twilight of the old regime, when a health ministry official sympathetic to feminism came to Recife. An SOS founder described the interaction:

[H]e was Coordinator General of the Ministry, and he asked to visit SOS. We received him with a lot of interest…somewhat fearful of that invasion, all of us suspicious. We received him, but not very well.… In the afternoon, there was a big debate here in a [state] government agency, the Pernambuco Development Council…and we were invited. SOS was there, but there were other people, from the union. It was the period when those moments of dialogue were beginning…and there was representation of civil society, but more as observers. [The Coordinator General] spoke about the importance of dialogue and said that it gave him enormous pleasure… to see seated there "my associates of SOS Corpo." He said that and we panicked. We left, running to SOS, and had an urgent meeting where we said that he had stated publicly that SOS was an associate [of the Ministry]. Girl, it was something. It caused chaos…[and people said] that we had to undo it. Earlier [during the debate itself], during the period for comments, the other two pushed me—they said, "You have to speak." And I was very delicate.… I spoke nicely, but I clarified that the partnership did not exist, and then ran to shelter myself among my autonomous comrades.

The SOS collective's resistance to this "partnership" was rooted in distaste for dictatorship as well as commitment to political autonomy. But the old regime was crumbling and the temptation to engage with a more democratic state was strong, particularly given the needs they were encountering. Despite their early misgivings, SOS members agreed to help design a new comprehensive women's health program, initiated by feminists within the health ministry, and they began training groups of state health professionals to increase their sensitivity to women's needs. Unlike the earlier maternal-infant care models, in which women were seen as no more than a "reproductive apparatus," the new *Programa de Assistência Integral à Saúde da Mulher* (PAISM [Program for Integral Protection of Women's Health]) treated women as "citizens possessing rights and as whole beings, where the body's history is linked to the life history," according to an SOS publication.[42] Approving of this framework, and seeing an opportunity to influence the medical care provided to their working-class constituency in the public health system, SOS members and other autonomous feminists put aside their doubts and launched into a collaborative relationship with the state.

In 1985, Brazil elected its first civilian president since the 1964 coup.[43] Responding to pressure from feminist legislators and autonomous women's movements, that year José Sarney's government created a *Conselho Nacional dos Direitos da Mulher* (CNDM [National Council for Women's

Rights]), whose mandate was to open new channels for women's organizations to influence state policies on gender.An activist from SOS Corpo was invited to join the National Council as a representative of broader feminist constituencies within civil society. Again, SOS debated the issue, but eventually accepted the invitation, swayed by the urgings of other women's organizations whose members saw it as important to counteract the influence of the Catholic Church on government policies.[44] Three years later, the Recife women's health organization, along with most of Brazil's feminist organizations, participated in a national effort to lobby for the inclusion of their concerns in the country's new constitution. In the process, as with its involvement on the women's council, SOS was drawn into debates on issues, such as the rights of domestic workers and of female agricultural laborers, outside the more limited sphere of health. The organization's feminist practices broadened. No longer centered only on constructing and disseminating knowledge of the body, SOS's practices now extended to making claims for rights to citizenship on behalf of a broad range of social sectors in a newly democratic polity.

The third process of realignment revolved around the nature of the group's constituency. Initially, SOS, in the tradition of radical feminism, was an organization explicitly devoted to working with women and fostering their identity and sense of power as women, as distinct from men. The value placed on being an all-women's institution was such that even a proposal to hire a male night watchman provoked controversy. But, over the years, SOS members increasingly found themselves working with mixed groups of men and women, as they began training state health professionals, holding workshops for other NGOs, working with women's organizations affiliated with labor unions and neighborhood associations, and encountering the personal and familial networks in which their female constituents were embedded. All of this was a long way from SOS's beginnings when, as one staff member put it, "It was unthinkable for you to have feminists, both in the governmental and the nongovernmental spheres, training men."

In one final transition, over the decade of the 1980s, what had been a collective of eight volunteers working out of their homes became a formal institution with a sizable office, some twenty-five staff members, and a budget of several hundred thousand dollars a year. At the beginning, the group studied feminist theory and practiced self-exams together as peers, everyone participated in all projects, and administrative tasks were shared. But, by the late 1980s, the group had begun a process of professionalization and the creation of formal hierarchical structures. Members became paid staff who specialized in certain tasks, collective self-help practices were abandoned, and study group sessions became more sporadic.

The process of institutionalization described above was both facilitated and demanded by the U.S. and European funding agencies that, after 1982, increasingly supported SOS's work. As its relationship with the state intensified and the demands on its time increased, the women's health organization faced growing internal chaos. In a process described in Chapter 6, the demands of Northern donors for order and financial accountability led to the creation of a new, more professionalized structure with a specialized administrative department; what was once a collective of volunteers became a formalized institution. The move both ratified and enabled SOS's deepening involvement with state entities, international funding agencies, and the broader transnational network of allied feminist organizations.

These four changes in SOS's practices allowed the organization to extend its field of influence, but they also put new perils in the path of a group of feminists who had set their sights on profound social changes—the perils of isolation from their working-class allies, incorporation into dominant agendas, and loss of radical vision. At the same time, the organization developed a kind of locally based power vis-à-vis transnational discourses. Their evolving practices put questions on the table that could not be addressed by the discourses of women and body alone. Increasingly their work revolved implicitly around notions of corporal citizenship, rather than bodily knowledge, and around the creation of and participation in a new kind of polity as gendered beings, rather than as women per se. SOS eventually brought this subterranean shift in conceptions to light, appropriating new discourses that gave it tools to confront the dangers that faced it as an expanding movement.

ENGENDERING FEMINISM, 1990–98

Gender is a useful concept to explain many of the behaviors of men and women in our society, helping us to understand a large part of the problems and difficulties that women confront at work, in political life, in their sexual and reproductive lives, in the family. That is why the women's movement discusses gender so much.

(Camurça and Gouveia, *O que é gênero? Um novo desafio para a ação das mulheres trabalhadoras rurais*, 1995b, p. 5)

In 1990, *SOS Corpo: Grupo de Saúde da Mulher* (SOS Body: Women's Health Group) became *SOS Corpo: Gênero e Cidadania* (SOS Body: Gender and Citizenship), reflecting the incorporation of new discourses that had a better fit with the NGO's changing practices and with its increasing orientation toward the state. "Gender" had appeared in SOS documents some years earlier, soon after the 1985 U.N. conference in Nairobi, where the term was already being used. It came into broader circulation among Brazilian feminists during the mobilization around the new national constitution in 1988, when they sought, through their proposals, to articulate women's concerns with broader social changes.

Though some feminists had begun to incorporate a gender analysis, in 1990 there was still little or no bibliography on or discussion of gender in the local universities in Pernambuco.[45] At a national level, debate on the concept was just beginning within the national social science association.[46] "Gender" was starting to make its way into the language of mainstream development and funding agencies, but, with a few exceptions, had not yet been widely institutionalized or clearly theorized.

One SOS founding member had read Gayle Rubin's work on the "sex-gender system" in 1980, but the concept of gender was not integrated into organizational discourse until 1990, when she read and translated Joan Scott's article, "Gender: A Useful Category of Historical Analysis," into Portuguese.[47] SOS subsequently organized both internal discussions and public debates for the Recife feminist community on Scott's theory.

The initial reaction to gender as an analytical category among participants in these discussions was mixed. One woman expressed the source of her frustration at the time:

> I thought ["gender"] was very strange and it took me a long time to incorporate this concept. Since it was very complex, with different interpretations from different authors...for me, not being a theoretician, this discussion was very complicated and I didn't identify much with it. And I was a little exasperated because in reality people began to use the term without knowing what they were talking about.

According to another SOS member, there were also political objections:

> People didn't want to abandon the old categories—subordination and patriarchy—and...they were not convinced. The reaction was that this is much too abstract. It doesn't talk about women's suffering....I think feminists [were] more nervous about gender... [because] they had to start thinking about men again....You cannot think of gender...without having to pay attention to men. And feminists reacted very quickly.

But the concept was compelling, for reasons discussed in this chapter, and Scott's approach, linked to other discourses on gender, was increasingly integrated into the work of SOS, as well as that of many other feminist organizations around Brazil, in a way and to a degree unprecedented among feminist movements in Scott's country of origin where "women" continued to dominate the language of activists.

Throughout the 1990s, the Recife women's health organization conducted "gender training" workshops and seminars for a wide variety of groups in Pernambuco and around the country, including "mixed" (male and female) NGOs oriented toward social change, feminist institutions, grassroots women's organizations, state employees, and international funders. They produced pamphlets and wrote articles on the subject, and planned projects to analyze the gender content of government policies and communications.[48]

But, except for these programs explicitly addressing the new conception, for the most part the move to "gender" did not signal dramatic changes in practice, but rather facilitated those that were already occurring. By 1990, SOS was already working with mixed groups of men and women in workshops and other settings, though most projects continued to be directed at women and all of its work was intended to benefit them. But gender offered a new tool for approaching these groups. Whereas in the 1980s health workers were trained simply to be more sensitive to women, in the 1990s they were educated about the power relations between men and women, and the ways gender structured not only health care, but work, families, the state, and other institutions as well.

SOS had already begun working within the state before the discursive transition, but the language and meanings of gender gave the organization added legitimacy vis-à-vis government institutions, as one staff member explained:

> Going to the government health service or in any other area of social policies and saying, "Listen, if you don't deal with this question, you aren't going to be doing anything.... [I]f you don't take into account that the impacts of policies are differentiated for men and women, that policy won't work." And for you to say that and be heard...I think that owes a lot both to the introduction of the concept and to the adoption of this perspective within Brazil in the form that it was adopted.... [H]ere in Brazil the impression I have is that we took... the gender perspective and used it to broaden political action.

In the 1980s, SOS had already expanded from its initial focus on sexuality to the broader field of health and reproductive rights. With the introduction of gender discourse, the institution moved into the arena of gender and development, while maintaining its central concern with health. This more encompassing approach gave greater capacity for negotiation with a wide variety of institutional counterparts—including funding agencies, and other NGOs, as well as the state. Given the wide-spread prejudices against feminism, the adoption of new and apparently more inclusive language also created the potential for deepening alliances with other social movements, such as unions and community organizations, which had viewed the pursuit of "women's" interests as parochial and divisive.

Some feminist activists have critiqued "gender" as a technocratic discourse linked to the professionalization of feminism, as well as to the development industry.[49] In the case of SOS, by 1990, when the new conception was adopted, the Recife organization had already begun to institutionalize and extend its sphere of influence. However, the arrival of "gender" did help to further consolidate this process by giving the organization expanded access to a development establishment alert to the latest trends in discourse.

The feminist critiques reflect the fact that gender is a contested concept and the meanings associated with it in the academic literature as well as in activist practice are diverse. In the case of SOS, Joan Scott was cited repeatedly by staff members as the primary inspiration for their interpretation of "gender":

> SOS understands gender as a social relation of power, developed at the level of representations, and…produced and reproduced through norms, laws, customs, institutions, [and] the ways individual action is structured. It therefore adopts Joan Scott's perspective.[50]

This interpretation offered far more possibilities from a feminist perspective than the one being implemented in the development world, where gender came to represent an inert, depoliticized category, rather than a power relation reproduced through a wide variety of institutions. In the context of development work, "gender" was often disconnected from the feminist project of social transformation, becoming a static variable used to measure policy impacts. Moser reported in 1993 that, where Gender and Development (GAD) units had been established, "gender" had all too often merely replaced "women" without any change in substance from the efficiency-based approach of earlier Women in Development (WID) programs.[51]

A similar process occurred in the Brazilian academy, where, according to Costa and Sardenberg, gender lost its initial meaning, often becoming a synonym for "women," which functioned to make feminist work seem more respectable and scientific. The result was a growing distance between the academy and women's movements, with some activists giving the pejorative label of "*genericas*" to those academics who tried to hide their politics behind a "gender" shield and some *genericas* criticizing the "lack of academic seriousness" of feminist scholars who sought to maintain their activist commitments.[52]

For SOS, shifting its discourse from "women" to Scott's particular approach to "gender" had a number of important theoretical implications. Whereas the earlier discourse, and the practices initially associated with it, implicitly placed both problem (patriarchy/women's oppression) and solution (women's knowledge of and control over their bodies) in the hands of one sex, "gender," as SOS generally interpreted it, focused on social relations as the problem and their transformation as the solution. Society as a whole, rather than women alone, was depicted as both object and agent of change. Women's health and bodily knowledge became vehicles for promoting broader changes, as well as ends in themselves.

Just as the category of "women" had earlier been to feminism what "working class" was to Marxist analysis, in the 1990s "gender" paralleled "class" in its theoretical power and ability to embrace all of society. From the new discourse, groups like SOS drew theoretical justification for a much more ambitious political project than that originally constructed around "women." Executive director Silvia Camurça described the universe they saw opened up by the new conception: "Working with gender requires us to act at the level of social contradictions, in the subjective arena, the field of politics, relationships, institutions, norms, laws."[53]

By stressing that gender relations were socially constructed, SOS moved away from an ahistorical conception of patriarchy as an entrenched system to a view of gender as potentially infinitely malleable. This allowed a shift in how men were conceived; from enemies, they were transformed into fellow victims of the current gender arrangements. Though they held more power in this system, by virtue of their own injuries, they also became potential allies. As one member explained:

> In our work with mixed NGOs, it gives a certain tranquility to people…to show a…possibility that men—concrete men—are not the villains and that gender relations also create certain difficulties for them. It's very interesting when we start to talk about norms: that men don't cry…that men are violent, that men always have to be ready for sex.…[P]eople feel relieved, because it seems like we are going to accuse them and suddenly we show that everything is a cultural construction.

Finally, in contrast to the universalizing quality that had been bestowed on "women," Scott's conception of gender relations created the possibility of recognizing differences among women through acknowledging the ways gender was inflected by other experiences, such as class, race, and sexuality. Indeed, SOS pamphlets and workshops made reference to the "great web of differences" among women, as well as between women and men. However, in practice, in the late 1990s, SOS primarily engaged with differences of class and gender, neglecting other social experiences. None of their projects explicitly addressed either race or sexual preference, for example. One longtime SOS member commented:

> SOS Corpo never discussed lesbianism adequately, at least in the same depth that it discussed other themes, never.... I think that it is really a resistance...a prejudice.... I think that race also was never discussed, though at certain moments there were certain choices of staff members to be contracted, choosing the black woman because it was necessary, it was good to have black people in the picture, but the issue of race...was never debated.

Though Scott's was their dominant interpretation of "gender," SOS members at times drew strategically on other sources of meanings for the term, based on the work of feminists from Latin America, as well as the United States and Europe. Moser's operational approach to "gender planning" was evident in their workshops with development professionals, eager for ways to implement their new understandings.[54] The conception of gender as a variable to measure the impact of government policies surfaced in their work directed toward the state. In the context of SOS's organizing with grassroots constituencies, the work of pioneering Brazilian feminists on the intersection of class and gender was an important influence.[55]

The process of appropriation of feminist theory from the North took place in the context of SOS's relationships with the array of other forces in its field of action at that particular historical moment. First, feminist relations with a larger social movement field in Pernambuco played an important part in shaping SOS's discourses. In particular, the dominance of class-based movements in the struggle against dictatorship in the 1970s meant that SOS feminists who came of age in that period absorbed inclinations toward revolutionary change, rather than piecemeal reform. When "gender" came on the scene, they were receptive to Scott's transformative approach. One group member explained:

> I think that ideas reach a certain place [from elsewhere], but they find a political, theoretical, and cultural base where they either settle in or they don't.... I think Joan Scott caught on so much here because feminists..., in general, have a Marxist heritage. Even though... radical feminism was very strong in Brazil...it didn't lose the commitment to a historical perspective on social transformation.

This perspective, along with the social inequalities in Brazil, led SOS members to direct their message toward the popular majority from the beginning, and, later, to give class content to their understanding of "gender." Their working-class constituency too pushed the Recife feminists beyond the limits of the discourse of "women" toward a language that could encompass their lives in families, communities, and class-based movements of both men and women.

The absence of movements around sexual preference and the weakness of black women's organizing in the region in the early 1990s meant that there was, at that point, little pressure to incorporate differences among women other than class in SOS's work. As the decade wore on, however, these omissions were increasingly challenged by black women and lesbians, as they began the process of constructing their own movements.[56] Though some of these activists kept their distance from white heterosexual feminism, others maintained a dialogue with SOS, seeking to push the NGO to expand its practices around gender. One Afro-Brazilian activist and SOS ally remarked:

> I think that the organization should be looking more closely at this racial question...you can't work on things in an isolated way. The gender relation isn't so simple. There is something that differentiates a black woman and a white woman. What is this something? What can we do so that we advance as a group, as black, white, and indigenous women?

SOS's discourse on gender was also influenced by its relationship to a changing Brazilian state. Democratization was accompanied by economic crisis in the early 1980s. After a brief period of feminist withdrawal into civil society, the dramatic lack of resources for health drew SOS's attention back to the state. Simultaneously, during the last years of the dictatorship, a number of feminists and fellow travelers infiltrated the Ministry of Health, offering SOS opportunities for intervention in the state not available to activists working on other issues. Over time, feminist pressure opened up other niches, such as the National Council on Women's Rights, and SOS and other feminist organizations also participated in the struggle to shape the new national constitution. Taking advantage of these openings meant working with both men and women, creating alliances, and developing proposals for broader social change. Scott's notion of gender offered a theoretical means of making sense of this new political panorama.

Finally, SOS's links to international funding agencies had a role in the emergence of a particular set of meanings around "gender." The early support these agencies gave SOS's work on women's health fostered the move toward the formalization and professionalization of the original collective of volunteers. These developments, in turn, allowed SOS to expand its visibility and transnational connections through participation in global networks, attendance at international conferences, growing access to and use of the Internet, and so on. Its insertion into global networks gave it access to the circuits through which gender theories and discourses were circulating and through which they reached Recife. At the same time, the pressure of funding agencies on all applicants for proposals with a gender component created a new demand for gender training by feminist "experts."[57] International grants enhanced SOS's capacity to respond, and the NGO quickly became one of the primary purveyors of such training in the Northeast.

In 1990, faced with the inadequacy of the organization's original discourse to articulate its evolving practices, for the second time, SOS drew on feminism from the North as a resource. But, at this juncture in its history, as an established organization with a leadership role at the national and international levels, SOS negotiated with foreign influences from a position of strength. The organization's leaders did not borrow discourses and practices directly from Northern feminist movements, but selectively appropriated academic theories of gender, rearticulated them as a set of activist discourses, and integrated them with their own pre-existing practices.

As a discourse, gender helped SOS recreate its identity, while broadening its agenda and bringing feminism to new constituencies. Nonetheless, the new conception, in itself, was vulnerable to manipulation. Increasingly powerful forces threatened to drain feminist gender discourses of their transformative content and corral them into serving technocratic ends. SOS confronted these dangers through recourse to the locally based discursive construction of "citizenship."

EXPANDING CITIZENSHIP, 1990–98

[O]ne of the fundamental elements in transformations of gender inequalities is precisely the recognition that by struggling to improve the concrete conditions of their lives, women [are] exercising their citizenship on a daily basis; they are acting in the political sphere and, beyond that, constructing through these actions a bridge between the public and the private.

(Camurça and Gouveia, *Cidade, cidadania: Um olhar a partir das mulheres*, 1995a, p. 33)

SOS did not let gender stand alone but, through its practices, linked the imported discourse to an idiom with a uniquely local meaning—that of citizenship. Placing gender in the context of this indigenous construction had a politicizing effect that opened up the possibility of navigating the treacherous shoals of success and maintaining commitments to gender and social justice.

"Citizenship" had its own travels and itineraries, which passed through the French Revolution, as well as the exclusionary naturalization acts that constructed the early U.S. version of the concept. In the 1980s and 1990s, while "gender" had a North to South trajectory, the discourse of citizenship resurfaced simultaneously in multiple locations around the world, taken up by nativist forces in the United States opposing the presence of undocumented immigrants, as well as by social movements fighting neoliberal attacks on welfare states, and by those pushing forward democratization processes from Eastern Europe to Latin America. In each location, it took distinctive forms—in some it was an ideological rationale; in others, it served as the tool of an academic critique; in yet others it expressed an inchoate aspiration or a revolutionary demand. The substantive meanings it held varied widely according to political circumstance.[58]

In Recife, unlike "gender," "citizenship" made no sudden dramatic appearance. Instead, it seemed to seep into the discourse of SOS Corpo, as if part of the surrounding air, its placement in the organization's name the first clear signal of its arrival. Though it surfaced frequently in writings and political slogans, grant proposals, and seminars, the concept was not often the explicit focus of study or debate; instead, "citizenship" was tacitly incorporated as a framework associated with certain practices.

The first practice was the dissemination of knowledge. In the 1990s, SOS grouped its documentation center, media liaison, and video distribution projects under the rubric "Information for Citizenship." Knowledge of the body and health practices took on new meaning; no longer only a vehicle for women's autonomy and empowerment, now they were also a means to full participation in a new social order.

In 1989, conservative candidate Fernando Collor de Mello won the presidency, and the national state retreated from commitments to gender equality made in the early period of democratization.[59] In response, SOS, like other Brazilian feminist organizations, shifted its efforts from fighting for the formal recognition of new social rights, to struggling for the implementation of those rights it had won in the previous decade. At the same time, its locus of political action expanded in two directions. From direct involvement with the state on a national level SOS moved toward both greater engagement with local governments and more concerted efforts to influence the national and local states through transnational organizing.

As neoliberal policies promoted decentralization as a means to shift responsibilities off the shoulders of the national state, changes in Brazilian laws gave local governments greater autonomy and additional resources. "Municipalities become…the basic political setting in which the daily construction of democracy and citizenship takes place, through negotiation and local agreements among groups with diverse interests," according to a publication edited by SOS in 1997.[60] With this understanding, the institution sent a representative to the Municipal Development Council, began working with women in neighborhood associations, and launched a newsletter, *De Olho na Cidade* (*With an Eye on the City*).

At the same time, the increasingly global nature of its targets and the possibilities opened by newly created feminist networks led SOS to accelerate its cross-border activism in the 1990s. By the end of the previous decade, staff had already attended a number of international events and they were participating in a raft of transnational feminist networks. In the 1990s, SOS assumed leadership of several of these networks and played an important role in the local, national, and international preparations for the U.N. Women's Conference in Beijing. The 1995 conference gave SOS an opportunity to help strengthen a newly founded alliance among local women's organizations, the *Foro de Mulheres de Pernambuco* (Pernambucan Women's Forum). The NGO worked with the Forum to spread the word about the Beijing event and, afterward, to lobby for implementation of conference accords through concrete legislative and policy changes at a municipal level. SOS also took part in a similar effort at a national level through the *Articulação de Mulheres Brasileiras* (AMB [Brazilian Women's Network]).[61] Global activism became a vehicle for expanding women's rights in Recife, which, in turn, served as a means of pressing claims on the state.

SOS's conception of citizenship included both elements common to feminist analysis elsewhere and contributions particular to the Brazilian context. Its overall concern was with pushing the boundaries of citizenship outward to incorporate rights that would allow women equal participation in both society and polity. In particular, the Recife organization, like feminist movements in the United States and Europe, sought the inclusion of reproductive rights in a broader definition of citizenship, a move that would "make the sphere of reproduction a site of the constitution of political subjects," and contribute to the dissolution of boundaries between public and private.[62]

Beyond a set of particular rights, for SOS:

> citizenship [was] also a "conflictive practice linked to power, which reflects struggles about who can say what in defining what are common problems and how they will be treated" [Jelin 1994]. In other words, the conquest of rights necessarily passes through the

recognition and action of political subjects, male or female, and the "right to have rights" [Arendt, cited in Jelin 1994].[63]

In this sense, the concept was closely linked to struggles for democratization being carried on by a wide variety of social movements in Brazil at the time.

Finally, "citizenship" meant not only guaranteeing the right of women and other disempowered groups to make decisions affecting their lives, but also ensuring the social conditions to allow them to take advantage of this right. Women who faced the dramatic conditions of poverty, illiteracy, poor health, and racism in Brazil, and in the Northeast in particular, would not have access to "free" political and reproductive choices without sweeping changes in social relations. In an article published in the academic journal *Revista Estudos Feministas* (*Journal of Feminist Studies*), SOS coordinator Maria Betânia Ávila wrote: "Feminism…should constitute itself as a permanent site of redefinition and insertion of these [reproductive] rights in the broader dynamic of the transformation of social inequalities."[64]

In this context, SOS's discourse on citizenship implied a trenchant critique of the dominant economic and political model whose effects in terms of misery and marginalization were increasingly felt in the 1990s among the women with whom they worked. In Ávila's words:

[L]iberalism…where the market is perceived as the institution that promotes possibilities for choice, and accumulation and competition are basic values that support it…could never incorporate the implicit issues in the notion of reproductive rights in an integral way.[65]

Full citizenship and the competitive market economy being championed by successive Brazilian governments were viewed by feminists as fundamentally incompatible, as they were by left movements around Latin America and beyond.

The shift in SOS discourse from "the body" to the kind of "citizenship" described above had important theoretical and strategic implications. The discourse of the body had first been linked to practices based on an inward turn toward oneself as an autonomous being. As organizational practice evolved, however, the body was constituted as the carrier of (reproductive) rights and, therefore, a subject of politics beyond the self. But the focus was still on female specificity, and the struggle was defined as the province of women.

The move to "citizenship", which grew out of this change in practices, established a broader framework in which bodily rights were to be claimed. It implied, in fact required, the negotiation of alliances with diverse groups that shared an interest in this inclusive vision. And it meant understanding how women *and* men, and the reconstructed relations between them, might be part of this vision. As with "the body," the emphasis was on gender difference, rather than sameness, but in this case, it was on the rights required to ensure that women, particularly poor women, had equal status as political subjects.

The new discourse of citizenship came, not from abroad, but from Brazilian movements struggling to push democratization beyond the narrow confines conceived by the elite. In the 1980s, as the authoritarian regime "liberalized" from within and formal democratic political institutions were established, the term began to circulate among the opposition.[66] "Citizenship" became a vehicle for a wide diversity of heretofore suppressed aspirations for social rights—from employment and land, to racial pride and culture, to health and sexual pleasure. As an SOS staffperson explained, it was also a means of rejecting old clientelistic practices:

> Citizenship, in the general discussion, means this: I am a person full of rights, which might not be recognized, but I have the right to be happy, to earn money, to study,…to have fun, to be healthy. I don't owe favors to anyone. I have to win this right for myself. To do that I have to have the right to participate, to express myself, to organize freely, to march, to carry out political pressure.

It was not surprising that the conception of citizenship constructed by an opposition with a Marxist legacy would also incorporate a rejection of neoliberal policies and emphasize the importance of social transformation as a necessary condition of political participation.

In spite of the local nature of citizenship as an oppositional discourse, transnational feminism—and the international funding agencies that facilitated access to it—also helped shape the specific content that feminists gave to citizenship. Both SOS founders' experiences with movements around reproductive issues in Europe and the United States and their participation in the international women's health movement during the 1980s contributed to their conception of rights. At a 1984 International Tribunal in Amsterdam, in a dialogue among women's movements around the world, struggles that had been narrowly focused around abortion and birth control in the Northern countries were broadened and reframed as reproductive rights.[67] According to Ávila, "In this new perspective, conception, birth, contraception and abortion are seen as interlinked events where the impossibility of access to any one of them puts the woman in a submissive position."[68] This approach, which defends the right of women to have, as well as not to have, children, is the one reflected in the meanings SOS gave to citizenship.

Finally, feminists' relationship to the state played a part in constructing an inclusive discourse of citizenship. During the 1980s, openings for feminist movements led SOS and other organizations to occupy spaces in the state and to participate in struggles for the formal recognition of social rights. Despite a series of victories, however, many of the programs that were won, including the women's health program, PAISM, were never effectively implemented. According to SOS analyses, this reflected intervention by the Church and private family planning agencies, corruption, and a lack of political will to address women's needs, based on the state's ties to economic elites whose interest lay in restrictions on social spending.[69]

Meanwhile, an accelerating economic crisis deepened the reproductive health crisis, particularly among those women already living on the margins. By 1991, one study found that nearly 70 percent of those using a contraceptive method in the Northeast used sterilization, an increase of more than 15 percent in five years.[70] This was one factor in what has been called the "demographic transition" expressed in plunging fertility rates.[71] The combination of worsening health conditions, the closing of doors to feminists at the national level, and the clear inadequacy of a truncated democratization process led SOS, with its links to women in the urban periphery, to adopt a conception of citizenship that embraced substantive social rights and that rested on an inclusive political vision.

In spite of its academic roots far from Recife, gender as a discourse offered much to local feminists. Its appeal to Brazilian movements in part reflected collective identities parallel to those being developed by feminists in the North. But the meanings carried by the discourse in Northeast Brazil deviated from those found elsewhere. As they fused "gender" with home-grown concepts of citizenship, SOS Corpo drew out its radical implications. By calling for the extension of democratization to incorporate substantive rights, "citizenship" challenged the basis of inequalities among women and provided a framework for alliances among movements based on class, race, sexual orientation, and gender, among others. Whether these alliances could be forged, however, remained a subject of ongoing contestation and negotiation.[72]

CULTURAL CONTENTIONS

Transnational cultural flows constitute one of the essential strands that knit disparate movements together in a counterpublic. But social movement discourses, such as "women's bodies" and "gender," can only relocate and set down roots through the work of agents who appropriate and translate them. Discourses need practices in order to exercise their power, and translators work in the space between the loose couplings of language and tactics, shifting first one, then the other, and linking borrowed discourses to more familiar political rhetorics and tactical repertoires.

Feminist movements in the global South, like their counterparts in Europe and the United States, play an active role in facilitating the movement of meanings across borders. Their relationship to hegemonic discourses from certain sites in the North is neither a matter of simple acceptance, nor of totally autonomous local innovation, but rather an ongoing process of cultural struggle to accommodate globally mobile feminist conceptions to their local political milieus.

As the feminists of SOS Corpo constructed a movement around women's health, they drew on transnational discursive resources that resonated with the elements of collective identity that they shared with European and American women's movements. But imported discourses brought risks of cultural imposition and dangers of depoliticization. SOS Corpo resisted these threats by selectively appropriating the language of Northern feminisms and resignifying its meanings through their practices. In the process, the women's health organization asserted a form of power based on its engagement with local constituencies and institutions—as it contended with the cultural and economic power of Northern feminisms and the international funding agencies that often promoted them.

But the local power of Northeast Brazilian feminists had limits. The experience of SOS illustrates the ways activists transformed feminist theories and discourses as they followed trajectories from North to South. Cultural flows in the reverse direction, however, were uneven. While "women's bodies" and "gender" had journeyed South and been appropriated by feminists in Recife, Brazilian constructions of "gender" linked to "citizenship" found more obstacles to travel in the reverse direction.

Revisiting the BWHBC nearly thirty years after its emergence revealed an organization dramatically transformed in many respects. Like SOS, it had professionalized and become a formalized organization. The one-time collective of middle-class white women had diversified internally and had stimulated the construction of a vast transnational network. No longer rejecting medical expertise, the Collective's materials had come, in some ways, to embody it, making the latest research available to allow women to make informed choices.[73]

In other ways, the BWHBC remained quite faithful to its original discursive orientation. Women's bodies remained central to its project; neither gender nor citizenship was anywhere apparent in its discourse. Where SOS used the language of "gender," the Boston Collective continued to speak of "women"; where SOS fought social exclusion and targeted the state, BWHBC continued to struggle against the social control of women's bodies and took aim at the institution of medicine; where SOS demanded citizenship and the "right to have rights," the Boston Collective continued to seek consumer empowerment and the right to control one's own body.[74]

The discursive approach of the BWHBC did not appear to be unique among longstanding feminist institutions in the United States. In the late 1990s, gender theories and discourses certainly pervaded the academic disciplines, and debates around citizenship were common in U.S. universities. These concepts could also sometimes be found among groups of immigrant women and women of color, whose ties across borders were more direct and less asymmetrical than those of mainstream feminism. But it was rare to find established U.S. feminist organizations outside the academy giving discourses of gender and citizenship the central place in their work that SOS Corpo and many other Brazilian feminists did.[75] From this perspective, discursive travel between activists in different parts of the counterpublic had a dislocated quality, with flows from North to South occurring far more easily and consistently than in the reverse direction, particularly in the case of the United States.[76]

On the one hand, it is clear that feminists in different locations engaged with different kinds of institutions. Organizing in the context of a newly democratizing state, such as Brazil, called for discursive strategies quite unlike those called for when organizing in the context of a vast private medical industry, like the one in the United States. On the other hand, despite these kinds of differences, Brazilian feminists were able to make creative use of discourses from the U.S. and European women's health movements, as well as theories from the Northern academy, even while adapting them to their own local conditions. How, then, is it that the obstacles to travel were greater in the reverse direction? What are the forces that have the power to close some borders and exclude, while ensuring that others remain permeable to cultural imports? And why does it matter for counterpublics of all kinds?

The barriers to conceptual migration from women's movements in the South to many of those in the North take a variety of forms. On a discursive level, the periphery and its intellectual products are often constructed in the North as both exotic and specific, while the center and its discourses and theories enjoy universalized status. In terms of politics, the class-conscious feminisms of the South find some echo in Europe, but little in the United States, where class is a category largely absent from movement practice.[77] And, in the economic sphere, inequalities ensure that distribution networks for Brazilian academic—and activist— theorizing do not operate with the same insistence and power as do those that disseminate Euro-American discourses and theories.[78]

Discursive travel and translation across internally diverse counter-publics are essential to the processes of dialogue and debate that produce strong oppositional alliances. The task becomes all the more urgent as social movements increasingly confront enemies that require coordinated efforts, shared strategies, or innovative tactical repertoires. In spite of their impressive accomplishments, the case described in this chapter shows that transnational feminist movements have only begun the process of constructing a counterpublic where horizontal discursive travel and mutual translation could challenge the fundamental asymmetries in global cultural flows, a space where movements in the North could benefit fully from the rich experience of feminists in the South.

The next two chapters shift perspective from discursive struggles to political negotiations among social movement organizations, addressing another strand of sometimes conflictive connection across the feminist counterpublic. Chapter 4 takes us to the *sertão*, introducing the MMTR and describing their relations with the male-dominated agricultural union movement. Chapter 5 then compares this local class-based alliance to the transnational connections developed by the rural women around gender, with SOS Corpo.

4

NEGOTIATING CLASS AND GENDER

Devalued Women in a Local Counterpublic

In 1984, local activists from the Rural Women Workers' Movement (MMTR), backed by the agricultural unions around the town of Serra Talhada, organized the first gathering of women from across the Pernambucan *sertão*. The movement itself had been founded two years earlier in a small local community, called Caiçarina da Penha, one of the first such efforts in Brazil. At the 1984 *Encontro*, thirty-three small farmers, sharecroppers, and landless workers from nineteen communities participated in discussions aimed, in part, at reflecting on the role of women in the rural union movement. Though all worked in agriculture, and many were heads of households, less than a third had had any prior relation to the union, reflecting the historic marginalization of women from the workers' movement, or, indeed, for some, from even an identity as worker.

At the meeting the women were asked to speak about their lives, and their testimonies, later recorded in an MMTR publication, were marked by the dual experience of class and gender:

> Oh my God, I am out of breath. I am a little excited because I never went out [before]. My husband is the one who comes here [to town] and I stay at home.... My husband goes out to shop, to take a trip, to do business, and I just stay home.

> I am nervous—I don't know what I am going to say. It seems like women suffer more than men. They have to raise the kids, make

the food, help in the fields. I am a farmer. I have to help because my husband doesn't have any loans from the bank.

I…work in the onion fields, you know? Onions right now don't bring in any money. My husband only has help from God and our health. So, I help him.… I feel good because I am strong. If it were only for the work of my husband, we would have died. That's why I know how to make a living.

…[W]hen we say that we help in the fields it's because we are helping the men and we don't get anything in return. When it's time to work, it's men and women's work; when it's time to get paid, the money belongs only to the man.[1]

Their words evoked both their embeddedness in families struggling for economic survival and their distinctive experiences as subalterns within a gender hierarchy.

At this initial *Encontro*, leaders asked participants to identify two kinds of problems: those they faced as women, and those they confronted as members of a rural working class. The group prioritized one issue to address in each category: as rural workers, they agreed that they suffered most from the lack of conditions sustaining a viable family agriculture; as women, they protested the unequal pay for male and female day laborers. More than a decade later, in the mid-1990s, members of the MMTR studied the concept of "gender relations" but also discussed sustainable agriculture; they organized around the impact of AIDS on women but also pressed the government to favor small farmers in its drought relief programs. While the specifics of the issues had changed, the insistence on linking gender *and* class struggles had not.[2]

Organizations and discursive communities straddle diverse political spaces, based on the multiple identities and experiences of their members. The MMTR was located at the intersection of two distinctive counterpublics—one organized around class relations and the other around gender, one rooted in the local, the other stretching across borders. The rural women were linked to other members in each of these publics in part by discursive connections—with one, ways of thinking about women's subordination and gender identity, and with the other, ways of thinking about economic injustice and class identity.

But counterpublics are held together not only by intangible cultural connections, but also by relations among organizations. While the kinds of discursive links traced in the preceding chapter may involve contention, conflict over discourses, by itself, produces few casualties in social movement alliances. Links between organizations, on the other hand, often take the form of negotiated exchanges and require careful diplomacy.[3]

Narrow institutional or other interests quite often undermine shared long-term goals. The fact that organizations participate in multiple publics and articulate diverse identities makes the creation of coalitions all the more complex. In contemporary counterpublics, at the level of political relations, collaboration coexists uneasily with contestation.

This chapter and the one that follows turn from discursive links to political alliances among social movement organizations. In these chapters, I examine the nature of the resources social movements use to negotiate with one another, as well as the way the process is complicated by their allegiances to distinctive counterpublics. This chapter considers the relations of the rural women's movement to the male-dominated agricultural unions in the 1980s. Chapter 5 takes up the MMTR's alliance with transnational feminisms, through its relationship with SOS Corpo.

RESOURCES AND RELATIONSHIPS

Throughout its history, the MMTR juggled political relationships with two organizations linked to distinctive counterpublics. On the one hand, the MMTR's roots in the local union movement revolved around issues of class; on the other, its ties to transnational feminism—sustained, in part, through urban institutions like SOS Corpo—reflected the perspective of gender. Each of these alliances provided important sources of identification and support to the rural women's movement; yet, in each, there were moments when political differences provoked disagreement or organizational interests clashed.

At those moments, the MMTR used creative forms of negotiation to defend its perspective or interests vis-à-vis rural men and urban feminists, while preserving its alliances with each group. In doing so, the movement drew on a variety of political resources—currencies that act as a source of influence or means of exchange with others.[4] Some of these currencies are both tangible and measureable—money, infrastructure, members, and social networks, for example.[5] Other attributes—such as leadership abilities, experience, forms of knowledge, or political discourses—are intangible and less easily quantified, but nevertheless they too can be deployed directly as resources in the context of social movement struggles.[6] These intangible currencies are often particularly important for movements, like the MMTR, which may be rich in organizing experience, but lack funding or sophisticated infrastructure.

Beyond these two kinds of *practical* assets, movements also draw on *symbolic* resources—qualities, such as legitimacy, authenticity, authority, or expertise, which emerge in the course of relations among social actors.[7] These cultural forms of power do not stand alone, but are loosely attached to more easily accessible practical assets, though not always in predictable

Table 4.1 Political Resources

Practical		Symbolic
Tangible	**Intangible**	
Money	Leadership ability	Legitimacy
Infrastructure	Experience	Authenticity
Membership	Knowledge	Expertise
Networks	Political discourses on race, class, gender etc.	Authority

ways. For example, a large membership is usually linked to legitimacy; access to funding, on the other hand, *may* help produce legitimacy, but may also undermine it. Symbolic resources may, or may not, be deployed by social movements in a calculated manner. Instead, qualities, such as legitimacy, may simply accrue to organizations by virtue of their practices and the larger social context. While volatile and apparently ephemeral, in certain circumstances, these qualities can become currencies of exchange and sources of power in their own right, as we'll see in Chapter 5.[8]

Organizations wield different configurations of political resources, which change over time. The MMTR may have been financially impoverished, but it was rich in human capital, with a skilled leadership, a substantial and fiercely committed membership, and longstanding personal and professional relationships within the union movement, as well as, increasingly, contacts among feminists in Brazil and outside it. The rural women's movement also had potentially valuable symbolic assets. By virtue of the poverty, marginalized status, and extent of its constituency, the organization could draw on discourses of class and regional legitimacy as forms of leverage with urban feminists. In its struggle with the unions, the MMTR evoked the legitimacy associated with its leaders' long experience and dedication as organizers in the class-based movement.

The value of political resources is contingent, acquired in the context of particular relationships at specific historical moments. In fact, they can only *become* "resources" under certain conditions. Organizational attributes in general are converted from taken-for-granted qualities into potentially influential forms of strategic leverage when power and inequality come into play. Their meaning is embedded in social relations. Most resources—and especially those that are symbolic—only acquire their ability to have effects in a context where different groups of social actors come to share the same sense of their value—and the same need or desire to possess them.[9]

In the MMTR's early years, during the 1980s, its array of attributes held far less value for its class comrades than for its gender allies. While the unions, for the most part, treated women as junior partners in a class struggle, feminist allies by and large encouraged their autonomy and promoted their leadership of what they hoped would be a rural gendered revolution. As a result, during this period, the MMTR employed a distinctive means of defending its interests and political agenda with each of its counterparts. In this chapter, I begin with the local, tracing the relations of the rural women's organization within the class-based counterpublic during the period of the 1980s.

MMTR and union members shared a class identity, a culture, and a conception of social and economic justice, as well as, in most cases, a roof or a bed. This was a political relationship constructed through often mundane, day-to-day practices, which provided an initial institutional and ideological framework. The MMTR's links to the unions gave the women's organization added legitimacy within local communities and access to resources from the state and other local institutions.[10] But the rural women struggled for recognition in what was largely a male union brotherhood that placed little value on their participation and often seemed to view their organization as a threat. In the early years, as devalued insiders in a dysfunctional organizational family, they maneuvered within its constraints. Though they spoke their minds, MMTR leaders also sought to preserve their links to the larger union structure. Rather than waging pitched battles, they exercised diplomatic skills, drawing on personal relationships, building support incrementally, and asserting autonomy quietly but forcefully.

The following three sections lay the groundwork for my argument. The first explores the roots of the rural trade unions and the nature of their relationship to the state; the second goes on to explore gender relations in the *sertão*; and the third describes the emergence of a rural women's movement from the unions in the early 1980s. The body of the chapter then examines the MMTR's strategic use of its political resources in its relations with the rural union movement in this early period. In the conclusion, I argue that the ability of movements to make effective use of political resources depends on the larger arena and sets of relationships in which they are deployed. In the late 1980s, the rural women's movement found limited receptivity to its gendered message in a male-dominated union movement, still largely confined within national boundaries.

THE LOCAL: RURAL UNIONS AND THE STATE

The rural union movement with which the MMTR was loosely affiliated emerged in the 1950s during Brazil's populist *Segunda República*.[11] Pernambuco was one of the earliest sites of resistance to capitalist modernization, which was driving peasants—particularly in the fertile coastal zone—off the land and into a variety of forms of wage labor. In the mid-1950s, Peasant Leagues used the tactics of direct action to demand land redistribution without compensation and to call attention to the shocking poverty and the nearly feudal power of the large landowners in the Northeast Brazilian countryside.[12] But by the end of the decade the Leagues were eclipsed by rural trade unions, which defended worker interests from within the state's corporatist structure and accepted its framework of a limited agrarian reform. By 1960, there were eight different rural workers' unions in Brazil, three of them in Pernambuco. In 1962, the state federation was founded; the following year FETAPE joined other state federations to create a national confederation of agricultural workers, CONTAG.

The early 1960s brought a surge of rural union organization in the context of the populist presidency of João Goulart.[13] In Pernambuco, the unions found support in the governor's office from Miguel Arrães, who saw a potential constituency among rural workers, as well as from the Catholic Church and left political parties. These forces opposed the radical anarchism of the Leagues and sought to offer a more moderate alternative. After a statewide cane workers' strike in 1963, Arrães brokered an agreement that recognized unions' collective bargaining rights, raised wages, and established norms for working conditions for the first time. However, only a year later, a military coup toppled Goulart, jailed Arrães, and brought a temporary end to activism. In anti-union "interventions," resources were seized by government forces and "subversive" leaders beaten, arrested, or, in some cases, killed, and replaced with those more disposed to quiescence.[14] The Leagues, along with the more radical local unions, succumbed to the repression.

But, despite the purges and often violent repression, the military regime, which maintained state power in Brazil from 1964 to 1985, chose not to abolish unions entirely. Unlike the other military dictatorships in Latin America, which crushed union movements, the Brazilian regime instead sought to forestall political challenges by reinforcing and extending state control over their day-to-day operations.[15] Legal provisions dating from an earlier period of dictatorship had put unions firmly under the thumb of the Ministry of Labor.[16] Mechanisms already in place included a system of *unicidade*, whereby local unions were given exclusive rights to represent a given category of workers in a particular area; a mandatory union tax, deducted from an employee's paycheck and returned to the union by the state; and a prescribed hierarchy of officially recognized organizations, from local unions to state federations to a national confederation. The military regime went beyond these pre-existing restrictions, curbing the right to strike and to negotiate salaries and, for a time, limiting union functions to legal counseling for individual workers and their representation in labor courts.

In tandem with its repressive strategy, in the early 1970s the state created Brazil's first welfare system for the countryside and offered the unions the opportunity to administer medical, dental, and, later, retirement benefits to those they certified as "rural workers," through a program known as FUNRURAL. The program had a profound effect, at once providing a massive infusion of state resources into an impoverished union movement, and reshaping it into a provider of welfare services, rather than a defender of worker rights. By 1980, more than half of the government's rural medical services were delivered through unions, a task that demanded a formidable proportion of officials' time, but also drew in enormous numbers of new members.[17] Nationally, between 1968 and 1980, the number of rural unions quadrupled. The trend was even more pronounced in the interior: twenty-three of the thirty-three rural unions in Pernambuco's *sertão* region were founded in the decade when welfare contracts were made available to their officials.[18]

The local unions' new role as provider of state-sponsored services had a significant political impact in rural communities. As one FETAPE leader explained:

> [W]hen people got sick, they filled up the headquarters of the union just with sick people coming to see a doctor in the union office. The union was more a clinic than a union…. If you asked where the workers' union was people would say, "You mean the old people's union? FUNRURAL?" People were confused. They neither knew what a union was, nor what FUNRURAL was. It was all the same thing.

According to a former official from the grouping of unions—or "pole"— in Pernambuco's central *sertão*, the unions' focus on service delivery meant that "the worker remains steeped in individualism….[H]e joins hoping to achieve some objective. Having achieved it, he thinks that he doesn't need [the movement] and he withdraws."[19]

As Pereira points out, for many leaders the bureaucratic work of administering medical programs and processing pension applications had far more appeal than the difficult and often dangerous task of confronting local landowners, or the seemingly quixotic struggle for agrarian reform. The proliferation of state resources in welfare programs increased the power of local union officials, offering the potential for patronage and the possibility of cultivating personal loyalties, which more confrontational activities did not. According to one trade union leader, "Without it [the government], we wouldn't be anything. The government has power. We need it."[20]

But other activists were more critical. Like the longtime state union leader cited above, they believed that the state had ulterior motives:

> [Putting] all this inside the unions was a way of involving the union leaders in "welfarism" (*assistencialismo*) and forgetting the true role of unionism. That's why I say that it was a decade of anesthetizing the union. They anesthetized the unions with welfarism. Many leaders… instead of struggling for land, for a better salary, for better living conditions, were only tied up with FUNRURAL, guiding people through the process of getting retirement [and] medical care. That took up all the union leaders' time; it aborted the union struggle.

A former local official from the central *sertão* also rejected the emphasis on service provision:

> The union that I know is there to defend; it isn't there to give rights to anyone; it's there to struggle for people's rights…. [T]he union is there…to give ideas, but not to do what the government has to do. That's my vision.

These more militant leaders, many of them with roots in progressive Catholic movements, struggled to balance the bureaucratic workload demanded by state programs with the political education they hoped would teach their members to reject passivity and defend their rights collectively. In some cases, helped by the force of circumstance, they succeeded. Along the coast, in the *zona da mata*, where sugar cane workers had mobilized before the coup, unions organized the first mass strike under the dicta-

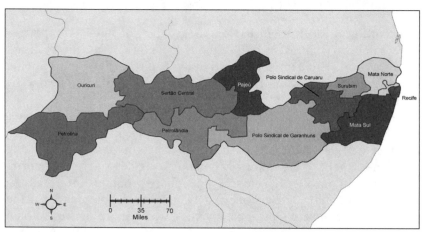

Figure 4.1 Rural Union "Poles" in Pernambuco. Source: FETAPE, http://www.fetape.org.br/index.php?secao=polo_SertaoCentral

torship in 1979. They won both wage increases and a system of tripartite bargaining that included unions, landowners, and the state. According to Pereira, massive annual strikes in the cane fields of Pernambuco for the next decade were one of the factors that led military leaders to orchestrate a gradual retreat and to move toward political democratization.[21]

Union membership in the central *sertão* was dominated by *minifundistas*—small farmers, tenants, and sharecroppers—with different sets of interests than the wage workers along the coast or the prosperous farmers in the *agreste*, the transitional region in between. In the interior, state-sponsored medical services had provided the primary motive for the creation of most rural labor organizations, and continued, in the 1980s, to play a fundamental role in sustaining membership and orienting most unions toward "welfarism." But the *sertão* also had an insurrectionary history of Robin Hood-style bandits and millenarian visionaries, and, as fiscal crisis and changing priorities undermined state support for union medical programs, challenges to the service-provision model began to emerge in some local organizations.[22]

Then too, the strikes on the coast had ripple effects in the *sertão*. This was particularly true in the central *sertão* where an accident of geography had created a humid micro-region around the town of Triunfo in which sugar cultivation and processing brought together large groups of workers. The historical memory of their confrontations with landowners in the 1960s, their subsequent repression, and renewed activism in the 1980s helped give a more politicized character to the unions of the surrounding arid region. There, active local unions defended tenant farmers, sharecroppers, and day laborers in conflicts with landowners over wages, land use, and water access. They fought large ranchers who had historically left their grazing lands unfenced, allowing their cattle to trample the crops of their impoverished neighbors. Unions set up encampments to protest the uncompensated displacement of some five thousand farmers by the government's Serrinha Dam project. And they marched on the state capital, Recife, to demand aid for victims of drought.

These struggles reflected a militance that went far beyond doling out welfare benefits to passive recipients, but even so, they necessarily took place on the terrain of the state. In some cases, target, in others, solution, the state not only bankrolled and regulated union activity in the 1980s, but also played a key role in defining how and for what workers chose to organize. Often, unions appealed directly to the state—for land, price guarantees, subsidized credit, drought relief, welfare benefits, and compensation for the displaced. But even when unions clashed with private landowners, once the untamed rulers of the rural zones, conflicts in this period rarely took place without government mediation. In strikes, the state arbitrated agreements; in struggles over loose cattle and trampled crops, the unions sought changes in the law.

This orientation toward the state on the part of unions reflected both the expansion of government authority over the previous half century into what were once private spheres, and its subsequent retreat in the face of global economic crisis and neoliberal politics in the 1980s. The rural unions, representing one of the most marginalized populations in the country, found themselves both struggling against the state and fighting a rearguard action to preserve and expand the meager protections it had once offered.

The rural union movement was rooted in the local in two senses. On the one hand, it was made up at its base of organizations that functioned at the municipal level, responding to the particular configuration of interests represented among members, who guaranteed unions their political legitimacy. On the other hand, the movement was also "local" in relation to global forces. A national hierarchy presided over a movement that was fundamentally entwined with the Brazilian state. Beyond that, the unions in the *sertão* defended a class of subsistence farmers whose "local-ness" was increasingly enforced by a global economy that threatened to make them obsolete. Taken together, the primarily local nature of the rural unions' institutional connections had a profound influence on the changing character of interactions between the unions and the women of the MMTR.

SERTANEJA STRUGGLES

Traditionally, Northeast Brazilian rural women were invisible in the public sphere. Subordinated within families throughout the life cycle, they passed directly from the authority of parents and brothers to that of husbands and older sons. Their sexuality was a primary object of surveillance; male family members monitored everything from necklines to skirt hems. In their relationships, rural women were expected to subordinate pleasure to procreation. "I was raised to multiply—to serve and not to be served," commented an older woman at a workshop on sexuality, in answer to a question about whether she enjoyed sex. The physical demands of constant pregnancy, as well as the subsequent responsibility for family welfare in the face of frequent scarcity, disease, and death, were heavy burdens for rural women. During my fieldwork, one woman in her seventies, whose experience was common for her generation, told me she "gave birth to thirteen and raised six."[23]

In the *sertão*, women's working lives were divided between *casa* and *roça*, home and field. At home, their fundamental domain, they were responsible for the multiple tasks involved in social reproduction—caring for children, cleaning, washing clothes, and preparing food, as well as hauling water and raising small animals to supplement the family diet and income. In addition, they labored on the family subsistence plot, along with men and older children. But neither women's domestic work nor their labor in the *roça* received social recognition. The *roça* was seen as an exclusively male arena by virtue of the exchange value it produced, and their responsibilities in the home were perceived as the natural order of things. Because of the gender division of labor, women were not defined as workers, despite the indispensable nature of their labor for family survival.[24] Ultimately, many women themselves internalized their own nonexistence as producers of value. One MMTR activist commented:

> Even today there are women who say, "No, I only stay home. I don't work." Now, she washes, irons, cooks, looks for wood…[and] works in the fields…harvesting beans, crushing corn, picking cotton, and she still says, "No, I don't do anything, really."

Their discursive erasure had significant material consequences for women's rights. Law and custom conspired to deny women access to land; in the vast majority of cases titles passed directly from father to son.[25] Even when they were hired out as day laborers, women's wages were tradition-ally half those of men. Until the mid-1980s, many local unions denied them full membership, and they could obtain government benefits, such as pensions, maternity leave, and emergency drought relief work, only by virtue of their connection to a male head of household.[26] Lacking official documents of their own, such as working papers and voting cards, rural women were denied their very identity and, consequently, their ability to exercise citizenship.[27]

But the *sertanejas'* burdens had contradictory effects. As one volunteer who helped initiate the women's movement explained:

> Culturally, women in the *sertão*…live in a relationship of deep sub-jection. But it has some peculiar characteristics. For example, the autonomy [they have through] raising the animals. It's a relationship of subjection and at the same time [they are] strong women. I don't know how else to say it…they are women born in the struggle for survival.

Survival was never more in question than during the cyclical droughts that plagued the *sertão* and it was women, the administrators of the family economy, who paid the most devastating psychological price, as food supplies shrank and families went hungry. With sons and husbands departing to seek work in the cities, often never to return, many of these women became *viuvas da seca* (widows of the drought) left with the full burden of the household on their shoulders. The independence imposed on women in the *sertão* during these extended periods of hardship led some to seek collective solutions.

THE BIRTH OF THE MMTR

The Rural Women Workers' Movement in Pernambuco was born in the early 1980s during one of the most severe and prolonged dry spells in memory.[28] As the agricultural workers' union mobilized in response, Vanete Almeida, the only female organizer in the central *sertão* region for the state union federation, FETAPE, began to question the long-time absence of women in union affairs:[29]

> I used to meet with a group of eighty, one hundred people and there wasn't one woman, except me....I only got closer to other women when there were meetings in the countryside, in the workers' homes. But the women didn't come to the living room, where the meeting was. I stayed in the living room, talking with their husbands, brothers or sons, and they were hidden in other parts of the house. When the meeting was over, I went to the bedrooms or the kitchen and talked a little with them. Sometimes, I was more daring. I sat at the table with the men and asked why the women weren't there too. They answered that the women were busy serving the table and, for that reason, couldn't sit there. This situation made me feel more and more anguished. I had to do something. So, I said to the men that I wouldn't continue to eat lunch with them, that I would go eat lunch in the kitchen with the women. My intention was to know why they didn't sit with us, why they didn't get close. So I decided to eat with them in the kitchen. It was really strange for them. They were kind of uncomfortable, but it was an opportunity for us to talk.[30]

In her travels to meet with union members on isolated homesteads, she slowly began coaxing women out of their kitchens, away from their husbands' watchful eyes, and into contact with other women. The first meeting, held in a church with a small group in attendance, focused on the drought and how the women were surviving it.[31] A volunteer who helped organize the meeting remembered the following incident:

> In the *sertão* the ideal of beauty is different.... A woman is pretty when she is fat. Fatness [is or] was the synonym of beauty, health, vigor. And I remember that on the sidewalk outside the church, a little before one of these meetings,...Maria, who was very thin,

leaned down and said to Vanete [the FETAPE organizer], "Oh Vanete, you are so pretty! You are so strong! I am so skinny, so ugly." And it was an expression of [the fact] that she was really experiencing hunger.

Almeida was joined, in the early years, by three other collaborators: a local union staff member, a sociology student and urban community organizer, and a FETAPE staff member in Recife.[32] These founders all shared geographical origins in the *sertão* and political roots in class-based movements: Three had been involved with political education projects based in liberation theology; one was a member of a left political party. All were from middle-class backgrounds and had both more education and more contact with the world beyond the *sertão* than the women they sought to organize.[33]

The four advisors who called the early meetings used a methodology influenced by liberation theology and the popular education movement in which the MMTR's founders had initiated their political lives. Employing consciousness-raising techniques inspired by Brazilian educator-theorist Paulo Freire, they spent their time "hearing, listening, creating together with the women, [allowing them to be] the main protagonists."[34] Rather than imposing their own particular views, organizers saw themselves as facilitating the development of others, "creating a space where women could speak."

The goal of these early discussions was to create a female identity, a process where the influence of church-based movements and the link to class-based social justice work were again visible.[35] As one volunteer remembered:

[W]e thought that for them to begin to speak, to express themselves, there had to be "specific" meetings [of women by themselves]. The discussion in the church [youth] group in which I participated… [was about] the importance of bringing people of the same social condition together, with the goal of constructing a social identity. I think [this idea] was also present when we said, "It has to be a meeting specifically for women."

If Joan Scott traveled from the U.S. academy to the *sertão*, Paulo Freire moved from the church to the kitchen. In effect, a methodology designed to empower workers as a class served also to empower the women within that class in terms of gender. In the end, it helped unleash a force that the class-based movements could not control.

The MMTR's location at the intersection of two distinctive counter-publics was visible in its practices over more than two decades. In 1984, after two years of grassroots organizing, the MMTR held the *Encontro* of women from different communities across the central Pernambucan *sertão*, described at the beginning of this chapter. Their discussions addressed the question: "Who are we?" According to one participant, the impact of discovering the self was so great that it reduced some women to tears. In fact, female identity was also new for some of the activists who launched the organization. One of them described her feelings:

> And me, I was there [in the movement], but I didn't even perceive that I was a woman. I just wanted to see things different, see a more just world. But for me, it didn't matter if you were a man or a woman. For me, it was the question of class, and inequality was just based on class.

As time went on, however, her ideas began to change:

> I started to go into internal shock. "But, my God, how is it that I [have been] in this union movement all these years and didn't even perceive myself," you know? The discrimination that I lived in the family, as a woman...and in the movement as well because I was a woman, and I was really small.... And so I began to go into shock: "And why did it take me so long?" And at the same time I said, "Well, but it isn't too late. Now I am awake. So I have a mission: to awaken other women."

MMTR organizers faced multiple obstacles in the struggle to build a movement. The first hurdle was logistical. Organizing and communicating with members were serious challenges because of the way the dry unproductive land in the *sertão* had given rise to tiny settlements, scattered widely across the landscape on rocky dirt roads. Almeida remembered traveling "fifteen or twenty kilometers to find one, two or three women."[36] Mail delivery to remote communities was nonexistent, and messages often arrived via union organizers, family members, or traveling priests. Funding for transport, food, and lodging for meetings was meager and materials often had to be begged or borrowed.

There were also less tangible barriers. Many rural women rarely or never left field and home. As a consequence, according to one organizer, many of them were afraid:

> Fear is something that really gets in the way. Even today it holds women rural workers back a lot. But when they lose this fear, they go a long way...because they lose the fear of speaking; they lose the fear of leaving the house; they lose the fear of the husband.... They begin, you know, to value themselves, to feel like people.

Organizers developed techniques to address some of the concrete ways that apprehensions were expressed:

> [W]e would go to their homes to pick them up and take them back, since they had never left home [before]. And we had to be really careful not to leave [anyone] alone, to always link up two or three from the same area so that they would begin to situate themselves and start to lose their fear.

But the fact remained that for most MMTR members to leave home, even to attend a two-day meeting in a nearby town, was a major achievement that involved having the cash to buy enough food to last through their absence, preparing meals in advance, finding childcare, providing for animals, leaving laundry and other chores done, standing up to disapproving neighbors and family members, and grappling with their own guilt, lack of self-confidence, and concerns about the very real dangers on the road.[37]

Male resistance was a significant obstacle. Initially, husbands and family members sometimes accompanied women to meetings, a practice that was tolerated in the hopes that they would discover that the movement was not a threat. But their presence often had a dampening effect, as one organizer explained:

> Once, we were in a meeting, in a union hall. There were a number of women and one couple. At a certain point, we asked Dona Maria Rosa, who was accompanied by her husband, what she understood about unions. She could have said what she wanted, even that she didn't understand anything. What we wanted was for her to speak. She was happy that we had asked her, but when she stepped forward to speak, all excited, her husband held her back and said: "Maria doesn't understand at all. The one who knows is me."[38]

Beyond these attempts to silence, many women lived with insistent surveillance by husbands, children, and neighbors who opposed even their attendance at meetings, whether within the community or in neighboring towns. One MMTR member reported:

> In the community there is criticism when we are going to go out. They say, "Hey, girl, where are you going? What is all this traveling?" They call us vagrants, idlers. "You have lost the love for your children, for your husband, for everything. You aren't that responsible woman you were before...."[39]

Another woman recounted, "As long as I lived with my husband, I participated with one foot in and one foot out because he questioned [me] a lot. I snuck out of the house many times to participate in the meetings."

For many, like this woman, these skirmishes escalated as they increasingly challenged gender norms:

I didn't accept being beaten and staying quiet...any more. I didn't accept him [controlling] my body.... If I put on lipstick, he would tell me to take it off and he took it off with blood, [by] rubbing [it with] a rag. If I painted my nails, he would say, "I'm going to crush them with a hammer," and I didn't accept that any more.

In a number of cases, these conflicts led to beatings, separations, and divorces, and, in at least one, to the violent death of a movement participant.

The women's motives for overcoming these obstacles to participation in the movement often began with curiosity and expanded to a thirst for knowledge and broader horizons. "I went because, since it was a women's meeting, you could...develop [yourself] a little more, clarify [your] vision as a woman," expressed one member. "We didn't have the freedom to go out anywhere, only when [your children] got sick and you had to take [them] to the doctor, or when you were going to baptize [them].... I got involved in the women's struggle in order to participate, to have the freedom of movement, and also to liberate myself," said another.[40]

In its early years, the movement carried out a wide range of activities. The drought of the early 1980s, like others before it, drove men to the cities in search of work, and left women as heads of household with no means to support their families. In many areas, the struggle for equal access to government-sponsored work projects played an important role in the initial process of bringing women together. "We visited the 'emergency fronts,' [the government work projects], and met with the men," explained an MMTR advisor. "There were no women working there, only men.... And we began to look for the women.... Where were [they]? Why weren't they [given employment] as well?"

The situation was so dire that the local unions filed a written protest. In response, the government offered to include women—as cooks for the all-male work crews. The women declined and MMTR leaders organized a group of them to visit the army battalion commander in charge of the projects to demand a chance to work. They eventually won the right to participate in all-women's brigades to dig wells and build dams. Once established, these brigades, each of which included three hundred to five hundred women, served as a fertile recruiting ground for the movement, and offered confirmation of women's capacities.

The lack of full membership in the unions denied women access to benefits such as social security and health care, as well as drought relief and emergency employment. The newly founded MMTR therefore pressed for full union membership rights and struggled to expand women's participation in leadership at all levels of the workers' organizations.

When the drought eased, the MMTR fought for equal pay for female day laborers in the *sertão*:

> The women worked a lot in the harvest.... [A]t the time it was the bean harvest.... It was raining a lot. The beans were in the fields rotting. We organized groups of women—we began in the periphery of the towns, which was made up of rural workers. The largest landowners and producers of beans went with their trucks to pick up workers in the city.... The women were there waiting for the truck and we met beforehand and [they] said: "My pay will be so much." They found out the price of a man's work and said: "We can go to pick your beans now, if you pay X. The same that you pay the men...." And [the landowner] couldn't get any men because they were already at another job. There was a lot of work [at the time]. And [the women] began to win. And it began to spread.... The women workers in the countryside began to do the same thing.[41]

Beyond these battles for economic rights, in many communities MMTR members addressed their needs in other ways. While in some places, women started income-generating collectives that produced soap and herbal medicine, or created community gardens, in others they focused on fighting for schools and day care, or for health and retirement benefits.

In gatherings in the *sertão*, at the initiative of advisors, MMTR members discussed women's role in family agricultural production, studied Engels' historical account of the relation between capitalism and women's domination, learned about women's struggles around the world from New York to Nicaragua, and began to unravel the secrets of human anatomy. At one meeting, organizers brought in a world map:

> It made an impact! Situating themselves, [hearing] that it was a picture of the world, which was round...this flattened ball. Where Brazil is...the Northeast.... Pernambuco.... Serra Talhada. They didn't know!... The testimony at the end was thrilling—[they were] situating themselves in geographical space.

The movement these women built reflected a dual purpose: In a globalizing world, they struggled both to stay "home" and to leave it. On the one hand, the MMTR defended its members' interests as representatives of a sector of small agriculturalists threatened with extinction by the increasingly powerful forces of global capital, a struggle they shared with the union movement. The organization sought to preserve a culture based on love of the land, and to promote the economic viability of small-scale farming, organized around the household, in an effort to keep its members in their home in the *sertão*, rather than seeing them embark on one-way journeys to urban centers.

On the other hand, the MMTR offered sisterhood to rural women in their efforts to break out of the confines of patriarchal family relations, a move that inevitably began with a struggle for freedom of movement—for the chance literally to leave home. This aspect of their struggle, as well as the claim to their own bodies, to social visibility as workers, and to a recognized place in the world, ultimately linked them with transnational feminist movements.

In this way, as globalization intensified in the 1980s and 1990s, the dual focus of this rural women's organization responded to its two faces: the exclusionary effects of global capital flows, and the liberating potential of transnational political and cultural connections. Though they struggled with the men in their lives for even the simple right to attend meetings, and many faced violence or abandonment as the price of their quest for gender equality, members of the MMTR also insisted on the need to strengthen solidarity within families and within unions to ensure their survival as a social class. It was this distinctive dual perspective that shaped the ways the rural women's organization negotiated its relations with both transnational feminisms and local unions.

NEGOTIATING THE LOCAL: THE MMTR AND RURAL UNIONS

Historically, machismo on the part of male leaders and family members, structural constraints related to the gender division of labor, and women's resulting lack of confidence in the public sphere had kept women from active union participation. Before the 1970s, in most municipalities, women could acquire union benefits only through their husbands. But the new decade brought FUNRURAL to the unions and, with it, new demands for access. In the 1980s, a generation of more progressive union leaders began pushing to allow women to join as full members. By the mid-1990s, according to union staff, 60 percent of the members in the central *sertão* region were women. But, said one union organizer,

"Quantity of members was not the same as quality." Many women signed up primarily to get access to medical services or the union certification required for retirement benefits; at the end of the century, most of the active participants and the elected leaders were still men.

MMTR founders responded to the absence of women from local unions. Rather than creating an autonomous women's organization, they sought to challenge and reinforce class-based institutions from within. In a 1994 publication describing the history of the rural women's movement, the authors wrote:

> We believe in the unions as important and strategic places for struggle for transformations in society. We know that, together with male workers, we suffer the same class exploitation. But we also know that it is women, because of their female condition, who suffer sex oppression and this oppression is neither understood nor taken on and confronted in the union movement.[42]

The MMTR's relations with their male counterparts in the unions "were always difficult," as one leader put it. However, the relationship with the unions evolved through a series of phases defined both by the MMTR's development and by changing historical circumstances that reshaped the larger political arena.

1980s: From Paternalism to Power Struggles

In the MMTR's early years, there was opposition to or apathy about women's organizing from some union officials within the central *sertão*, but other local leaders played a key role in facilitating the movement's outreach. One union delegate helped find locales in his community for the first women's meetings; others traveled with MMTR founders to remote communities to help talk with women, to calm husbands' opposition, or, later, to visit the women's emergency work brigades.

A number of unions provided resources for transportation, food, and publicity, and the union's radio program, *A Voz do Trabalhador Rural* (*The Voice of the Rural Worker*), was an important means of disseminating information about women's movement activities. According to a female union staff member and MMTR activist:

> [In my union]…at that time, there was enthusiasm. For the men it was very good; [they were] all happy and satisfied, going to take the women to Serra Talhada, coming back and then going to pick them up. There were a thousand things done to facilitate the women going to the meetings.

While the opponents of women's organizing were generally linked to a more conservative and clientelist form of union politics, its supporters, many of whom had been part of progressive church-based movements with MMTR founders, saw women's participation as part of a broader project to democratize and revitalize the unions. For some, like this former local leader, it was also a personal commitment:

> Look, my life without women isn't worth anything.... If my daughter is a human being, my wife is a human being, my mother is a human being, they have vision. They know things, they learn things, and why should I stop them from participating in what they think is best? Women particularly need to participate in this struggle for integration into the universe. They should participate, understand, struggle, and be strong. Because I understand that any struggle, any movement...without women only goes halfway, or less than half. It won't achieve its main objective.

While rural women found sympathy among some local leaders, such as this man, the reaction at the state level was more patronizing. A former FETAPE staff member described the response when she and another founder took a proposal to state federation leaders, requesting financial support for an MMTR meeting:

> [F]irst, they had before them two women who were not intimidated by the male space. We were already involved in the work; we were necessary, important. So, from the start, we were persons to be received with respect. Second, we had sincerity—we weren't bringing [them] a political party proposal, because they wouldn't accept any such hypothesis, though they got along well with the parties. But there was laughter. Laughter!

Though at least one director argued that educating women would strengthen the organization, and FETAPE approved the MMTR proposal, it was clear that the majority did not take the women's initiative seriously. The limited backing that they offered appeared to be mainly a result of personal relationships with the union staff members involved, rather than a commitment to the principle of women's participation.

In fact, according to a former state official, the laughter veiled substantial suspicion and hostility: "A lot of union people [thought] that this business of women meddling in the union was a matter of wanting to take over.... There was a lot of jealousy." With time, this fear would emerge and take institutional form.

As the decade wore on, the MMTR began to attract members and come into its own politically. The movement spread to other communities

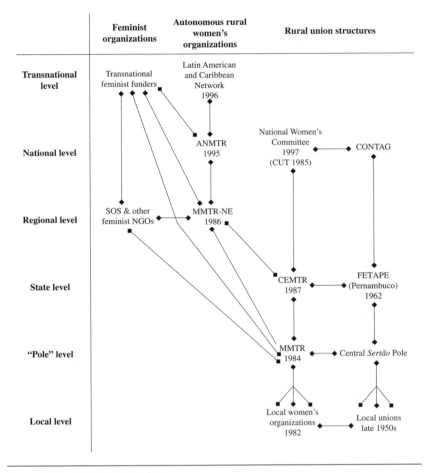

	Feminist organizations	Autonomous rural women's organizations	Rural union structures

Transnational level — Transnational feminist funders — Latin American and Caribbean Network 1996

National level — ANMTR 1995 — National Women's Committee 1997 (CUT 1985) — CONTAG

Regional level — SOS & other feminist NGOs — MMTR-NE 1986

State level — CEMTR 1987 — FETAPE (Pernambuco) 1962

"Pole" level — MMTR 1984 — Central *Sertão* Pole

Local level — Local women's organizations 1982 — Local unions late 1950s

Figure 4.2 The MMTR's Institutional Nexus

in the central *sertão* and inspired organizing throughout Pernambuco. MMTR advisors and elected leaders tirelessly criss-crossed the state, giving workshops, advising new groups, and, in 1987, helping organize a statewide meeting attended by 220 rural women workers. After that gathering, a FETAPE Women's Commission, the *Commissão de Mulheres Trabalhadoras Rurais* (CEMTR), was founded.

By that time, contacts had also been made with counterparts in other Northeastern states; in 1986, the first regional *Encontro* had launched the MMTR-NE, a nine-state network of rural women's movements. The MMTR in Pernambuco played a key role in the new organization. One of the MMTR's founders described the process of creating the regional organization:

There was organizing work being done in Paraíba and Pernambuco.... The two movements began to meet and we discovered addresses, finding out that in such and such a place there was a woman who was working and we went looking for them. The beginning of work in the Northeast was very difficult, super difficult to find a person way out there in that region, bringing her to a meeting, often without having the conditions, without having the money.... Paraíba was on the same footing as we were.... Then we discovered Piaui. Then later we discovered Rio Grande do Norte and we continued discovering. One state discovered a neighboring state and brought the address and we communicated and sent nice letters, telling them about the importance of us meeting, and we went on stitching it together for years and years and years.

Most of the movements affiliated with the regional body found support from NGOs and church-based organizations; only the MMTR and the state organization, the CEMTR, were linked to trade unions. However, though the women's organization in the central *sertão* worked closely with the unions, it was autonomous and had alliances beyond them. As will be discussed in the next chapter, the MMTR found backing from urban Brazilian feminists, and international funders, as well as from religious and political sources closer to home. Its success in attracting both rural women and a diverse panorama of allies gave the organization an independence that made the unions increasingly uneasy.

At the local level, though some male supporters were loyal, the passive opposition of others turned to overt hostility as the movement gained adherents. No longer were some union leaders so willing to help with transportation and other resources, and messages sent via their delegates were not always delivered. The potential of greater female union participation, which had initially attracted some leaders and dismayed others, was disappointing to both groups. To the extent that the numbers of women in leadership had grown, the fears of some were confirmed. To the extent that growth was slow, the hopes of others were frustrated.

In the state federation, condescension gave way to heightened tensions. These surfaced in conflicts over state resources and priorities, but were also visible in the relations between the MMTR and the state women's organization. Though the *sertaneja* movement had helped launch the CEMTR, the latter was a commission of FETAPE, led by one of the union's elected directors and advised by staff members based at the headquarters in Recife. As part of the bureaucracy of the union, the CEMTR had a more limited set of goals than the MMTR. The FETAPE commission sought to incorporate women into union activities and to support local women leaders, while the MMTR aimed to build a broader movement for rural women's empowerment, based on both class and gender.[43] Though supportive of the union, MMTR members resisted being bound by its narrower vision and defended their political autonomy and right to make alliances outside the union movement. For those with loyalties to the union as an institution, or to their own power within it, this was a potential threat.

MMTR Strategies: Personal Networks, Political Maneuvers

At a local level, the MMTR's ability to use its political resources to sustain its independence was based in large part on its strategic ability to build support among certain sectors of union leadership. Armed with their accumulated credibility as committed organizers, the organization's founders made concerted efforts to involve officials in unions where women were beginning to organize, getting together with them to share and discuss the agendas for upcoming rural women's meetings, and occasionally inviting them to participate in larger MMTR gatherings. The personal relationships they constructed with some receptive male leaders not only forestalled opposition at a local level, but were also key to the movement's efforts to advance its agenda in the state federation. As one movement participant described it:

> Vanete [FETAPE staff member and MMTR founder] already had the skill of involving male union leaders in discussions of proposals. So she came [to the state federation] with the backing of the Central *Sertão* Pole.... [I]t wasn't a clientelist friendship. It was a friendship of comrades who support and trust one another, so it was strong backing.

Beyond that, in its negotiations with the state union movement, where the resistance to its gendered message was more entrenched, the MMTR also had the advantage of its location in the interior, beyond the geographical area of highest priority for the Pernambucan union leadership. What might not have been tolerated in the more proletarianized coastal region, where the union had made its name, was to some degree overlooked in the distant *sertão*. At the same time, the unions in the central *sertão* subregion had produced a series of respected national leaders and, in the 1980s, were part of a powerful national opposition bloc, earning them a special status within the state bureaucracy.

MMTR leaders proved adept at making use of both location and personal networks as they moved from local, to state, and then national arenas. At each level, they painstakingly built alliances before moving on to the next, avoiding overt conflicts unless absolutely necessary to defend fundamental principles. The MMTR held its first gathering in the central *sertão* only after they had gained local union support built on working relationships.

At a subsequent FETAPE meeting, a glossy report appeared on each director's seat:

> Since we didn't have space to present the report during the meeting, we distributed a number of copies in silence, without saying a word, during one of the breaks. When the men picked up the copies, they made comments like: "What a nice report!" "What an important meeting!" After that it was impossible to avoid a discussion about the reality of the organization of rural women. The "divisionist" argument still appeared, but, in the end, it was clear that they couldn't stop the women's organization.[44]

State support was later won for a second *Encontro*, to which women's representatives from other parts of Pernambuco were invited. Clamoring from around the state then managed to extract FETAPE resources for women's organizations throughout Pernambuco as well as for the state women's commission.

In 1985, the MMTR used this same "leapfrog diplomacy" to fight for change in the national rural workers' union confederation. Taking proposals made by members in the first gathering of women from the central *sertão* the year before, MMTR advisors wrote a resolution advocating that CONTAG take on four commitments: to "encourage 'specific' meetings for rural women workers"; to "promote training for female leaders"; to "raise and give backing to women's specific demands"; and to "encourage women to become rank and file delegates (*delegados de base*) and to assume leadership positions."[45]

Believing that the resolution had more chance of passing with official support from FETAPE, MMTR advisors devised a means of winning the state federation's approval:

> "We...thought of the following strategy," said one of the organizers, "to come [to Recife] with a commission of male union leaders from the Central *Sertão* Pole to present the resolution to FETAPE to be included with the resolutions to go to the Congress...." The local leaders agreed to help, she explained, "because things came so strategically set up that there was no way to say no...." They received the proposal "very respectfully...without any laughs." MMTR representatives, in fact, were not even present this time, "because it was also part of the strategy not to be there.... [T]he strategy was for the men to take [the resolution.]"

Despite the respectful reception, the MMTR was informed that the period for including additional proposals from Pernambuco was closed. However, they did win a promise from the state leadership not to oppose the resolution when it was brought to the floor by representatives of the women's movement.

At the CONTAG Congress in Brasilia, the MMTR worked hard to pass the proposal:[46]

It was a really tough fight! Really tough. We had to hold discussions in the middle of the night with the resolution in hand, showing its importance. [We] distributed five thousand copies to the whole Congress. We chose one of our best leaders, who was president of the Itapetim union [in the *sertão*], and she was the one who defended the resolution. And it was really hard because at the time unionism had many difficulties, many diverse points of view; there were already polemical issues and we entered with one more polemical issue inside [the unions].[47] But it was accepted and we won a victory. Then we took that resolution, put a stamp on it, saying, "Approved in the IV Congress…," and distributed it all over Brazil so that everyone would know that that little piece had been approved.[48]

The women of the MMTR, for the most part, successfully maintained their right to define a gender politics independent of the rural unions. But they did not achieve this either by open confrontation or by counterposing the women's agenda to that of their male comrades. Instead, they waged what one participant called "a covert struggle." Her comment came in the context of describing the controversy over a photo exhibit on women workers, which the movement had proposed to display at a statewide union meeting. MMTR activists encountered vociferous opposition to the idea from the FETAPE leadership:

Everything was a struggle—even the photo display!… [T]here was resistance from [the wife of a prominent leader] because of jealousy, you know, political jealousy. There was resistance from the men. There was political resistance to anything coming out of the Central *Sertão*. It was a covert struggle, a very covert struggle.… From the public point of view, everything was fine, but in the intimacies of the court, it was very difficult. Really difficult.

In the 1980s, the MMTR confined its contention to the "intimacies of the court," lacking the strength to take on its opponents in more public fashion. The rural women's movement called on local resources—personal relations with municipal colleagues, political backing from their broader sub-region, and tacit support from the state organization—to leverage change within the CONTAG national hierarchy. At the local level, they were most successful when they encountered elected leaders who shared their vision of a democratic and participatory movement—and saw symbolic and practical value in the active constituency that the MMTR represented. These same male leaders, and their accumulated credibility at higher levels of the union movement, then became a resource in the struggle for gender equity. In this way, the rural women's movement made slow but important gains in this period, laying the groundwork for its emergence as a force to be reckoned with in later years.

NEGOTIATING WITHIN LOCAL LIMITS

Rural women in Northeast Brazil stretched across class and gender counterpublics, engaging with social actors in both spaces and creating their own unique discourse and set of practices. Their dual location was not a comfortable one. As the MMTR drew on conceptions of women's empowerment that circulated in the transnational feminist public to challenge longstanding local practices of gender inequality in the *sertão*, its members encountered first derision, then active resistance from many of their male union counterparts.

On the one hand, the women faced an entrenched system of gendered power, sustained by rural women's invisibility as workers and discourses of their incompetence in the male-dominated public sphere. As one MMTR member commented:

> There are so many difficulties that I suffered as a woman within the union movement that I don't even know how to express which were the greatest.... I feel that, at some moments, people do not believe that women are equipped to participate because they don't believe in [our] force, [our] capacity, in our understanding.[49]

On the other hand, the challenges faced by the rural women's movement were directly related to the unions' cozy relationship to the state during this period. First, the kind of patronage-based relations fomented in many unions by access to state welfare funds were threatened by active participation of any kind, including that of women. Second, with rivals eliminated by *unicidade*, and with funding guaranteed by virtue of membership rolls, no matter how inactive, there was little incentive for male leaders to cede political space to new social actors. Finally, given that rural women had historically been confined to the private sphere and lacked full citizenship status vis-à-vis the state, the unions' focus on struggles on state terrain left MMTR members unequipped for battle.

In countering these excluding forces, the rural women's movement wielded an impressive array of political resources: an enthusiastic and growing membership, a leadership experienced in grassroots organizing and immersed in rural social relations, and personal networks that linked leaders with local and state union officials. These more directly accessible resources were linked to symbolic forms of legitimacy that carried some weight within the class-based counterpublic. From the transnational feminist counterpublic, MMTR members drew other kinds of resources, including discourses of gender, which they articulated with conceptions of class more familiar and less threatening to those schooled in workers' struggles. They also cultivated contacts with feminist movements near and far, which offered new forms of knowledge and pedagogies, as well as financial backing for their organizing.

Resources, however, only exist as such, with the capacity to serve as effective forms of leverage or currencies of exchange, when all parties accord them equal value. In the 1980s, rural unions were still largely confined within the space of the nation-state, and most leaders gave little importance to the MMTR's global gender resources. The victories won by the women's movement relied instead on skills and relationships rooted in the *sertão*. But the MMTR's links to the local male-dominated union structure were tenuous and ephemeral. Leaders came and went, and priorities could shift. As long as the prevailing view was that women and gendered resources had negligible value in terms of the rural unions' larger aims, the MMTR would have limited leverage to bring to bear in negotiations with them. As the next chapter will show, the women's organization encountered a different set of valuations in the feminist counterpublic. And, as the union movement too became entangled with global forces, the symbolic resources of the rural women's movement gained new value. As a consequence, the MMTR's political capital in the class-based counterpublic would grow and its covert strategies would become overt confrontations.

5

THE LEVERAGE OF THE LOCAL
"Authentic" Rural Women in Global Counterpublics

After almost a decade of collaboration, in 1992, the MMTR accepted a request from SOS Corpo to be part of a transnational research project on reproductive rights. SOS staff came out to the *sertão* to hold focus groups and conduct interviews with members of the MMTR from seven municipalities in the central *sertão*, eliciting tales about their experiences of sexuality, reproduction, and gender relations. A team of Brazilian researchers, including SOS members, analyzed their findings, in conjunction with data from studies of domestic workers in Rio de Janeiro and housewives in the *bairros* of São Paulo. Their research on working-class Brazilian women's experiences was later published in a book, which was coordinated by a U.S.-based academic and an NGO consultant and included material from seven countries around the world.[1] The article from Brazil theorized working-class experiences, making them accessible to academic audiences outside the country. SOS received national and international recognition for its work, made possible through its connection with the MMTR in the *sertão*. In recognition of the rural women's contribution, in 1996 the NGO "translated" its conclusions into accessible language, and staff members took them back to the *sertão* where they used the methodology of popular education to share them with their research subjects.

MMTR members and advisors expressed satisfaction with this series of interactions. Red flags went up, however, when leaders of the nine-state regional organization, the MMTR-NE, inadvertently discovered several years later that SOS was holding a one-week course on rural women for

NGO representatives—at a cost of $200 per student. The rural activists had been neither informed nor invited to participate.

> "How are they going to discuss rural issues if *we* are the ones who live that reality? We're going to *pay* to attend? We're the ones who taught them!" asserted one outraged member.

> "They appropriated all of our production—the reality of the countryside," said another. "It's hard for us to get money and we aren't even invited!"

The outcry simultaneously reflected both a new sense of entitlement and feelings of betrayal.[2] On the one hand, as these women saw it, in using their experiences as the basis for a fee-based seminar, SOS had appropriated the very "local-ness" of the rural women for its own selfish purposes. In a sense, SOS had violated the terms of an implicit agreement made with the MMTR to share their respective resources in the pursuit of common—rather than particularistic—goals. For MMTR members, the episode left a bitter taste, making starkly evident the differences in power between the two organizations, and the vulnerability associated with their social class and rural location.

On the other hand, there were hints of a new kind of empowerment in their angry words. In this discussion, the women expressed the insight that their life stories were the outcome of their labor—both the labor of living and surviving in impoverished conditions and the labor of organizing themselves and producing an account of their experiences for the outside world to consume. The conflict with SOS revealed that their "products" had value. They were "tradeable" in a certain kind of marketplace and, perhaps, could be bargained over.

INTERSECTING COUNTERPUBLICS

Organizational ties are one of the fibers that weave together distinctive sectors of a counterpublic. These ties require political negotiations to sustain them—negotiations that are fraught with power as well as solidarity. In the previous chapter, we saw the rural women's movement struggling with male union comrades in a class-based counterpublic over gendered inequalities; in the incident described above, MMTR members were contending with the class differences that divided them from their allies in the transnational feminist arena.

Power within counterpublics is destabilized by the intersections between them. Each of the counterpublics in which the rural women participated offered them distinctive perspectives on the world they lived in;

their location in one provided discursive tools to critique the inequalities in the other. As gendered subjects, they challenged male domination in the unions; as members of a rural working class, they confronted feminist elitism and privilege when it threatened to appear.

From each arena, they also drew other practical and symbolic resources—including personal relationships, forms of knowledge, and discourses of legitimacy—for use in struggles to assert their own unique point of view in relation to more advantaged social actors. Resources, however, as I have argued, don't always hold their value from one political context and historical moment to another. Power relations and systems of valuation are organized in distinctive ways in publics concerned with class and with gender injustice, for example, and they change over time. Social movements struggle to expand the arena in which their assets hold value, but they also adapt their strategic approaches to the situations in which they find themselves.

The global discourses of gender and contacts in the feminist world that the MMTR drew on had limited influence with most rural union leaders in the 1980s. But, as this chapter will show, their local class-based resources reverberated with much more power in the transnational feminist counterpublic, allowing rural women to claim an authority, which they lacked among their male allies. And, over time, as the unions too entered global circuits, where gendered resources had greater worth, the balance of forces would shift in the class-based public, and the MMTR's painstaking strategies would begin to bear fruit.

NEGOTIATING WITH THE GLOBAL: THE MMTR AND ITS FEMINIST ALLIES

While the commitment to a class-based struggle linked the MMTR to the rural union movement, its commitment to transforming gender relations created the possibility of alliance with feminist organizations. The educated urban women who founded NGOs like SOS saw their mission as helping build a multi-class movement by bringing feminist knowledge and pedagogies for consciousness-raising to women of Brazil's poor majority. Whereas the rural unions were rooted in local communities, feminist NGOs became points of entry for transnational feminisms, acting as conduits for and interpreters of discourses and practices from abroad to the working-class women's organizations, including the MMTR, that made up their constituency. For the MMTR-NE, the regional umbrella organization, NGOs also served as bridges to international funding circles.

Though the alliance brought multiple benefits to the rural movement, class differences and clashing organizational interests sometimes produced tensions. Just as in its interactions with the male-dominated unions, the MMTR encountered power from a position of disadvantage in its relations with urban feminist organizations. But cross-class rural-urban political relations with feminists proved easier to navigate than cross-gender relations within local unions. In its negotiations with globally connected feminists, the rural women's movement found a kind of leverage in the local that had little meaning in inter-union battles. Rather than the slow and hidden struggle of insiders in a dysfunctional union "family," relations with the NGOs had the character of bargains struck among unequal allies in an often openly conflictive process. Even though urban Brazilian NGOs offered the MMTR feminist discourses and practices, and, later on, contacts in the international funding world, the MMTR controlled a local resource that was precious on the global market: access to and knowledge about the lives of its grassroots constituency.

1980s: Controlling Access

The MMTR made contact with SOS Corpo in the mid-1980s. The Recife NGO had been working on women's health issues for several years and was already an active participant in transnational networks and international feminist events, such as U.N. conferences. From the early moments of their links with SOS, MMTR activists and advisors engaged in a series of political negotiations around the conditions of access to their rural constituency.

SOS staff members, like those of other professionalized feminist institutions around Brazil, were eager to establish a relationship with working-class members of grassroots women's organizations like the MMTR. In large part this was based on SOS's origins in the context of left opposition movements in the 1970s, as well as the ongoing commitments of its members, and, later, staff, to the construction of an inclusive feminist movement.[3] The chance to see their class and gender politics embodied in a broad cross-class movement gave NGO personnel a powerful incentive for constructing solidarity with rural women that was linked to the political side of the organization's "hybrid identity." But access to working-class constituencies, and the legitimacy that it could provide, were also increasingly essential to SOS's institutional growth and stability and its success in the world of policy advocacy and implementation. Despite substantial economic inequalities, therefore, the encounter between SOS and the MMTR was not a unilateral transfer of resources from urban feminists to rural women. Instead it was an exchange of SOS's transnational resources for access to a local symbolic one—the political legitimacy represented by the MMTR's sizeable and active membership.[4] Beyond the instrumental bargain, the relationship gave both sides hope of creating a broad-based movement capable of transforming gender and class relations.[5]

The four activists who founded and advised the MMTR in its early years had their deepest roots in class-based movements—rural unions and political education projects based in the progressive Catholic Church. Their prior relations with and perspectives on feminism varied. Some emphasized the organization's independent origins:

> "Listen," said one woman, "when we began the work with women, I didn't have any idea of feminist groups and feminism—none!… [W]e began to work on it because we noticed and felt the absence of women. It didn't have anything to do with the feminist question."

For this woman, feminism meant a self-conscious ideology, institutionalized in organizations. She argued that, in their case, gender consciousness emerged from experience, rather than through contact with explicitly feminist organizations.

Others, like a supporter who had encountered feminist activism in Recife, described feminism as a set of pervasive discourses:

> The great women's social revolution that had its high point in the decade of the sixties penetrated people and places in a thousand ways…. Nothing comes out of nowhere. [T]hese ideas formed a wind that blows around the world.

This wind, she argued, blew across the *sertão*, fusing with local practices and raising new conceptions of women's rights and capabilities.

Regardless of these differences, however, all of the founders had kept their distance from what they saw as a middle- and upper-class feminist movement. Their primary concern in their early organizing efforts was with building an identity among rural working women that was female, rather than feminist.

As we saw in Chapter 3, women's bodies were the starting point for both Euro-American second-wave feminism and its urban Brazilian counterpart. The MMTR's first encounter with transnationalized feminist NGOs occurred in the mid-1980s and also revolved around the body. One of the goals of the first local meeting of the MMTR was building a sense of self-worth among the participants, both as women and as workers, which would allow them to become full political subjects. In the discussion, organizers soon came up against the shame and lack of information that most rural working women had about their own bodies. In the words of Almeida: "The women that I work with didn't perceive their own bodies at the beginning. They had a body that did not belong to them. Their bodies belonged to the children, to work and to the husband."[6]

Seeing knowledge and ownership of one's body as key to self-esteem, MMTR founders decided to borrow some anatomy slides from a local priest and show them at a gathering. The women watched in total silence, in the dark. It was only during the evaluation that embarrassment evaporated and the words spilled out: "I didn't know....I had never seen...." Afterwards, struck by the women's enthusiasm, leaders organized further discussions of the body. But the obstacles were great:

> They were super nervous. They spent the whole time laughing, you know? They didn't want to respond to things. For example, we asked the names of the organs, what name they knew them by and they gave us peals of laughter, you know? They had...a lot of difficulty in talking about the body. There was one that I remember well, that when we—first they touched themselves, then another woman would touch her face, her hands—[this woman] said that the sensation was as if she was being pierced with nails, it was so difficult. Only later did they manage to relax, but some of them were really tense. They had a lot of difficulty.

Feeling their expertise limited, advisors decided to seek outside help to work further with the issues surrounding the body. This choice led them to SOS Corpo, which was already carrying out workshops on women's health and sexuality in Recife and elsewhere. Even then, however, the rural movement's organizers were cautious. Some time earlier, a disastrous workshop had been given in a neighboring area by urban feminists who had inadvertently succeeded in mobilizing men in the community against the local women's group, and MMTR organizers had made a decision to avoid overtly feminist language. The structure of the family and its "rigid sexual morality" had to be approached with care, they felt. One founder reflected:

> [SOS] came in after five or six years of work, I think, when we were already sure that...now the women would be able to tolerate any kind of discussion. And at the beginning the doses had to be really small. You couldn't talk so openly about things.

When SOS was invited to give a workshop at a 1986 meeting in the *sertão*, specific guidelines were given. An MMTR advisor remarked,

> "We said that we had to be careful so that it wouldn't be a discourse that came from on high, you know?...[T]hat is, we had to do a good job articulating the feminist discourse with [the rural workers'] discourse. So we talked and said, 'Look, this is what we want from you.'"

Before SOS staff arrived, to avoid intimidation or miscommunication, members were warned that the workshop facilitators were urban women who might use unfamiliar language. "You ask—say you didn't understand," members were told. "These people know about the subject…but they don't speak like we do. They don't have experience [in the *sertão*]."

But even with all these precautions, SOS's first workshop did not directly address issues of the body. Instead, facilitators helped MMTR members construct a visual "lifeline"where the significant events in their lives, as they defined them, would be depicted. As it turned out, many of these events were linked to sexuality and bodily experience—menstruation, loss of virginity, pregnancy, childbirth, and menopause. Two years later, SOS came back, this time to lead an activity entitled "The Body and Destiny," followed, in subsequent years, by workshops on women's health, sexuality, and the body and power.[7]

1990s: Bartering with Power

As SOS deepened its ties with transnational feminism, new tensions arose in its relations with the rural women's movement. Within the central *sertão*, there were a series of uncomfortable incidents in which *sertanejas* expressed their displeasure when they felt boundaries were being crossed by their urban allies. In the minutes of one meeting, members made a forceful critique of an SOS representative who had come to lead a workshop in the *sertão* for "not understanding the reality of the interior and its difference [from the city], forcing participants to talk when they did not want to."[8] At another meeting in the late 1990s, members challenged an SOS representative who lectured them on the necessity of "marketing" their movement's message through the mass media. Participants injected skeptical commentary throughout her presentation and, during the evaluation period that followed, criticized the "lack of dialogue" about her proposals.

At the regional level, in the MMTR-NE, the tensions took a different form. First came the incident described at the beginning of this chapter. At the same meeting, another similar issue provoked controversy. In 1995, SOS and the MMTR-NE had collaborated on the production of a pamphlet entitled "What is Gender? A New Challenge for Rural Women Workers' Action."[9] The pamphlet included an introduction by Almeida describing the process: "We tried to simplify the concept and come as close as possible to the world of the workers," she wrote. "The primer was constructed step by step, with the evaluation of the rural workers of the Northeast, and it was a joint apprenticeship."[10]

Several years later, at a workshop in São Paulo, an MMTR-NE member encountered another SOS publication on gender for popular audiences, part of its "Notebooks" series, on sale for about $8. The title of the new pamphlet had moved from the inquisitive to the declarative: "What is Gender?" was replaced with "What Gender Is." The subtitle linking the topic to rural women workers had disappeared. The text was quite similar, but lacked the drawings of women working in the fields and references to rural gender relations, and the style and point of view had shifted subtly in the direction of greater distance and more objectivity. "Through our own experience, we know that we are the ones who receive lower salaries and it is our work which is devalued," in the old version, became "Daily observation shows us that it is women who receive the lowest salaries and it is their work which is devalued."[11] In place of Almeida's introduction was a new one by the SOS authors, crediting women's movements for the spread of the language of gender, and informing the reader that the current publication was an adaptation of the earlier co-production with the MMTR-NE. The new pamphlet was dedicated to the rural women workers' movement.

Despite the sentiments of the dedication, the members were indignant. The sudden appearance of the new version, without prior communication with the rural women's organization, seemed to confirm their feeling that their movement was being used by a more well-to-do ally for its own ends. "We can't manage to sell ours and [then] those intellectuals go and make one and sell it," one of the women complained.[12] "Our primer became an SOS text without consultation with the MMTR," said another. Several advisors accepted SOS's right to produce the pamphlet, but expressed shock and concern that there had been no communication about it, despite their frequent visits to the SOS office in Recife. In the end, an angry letter was fired off, using strong language to protest what was deemed "foul play" and reminding SOS of their historically close partnership. The urban NGO responded quickly, and face-to-face discussions about both issues, as well as about future working relations, ensued.

In each of these incidents, rural women assertively defended their rights in a relationship with more economically privileged, though well-intentioned, urban feminists. They insisted on their prerogative to control access to their membership, as well as their right to speak or remain silent in the context of cross-class encounters. As they became aware of the value of their "production" to others, they claimed ownership of their own stories and locally grounded expertise.

Regardless of the repeated tensions, however, the relationship, according to one of the MMTR founders, was basically a positive and reciprocal one:

Whenever we asked for their support, they were always very open to participate. And…we always sat down together to plan. If they planned alone, they would send us the proposal for us to check and give opinions. After the *Encontros*, we evaluated how it had gone, what had worked. Our relationship was always very good.

Both the MMTR and its Northeast regional umbrella organization maintained a long and collaborative, if at times thorny, relationship with SOS Corpo, based on what organizers described as mutual respect and the willingness of the urban NGO's staff members to work within the framework established by the rural women. When they stepped outside the bounds of what MMTR members viewed as acceptable, differences were negotiated between the two organizations.

The global context conferred new worth on local knowledge and experiences hitherto taken for granted by male, class allies in the *sertão* and, perhaps, even by rural women themselves. Through their encounters with transnational feminists, they came to view their narratives and identities as products of their own efforts, resources with value that could be exchanged—or expropriated by someone more powerful. The vigorous defense of its interests by the rural women's movement, SOS's ready responses, and their joint efforts to pursue common projects, all formed part of the larger struggle to maintain their alliances in the face of potentially destructive class inequalities.

MMTR Strategies: Open Exchange vs. Covert Maneuvers

The MMTR used covert strategies and the power of personal relations in struggles with unions, but its dealings with urban feminists were characterized by overt conflict and directly negotiated solutions. What was behind these differences and what sustained the rural-urban feminist alliance in spite of the obvious power differentials? Why did transnational "sisterhood" seem to have more flexibility in this period than the fraternity of class?

With the unions, the rural women's movement maneuvered within a patriarchal and still largely clientelist local institution entangled with the Brazilian state; with urban feminists, the MMTR engaged in negotiations in a transnational sphere increasingly shaped by the forces of the market. The differences in context conferred different valuations on the rural women's resources: In effect, they had more leverage with SOS than they did in their relations with the unions. Agricultural union leaders, for the most part, saw little of value in what the MMTR had to offer as a women's organization; their realm of action was the political system within Brazil where global gender discourses as yet carried little weight. In fact, the history of U.S. intervention in Latin America had helped to generate nationalist feelings among those who identified with the op- position, and the construction of feminism as an import from the global North—however inaccurate—tainted it in the eyes of many left-leaning union cadres. Organizing experience gave MMTR activists some amount of clout, but their status as marginalized working-class actors was of little interest to a union movement already saturated with these qualities, and their gender carried a negative valence for many union leaders. For the MMTR, working personal connections behind the scenes was, for the time being, the only alternative.

In contrast, the rural organization was able to strike an implicit bar- gain with SOS Corpo, a bargain based on a kind of exchange: access to the global (transnational discourses and, later, the world of international funding), on the one hand, for access to the local (a working-class con- stituency and its knowledge and experiences), on the other.

What value did this rural constituency hold for urban feminists with all their economic and educational advantages, and their national and transnational connections? As Alvarez notes, women's NGOs in Brazil were born out of political commitment, and their members shared a critical feminist identity. For organizations like SOS Corpo, links to the MMTR, with its significant social base among rural working-class women, helped reaffirm core values. Movement members' testimonies, such as "I learned to value myself, something that I didn't know how to do," or "I am not going to earn half [the pay that men earn] anymore.... I'm not half, I am whole," reflected a gendered consciousness that held inspiration for feminists hoping to build a broad-based alliance for social change.[13]

Beyond that, the MMTR also offered a resource that had a potential in- strumental value, largely created, if not imposed, by the global context.[14] Its constituency of working-class women gave the rural organization a form of class legitimacy—a symbolic resource much needed by feminist NGOs in their relations with other social actors. These actors included both class-based social movements and the state at home and, increasingly, development agencies and feminist counterparts abroad. Given Brazil's vast inequalities of wealth and power, NGOs that claimed to espouse goals of social justice but lacked a social base among the disenfranchised had far less appeal to the organizations and institutions that guaranteed their material and political survival than did those that could claim access to this kind of constituency.[15]

The fact that the MMTR's members were poor *rural* women, ostensibly "backward" and apparently uncontaminated by global flows, gave them an added aura of "authenticity" particularly sought after by Brazilian

NGOs under pressure to demonstrate their political reach to skeptical Northern audiences. The need among NGOs for the legitimacy and authenticity that working-class groups like the MMTR could offer was intensified by the increasing competition for international funding at a time when Latin American NGOs were multiplying and public apathy, or even hostility, toward foreign aid was growing in Europe and the United States. As we shall see in the next chapter, these shifting circumstances threatened to push the relationship between professionalized feminists and their grassroots allies further toward relations based on pragmatic organizational interests, rather than shared political goals.

The global connections of NGOs like SOS Corpo, as well as their own feminist politics, gave them a particular interest in sustaining relations with the rural women's movement that the locally rooted and male-dominated rural unions did not share. Given the latter's relative national boundedness and reliance on the state during the 1980s, the value of legitimacy by association with female Brazilian working-class constituencies was largely irrelevant. The machismo of many union leaders and their implication with bureaucratic welfarism meant that there was also little political impetus toward backing women's struggles. The new decade, however, brought winds of change to the *sertão*.

THE 1990S: GLOBAL WINDS ON LOCAL TERRAIN

In the 1990s, the MMTR's relationship with the local unions began to change, growing increasingly similar to the movement's relations with urban feminists. On the one hand, the unions more often professed their support for women's issues; on the other, the MMTR's covert maneuvers gave way to direct confrontations with union leaders over policy differences. Both of these developments were consequences, at least in part, of the growing presence of global forces and changes in the balance of power in the political arena of Brazilian social movements.

By the last decade of the century, economic globalization had transformed the rural interior and diversified its social composition as well as the political and economic interests represented there. While a few large producers and land speculators flourished in the new economic order, and some small farmers found a niche in links to agro-industry, many more encountered hard times, often leading to their expulsion from the land into the growing ranks of the landless crowding the periphery of towns and cities. New categories of work were created in response to growing mechanization in the export sector, but year-round salaried employment was hard to come by. The interests of permanent and temporary workers, field hands and tractor drivers, traditional subsistence peasants and modernized contract producers serving a global market, landowners, tenants, sharecroppers, squatters, and the landless jostled together uncomfortably in the confines of the geographically-based unions.

Representing this diverse panoply of often competing rural interests grew increasingly difficult, leading some to speak of a "crisis of the current union model."[16] Local activists complained of a lack of grassroots participation, a unionism "more in the leadership than the base." With democratization of the larger political system, internal debates about restructuring the unions began to emerge. Opposition slates, allied with the rival left-leaning CUT federation, challenged long-entrenched leaderships. While some argued that the municipally-based and locally-controlled form had outlived its usefulness in a world where economic power was more and more concentrated, others pushed for union organization by economic sector or for separate associations of small producers and wage workers. As the neoliberal state reduced its social commitments, a significant movement challenged the unions "welfarism" and dependence on the state.[17]

Giving particular urgency to these internal debates was the appearance, in the late 1980s and 1990s, of new movements speaking for the diverse interests generated by economic globalization and democratization. The competition from landless movements, cooperatives and small producer associations, race-based initiatives, and movements to defend drought victims and those displaced by public works projects, as well as the MMTR and other women's movements, undermined the unions' claim to be the sole representative of the *sertaneja* working class.

As state commitments to union-sponsored welfare programs shrank and clientelist relations were challenged from below, leaders scrambled to shore up traditional bases of support by other means, as well as to respond to new demands. In place of the old centralized and hierarchical structure, in the late 1980s and early 1990s unions began to introduce Secretaries of Social Welfare, of Agricultural Policy, and of Agrarian Reform into their leadership bodies, each designed to address the particular concerns of a different sector within the membership. In this period, national and state union leaders also launched campaigns and educational programs targeting specific subgroups, such as the landless and women.

Many of the organizations articulating new claims in the countryside from outside the unions were NGOs, part of a burgeoning sector fed by another global force—the extension of international funding into new arenas. Though the resources provided by foreign donors sometimes supported organizations perceived as union rivals, they also often fed NGOs that collaborated with the unions, provided employment for former activists, and helped foment class consciousness in the countryside. On occasion, unions themselves benefited from international grants. In 1997, for example, the state union federation sponsored a multi-year project, bankrolled by the U.N. Population Fund, to train union members as educators on issues of reproductive health.

International funding often came linked to discourses of gender and feminist politics associated with movements in the global North. More broadly, by the 1990s, feminism—whether from within or outside Brazil— had penetrated many of the institutions with which rural unions maintained relations. In the mid-1980s, the state had established the *Conselho Nacional dos Direitos da Mulher* (CNDM [National Women's Rights Council]). Left parties, such as the Workers' Party, formed women's secretariats or commissions, as did urban unions in Recife, including those of bank and social security workers.[18] In the *sertão*, NGOs dedicated to sustainable development promoted programs with a gender component.[19]

Not only was the discourse of gender in the air more generally, but the MMTR's hard work was beginning to pay off. By 1998, women's groups in communities across the *sertão* were carrying out campaigns, organizing workshops, and pressing for space in their local unions. The number of women among elected local union officials had grown, especially among members of politically progressive opposition slates, as well as among those active in other social movements.[20] The autonomous regional umbrella organization, the MMTR-NE, in which the MMTR played a leading role, was now linked to a national network of rural women's organizations, and both the local and the regional organizations had extended their support network to include urban feminist NGOs as well as collaborators from churches and other civil society institutions. In 1996, the MMTR won recognition from the state, when founder Vanete Almeida was named to the CNDM, the first rural workers' representative to become a member of the Council.

Along with these achievements within Brazil, the local and the regional rural women's organizations were beginning to make connections outside the country. To different degrees, both had begun to win the attentions of international funding agencies. These sources helped the rural women organize workshops and events and produce posters and brochures that put union propaganda to shame. Foreign donors also facilitated their entry as actors in the transnational feminist public: With international backing, the MMTR-NE was able to send two members to the U.N. Conference on Women in Beijing in 1995 and to organize the first Latin American and Caribbean Rural Women Workers' Encounter in 1996.

In this new context, the rural unions' relations with the MMTR and the MMTR-NE began to change. Opposition to women's organizing and leadership per se went undercover. According to one union staff member sympathetic to the MMTR:

> At the beginning we...suffered some difficulties, some obstacles— first because of the cultural issue itself. There were only men in the leadership. Suddenly, women began to appear, participating. They began to threaten the power that was his, [a feeling] that still exists today, I won't deny it.... Now today it's much more discreet.... The ones that still reject [women's participation in leadership] do it in a way that is more discreet—at least they don't take a stand openly.

Leaders began to take the concerns of rural women more seriously— or at least to give them greater lip service—and to incorporate "gender" into their discourse. The establishment of state commissions, such as the CEMTR in Pernambuco in 1987, was an early sign of the change. So, too, were national initiatives, such as the launching of a Rural Women's Commission by the CUT in 1990, and the organizing of a National Meeting of Rural Women Workers by CONTAG in 1991.[21] The state federation's project on gender and reproductive health in 1997, referred to above, and a seminar, entitled "Gender, Generation and Family Agriculture," held the following year by the unions around Serra Talhada, marked the dissemination of the discourse. By the end of the decade, rural women's movement leaders were complaining that, rather than dismissing them, the union was taking credit for their initiatives.[22]

At the same time, when conflicts between unions and the women's movement surfaced, power was more clearly at issue. Referring to FETAPE leaders, an MMTR founder had the following to say:

> At the beginning they said that a women's organization was unnecessary, that when women wanted to join, they would join, that it wasn't necessary [to organize them], that this work was divisive—that it would divide men and women. They never supported it. When the work began to take off [and] began to be important..., [when] it became visible and everyone was praising it and thinking women's participation was important, then there wasn't much that FETAPE could do and [they] said that they supported it. But even today there are difficulties. They support some things, criticize others, and put obstacles in the way of other things.... And this relationship between autonomous movement and union movement is...difficult because it carries the question of power.

Another activist described it this way:

Today, I think the movement has grown and we are living in another stage. There are other conflicts. The conflicts aren't those [from before].... They are more forms of contestation, of movement against movement. It's a power struggle, we can't deny that. It's their fear of women, of women advancing. It's *men's* fear now. Back then it was *women's* fear. But today we perceive—they don't say it, but it's clear in their actions—that it is really fear. So, today the difficulties are different.

One of the arenas where struggles around institutional prerogatives and authority were most visible was in the relationship between the FETAPE women's commission, the CEMTR, and both the local MMTR and the independent nine-state regional organization. The latter in particular, according to one of its advisors, was a "fishbone in [the unions'] throat." A leader of the CEMTR criticized the relationship of the MMTR-NE to a network of rural women's movements that also operated outside the union's authority:

We have a working partnership with the MMTR[-NE]. But from time to time there are some divergences because the MMTR[-NE] has a national network that discusses things there up above.... Then the people from the MMTR[-NE] come with some things already prepared for us to carry out and we, as a movement, as a commission, also wanted...to contribute in the discussion, to be there in the discussion as well.[23]

MMTR-NE leaders, in turn, complained that the union-affiliated women's commission, technically a member of the regional body, chose not to participate in regional and national activities. While rejecting the idea that their movement divided the working class, one activist defended its institutional autonomy:

[I]t's another space that we have. [In this space], many women workers have full autonomy and liberty to discuss and carry things out, to be independent of having to ask for the backing of the union movement. That's the big difference....We don't have to ask anyone for authorization. In the union movement you discuss, but at the moment of defining things, even if you are from the women's organization, you have to take it to...the union or federation leadership [and] you have to wait for approval. The meeting only happens if they give their stamp of approval.

In the face of the continued differences with union and CEMTR leaders, the MMTR and its regional counterpart deployed an increasingly assertive and direct strategy that reflected the political changes in the larger context and, in particular, the growing incursions of the global on local ground. Earlier, they had sought to protect women from male intimidation, but in the mid-1990s, both organizations demonstrated their confidence by beginning to invite male union members to participate in certain activities, such as the MMTR workshop on gender described in Chapter 1, or a 1998 MMTR-NE meeting on "The Body, Gender, and the Preservation of Land and Water."

Meanwhile, the movement's goals had expanded. More and more it entered union terrain, addressing broader themes, such as sustainable agriculture and government drought relief. Members insisted on holding their own meetings to discuss these important issues and often took independent stances. One former local union official sympathetic to the MMTR described a conflict that illustrates the movement's new approach:

> In 1992 we had a difficult period of drought and of negotiation with the government.... FETAPE made a proposal to have a meeting in [this area] with the mayors of the municipalities, city council members, and state legislators (*representantes e deputados*)—the bulk of them were PFL [a conservative party] here in the interior. In the *sertão*, people [in the unions] strongly disagreed that they should be present because they weren't going to collaborate. It was very difficult. There was a meeting all day long here and [the local unions] ended up approving [the politicians'] presence at the [proposed] meeting.... And the next day, as a result of these things, there was a meeting only of the women.... And when the women sat down and passed around the agenda of the meeting and what had been agreed, they totally disagreed and there began the fight.... They thought what had been accepted by the leadership was absurd.... [They took a] stronger and more radical position and put forward proposals about all this. When this was conveyed [to the unions], they began to reject [them]: "No! Why didn't you come that day?" And there it began. There was almost a total break and there was a lot of fighting too. I think that this difficulty still exists today.

Women in the MMTR were able to take a more assertive, even confrontational, stance because, in the 1990s, their participation had greater value to the union leadership than it had had in the movement's early years. Beset by difficulties partially induced by economic globalization, the union found itself obliged to reach out to new constituencies. Women were of particular interest for two, apparently contradictory, reasons. On the one hand, the women's movement had made powerful global connections through its insertion into feminist networks. Unions lagged behind in these transnational relations, and the MMTR's achievements in this sphere—as well as the movement's growing stature within the state—made union leaders sit up and take notice. On the other hand, once class-based movements themselves began to engage with global flows of discourses and resources, many of the same factors that influenced MMTR relations with NGOs like SOS Corpo came into play. Paradoxically, in this new context, the unions came to value both the very local-ness of the rural women's movement and its constituency of working-class women. While the more enlightened union leaders had longstanding political commitments to gender equality, now even the hostile or indifferent had compelling instrumental interests in women's participation and the language of gender-based rights, commodities that, in their symbolic form, might earn them access to funding and the approval of important transnational allies.[24]

"SAINTS FROM HOME" GO GLOBAL

The politics of the Pernambucan rural women workers' movement reflected its location at the intersection of two counterpublics, one organized around class and the other around gender relations. The discourses of gender transmitted, in part, by its urban feminist allies took new forms as the MMTR interrogated them in the light of rural women's own experiences as family farmers, community members, churchgoers, and union activists. Discourses of class also suffered changes as they were filtered through gendered identities. In the words of one member:

> We worked for the boss. We were enslaved. We accepted whatever he wanted…before the Women's Movement. We women don't want to be enslaved any more, nor to suffer the advances of the boss. [When] the boss tries to seduce us now we know what to say to him: You have the land, my body is mine.[25]

But these apparently easy conjugations of class and gender both reflect and conceal political struggles with allies in both of the counterpublics with which the MMTR was affiliated.

There is a saying in Brazil, "Household saints (*santos de casa*) don't work miracles." Only foreign saints have traditionally had that power. In its early political relations with Pernambucan unions, the rural women's movement found limited leverage in its own, all too familiar, local resources. But, in the context of the global, the refrain was turned on its head. In negotiations with transnationalized feminist NGOs, it was the very local character of the MMTR that worked miracles, producing a legitimacy and authenticity that won attention from more socially and geographically distant allies. And, as global winds blew through the Northeastern *sertão*, drawing rural unions into their updraft, local power relations too assumed new forms.

While the global conferred new powers on the local, it also brought ominous changes that threatened to undermine the political links of solidarity between social movements in their respective counterpublics, shifting them onto the terrain of the market, where instrumental relations ruled. How both the rural women's movement and its urban feminist allies navigated transnational economic relations is the subject of the following chapter.

6

FEMINISTS AND FUNDING
Plays of Power in the Social Movement Market

In 1995, an uncommon encounter between local Brazilian women's organizations and international funding agency representatives took place. What was unusual was not the contact between the two parties per se; foundation program officers made frequent site visits to applicants and grantees, and members of the latter groups often traveled North in search of much-needed funds. But on this occasion they gathered at a beachfront hotel near Recife to discuss, not the minutiae of evaluations and grant applications, but broader questions around the politics of gender and development aid.

While the economic power of the agency representatives in attendance might have been expected to dampen dissent, at least one invited speaker gave voice to the underlying tensions. Vanete Almeida, the founder of the MMTR in Pernambuco, used her spot on a panel to read the riot act to the assembled development agency representatives. Accusing them of a "colonizing mentality," she criticized their arrogance and disrespect for the MMTR's dignity and autonomy. She took aim at sudden changes in agency guidelines that left grant recipients without resources, the imposition of quantitative criteria to measure qualitative changes in consciousness, and unreasonable demands for immediate results in what was of necessity a very long-term process. "It is the women themselves," she said, "who should decide their own course and evaluate their experiences. The role of the agencies is to give them the conditions to do so."[1]

SOS Corpo, the Recife-based nongovernmental women's health organization, unlike the MMTR, had had a prominent role on the committee organizing the event and its personnel were visible staffing registration desks, organizing panels, and hosting cocktails. On the second day, SOS assistant coordinator Silvia Camurça participated in a panel on "Gender Politics in Brazil," discussing the theoretical roots of the NGO's conception of gender and the ways that it had been incorporated into organizational practice. Her approach was analytical, almost academic at times, though she cautioned that "[t]heory cannot substitute for action," as she described SOS's role in contributing to the creation of women's organizations and supporting the process of change in the law, as well as in daily life. But the tone and target of her remarks were quite different from those of Vanete Almeida. Rather than directing her remarks at the development agencies, Silvia ended her talk with a call to the non-feminist NGOs present to do more to integrate gender into their analyses of development.

The contrasts in tone, message, and audience of the two speakers, and in their organizations' roles in the event, reflected, in large part, the differences in their location within the political economy of international funding, a phenomenon that has increasingly shaped both the nature of social movements in Brazil and the relations among them. Whereas SOS attracted foundation backing early on in its development, and rapidly became dependent on external grants for institutional support, the MMTR received only small amounts of money for specific projects and struggled to make itself visible to distant donors.[2] Their distinctive links to foreign funding reverberated in the strategies and structures of each organization, and in their relations with one another.

At the same time, some of those distant donors were themselves participants in the feminist counterpublic, seeking to support movements around the world with which they too identified. Their links with feminist grantees in Brazil were economic but, as this chapter will show, the material reality of funding flows also had a powerful discursive dimension. The money disbursed by feminists in agencies in Europe and the United States came encased in particular kinds of meanings and practices, which both helped to sustain feminist movements and threatened the character of their relationships.

This chapter explores economic ties in the feminist counterpublic, focusing on the ways that power was embedded and contested in relations between feminists in European and U.S.-based development agencies and the two women's movements in Northeast Brazil. In their relations around flows of material resources, I argue, feminist movements faced grave risks, both for their political autonomy from more powerful forces and for the possibility of relations of solidarity with one another.[3]

THE RISE OF THE "SOCIAL MOVEMENT MARKET"

In the global North, international development agencies mushroomed in size and numbers in the 1980s and 1990s, channeling a growing portion of state, as well as private, foreign aid from the United States and Europe to NGOs and, to a lesser extent, to grassroots movements, in the global South.[4] A small part of the overall flow of development aid was dedicated to "Third World" women.[5] Since the 1970s, feminist movements in the North had pressed for the support of women's projects abroad. As they succeeded, feminists were hired to administer women's funding units, which occupied what was still often a fairly marginal space within agencies. Despite the economic power they represented, these Northern feminists shared some aspects of collective identity with and saw themselves as allies of the Latin American, Asian, Middle Eastern, and African women whose projects they funded. In this sense, they constituted another node in the transnational feminist counterpublic, and the relations of affinity between them and their "Third World" grantees complicated the plays of power between North and South.

The quantities disbursed by supporters in development agencies to women's movements in Brazil were small in relation to overall foreign aid budgets. Nonetheless, the funds were an indispensable condition of survival for many movements, given the lack of local philanthropy and scarcity of state support. At the same time, the unequal distribution of these resources aggravated previously existing hierarchies among women's organizations, granting visibility and power to some, while marginalizing others.

The extension of development aid across borders and into new sectors in recent decades has accompanied, and in some ways paralleled, the globalization of investments. In both cases, economic resources confer power on certain actors—largely located in the global North—and favor some in the South over others; in both cases, as well, money is entwined with political and cultural meanings. Along with funds from donor institutions come discourses and practices that help shape the terrain on which recipients conceptualize and carry out their work.[6] Many of these discourses and practices echo those of global capital in different form; the effect is to draw social movements—and professionalized ones in particular—ever closer into a web of market-like relations, which threaten to replace political solidarities and shared moral values with instrumental relations based on institutional interests.[7]

In this way, I argue, funding flows may create a kind of parallel "social movement market," which influences both the internal functioning of particular organizations and their relations with allies in the counterpublic. Like its capitalist counterparts, this shadow market is characterized by competition for scarce economic and discursive goods, by instrumental relations among participants, and by commodified exchanges whose benefits accrue unequally to some parties more than others. Not only do movements and organizations buy and sell tangible products to one another, but they trade in skills, constituencies, and forms of knowledge, as we saw in the preceding chapter. Political relationships themselves can be transformed into objects of exchange within hierarchies of power.

The social movement market has similarities to its capitalist cousin, but its participants begin with a different set of objectives, which themselves are internally contradictory. Social movements may sometimes pursue institutional "profits," which guarantee survival or extend organizational power, but they also seek political transformations that transcend their own narrow interests. The internal tensions between these two kinds of goals mean that market relations within a counterpublic are unstable and frequently challenged. At the beginning of the twenty-first century, this new form of market is not a totalizing or necessarily permanent condition; it is instead a dimension of social movement relations that waxes and wanes as it confronts still powerful sets of alternative values and resistant political modalities. Flows of international funding have facilitated the spread of the social movement market, yet protagonists on both sides of the aid relationship have struggled to counteract its toxic effects on the solidarities within counterpublics.

This chapter examines feminist engagements with and struggles against the social movement market through the experience of SOS Corpo, one of those feminist organizations that came to enjoy the largesse of international donors. The case of the MMTR will serve as a counterpoint, offering a distinctive vantage point on the relations between feminist funders in the North and grant recipients in the South.

CONTESTING COMMODIFICATION IN BRAZIL

In the last few decades, the tendency toward the commodification of politics was exacerbated in Latin America by the openings for some organizations inside the state, a by-product of the democratization process, as well as by the new availability of resources from the North. In Brazil, organizations like SOS Corpo seized these opportunities to enter the state apparatus as a means to influence policy and address the urgent social needs being generated by global economic dislocations. Meanwhile, from outside the circles of power, working-class movements like the MMTR struggled to defend their constituencies against economic crisis and state neglect.

Their different relations with international funding agencies and the state led the two organizations along divergent strategic paths. SOS embraced formalization and professionalization in the service of femi-nism, defining itself as an NGO and structuring itself accordingly, while the MMTR defended its status as a social movement rooted in the rural working class with a relatively loose form of organization. Over time, SOS took on many attributes of its donors and was increasingly both subject to and adept at using the logic of the market to advance its femi-nist agenda. The MMTR retained its character as a grassroots movement and continued to resist market modalities, while suffering the effects of limited resources.

One of the potential casualties of international development aid was the connection between SOS and the working-class communities, includ-ing those of rural workers, in which the NGO had initially grounded its research and educational work and for which it continued to advocate. Different relationships to international funders not only exacerbated the economic divide between SOS and the MMTR, but also knit them together in new ways. Once allies across class, in the context of a social movement market, the urban organization became a kind of feminist broker, while the rural movement was transformed into its client. Though they struggled to sustain their cross-class collaboration, the relationship confronted new tensions.[8]

The literature produced by development agencies is full of refer-ences to "partnership" between donors and recipients, a formulation that obscures the power relations inevitably involved.[9] The use of terms like "international cooperation" by grantees equally glosses over the uncomfortable inequalities with their Northern supporters and allies. The scholarly literature, on the other hand, has often taken the reverse position, conferring nearly absolute power to shape recipients' discourses and practices on those who control the purse strings and obscuring the complex forms of negotiation through which "beneficiaries" work to assert their agendas.[10]

This study shows that the disparities of economic power between feminists in the South and sympathetic benefactors in the North do indeed play a significant role in influencing the structure and political orientation of feminist organizations, in a multitude of ways. Beyond that, they also have deleterious effects on internal movement relations, fostering the commodification of women's movements' alliances across the counterpublic.

However, I also found that feminist NGOs and grassroots women's movements are not without power of their own vis-à-vis the funding establishment. Shifts in strategy are the result of political choices, albeit in the context of narrowed options. Though accepting international financial aid may have unintended negative results, it does not, in itself, signify the abandonment of feminist goals.[11] Even in the face of stark material inequalities between North and South, SOS Corpo and the MMTR defended their autonomy from financial backers and allies, whether by waging pitched battles or by engaging in transnational dialogue. And, despite the differentials of power between professionalized and grassroots movements, the two organizations constructed alliances with one another that strengthened their bargaining positions with Northern allies and mitigated the commodifying effects of the social movement market.

SOS CORPO: FEMINISTS AND FUNDING

The Slippery Slope

The entanglement of SOS Corpo with global funding circuits evolved in distinct phases, from an initial moment of self-sufficiency (1980–82), to growing dependence on international funders (1983–89), and, finally, to participation in transnational dialogues with its powerful economic allies (1990–98).

The year 1980, when SOS was founded, fell at the midpoint of *abertura*—the gradual political opening of the dictatorship that eventually led to its dissolution. The *abertura* period saw the last gasp of the state-led economic strategies of import-substitution, investment in infrastructure, and national integration on which the previous regime had been founded.[12] For SOS, as for the MMTR, the early 1980s were marked by autonomy from the state and independence in terms of economic resources.

As the decade wore on, democratization gathered momentum, moving from local, state, and congressional elections in 1982, to presidential elections in 1985, to the rewriting of the constitution in 1988. As the state opened up, so too did the economy, with rising levels of foreign debt, a reduction in protective tariffs, and declining state intervention.[13] The resulting combination of recession and massive inflation took their toll on the poor majority as unemployment rose and the real minimum wage plummeted. The percentage of Brazilians living below the poverty line grew from 24 percent in 1980 to 39 percent in 1988.[14] Meanwhile, the relationship of the Recife feminist NGO to international donors paralleled that of the larger Brazilian economy vis-à-vis global capital. While the MMTR remained largely on the margins of these flows, SOS's growing dependence on funds from international development agencies transformed the shape of the organization and brought new challenges on a variety of fronts.

The 1990s saw the intensification of the economic crisis that had begun in the previous decade. As elsewhere in Latin America, the neoliberal policies of the Brazilian government endorsed the dominion of the market and accelerated the shrinking of the state's sphere of action. Structural adjustment was the price of debt rescheduling: Government services were cut, public enterprises from energy to telecommunications were privatized, and state regulation of foreign capital was relaxed.[15] Foreign investment increased and inflation declined to some degree, but the poor continued to pay the price of the country's insertion into global markets. SOS, meanwhile, adjusted to the new conditions, adopting a leaner, more competitive profile as it entered into global negotiations with international development agencies.

The educated, middle- and upper-class women who founded the organization in 1980 all worked and had some access to resources. In the first couple of years their expenses were few and SOS functioned as a movement of volunteers who financed projects largely out of their own pockets and those of acquaintances in the opposition party of the time—the *Movimento Democrático Brasileiro* (MDB [Brazilian Democratic Movement]). The group made its first formal funding request in 1980, in the form of a letter to a few potential supporters, including a woman that some of them had met as exiles in France, who was involved in family planning and women's health issues, and a small women's health organization in Washington, DC. Also in this early period a German development agency provided a small amount of funding for a slide show, and SOS used some of the money to establish the legal status needed for more significant grants. Already the search for international funding had required them to initiate a relationship with the state, a dynamic which only intensified over the years to come.

In 1982 this strategy paid off in the form of the organization's first big grant, from the Ford Foundation. With this achievement, SOS entered a new phase of development. Over the next two decades, like other feminist NGOs in Brazil, SOS diversified and expanded its contacts among international agencies, becoming increasingly dependent on them to support a more and more ambitious roster of projects and a growing infrastructure. By 1987 the institution had sizeable grants from several different sources; ten years later, it had a total annual budget of some $500,000, more than 80 percent of it from international development funders. By 1999, the budget had risen to over $700,000.[16]

SOS's fundraising success was due in part to the legitimacy earned through its outreach in working-class *bairros* around Recife, a feature of no small interest to development agencies hoping to multiply the effects of their overseas investments. The cultural capital of its articulate and highly educated membership, who were able to parlay their accomplishments into attractive funding proposals, also played a significant role. But, most important, SOS's rising fortunes were the outcome of a convergence between its area of interest and the concerns of the international funding establishment.

Since the 1950s and 1960s, agencies such as the Rockefeller and Ford Foundations, the International Planned Parenthood Federation, the Population Council, and USAID had been fomenting population control as a vehicle to alleviate poverty and prevent political instability in the Third World.[17] Interest in women as targets of development intervention initially grew out of their role in fertility control and, from the point of view of population control advocates, their potential as protagonists in the struggle against poverty.[18]

In the late 1970s and early 1980s, the influence of feminist movements in the North was beginning to be felt in the field of development, and agencies responded with support for women's projects abroad. Feminist concerns with reproductive rights overlapped to some degree with those of population control advocates and, in response to pressures from the international women's health movement, the more forward-looking agencies, including the Ford Foundation, made a shift to funding reproductive health projects directed at women.[19] SOS was one of the beneficiaries of this move.[20]

The group's first grant from Ford, in 1982, was for a study on the "Causes and Conditions of Voluntary Female Sterilization in the Recife Metropolitan Region," an effort to understand why a shockingly high percentage of women of childbearing age in the area had apparently "chosen" such a drastic form of birth control. Though the Recife feminists began from the seemingly private experiences of individual women, the process of pursuing this question soon took them beyond their initial formulation. In the final report on the study, the coordinator of the project put it this way:

> In the lives of all those women, choices with an apparently intimate and even affective content linked to the body appeared to be articulated with a much broader play of forces: the state, class relations, power in its different expressions—micro or macro, public or private.... At the end of the study, we had the sensation that we were touching the core of the question: We were reaching the terrain of the political.[21]

Soon after, SOS entered that terrain, taking advantage of selective openings in the state to collaborate with the Ministry of Health on both design and training elements of a new national women's health program.

The budding relationship with international funders reverberated in these opportunities for feminists to penetrate a newly democratizing state. The Ford funding, renewed in 1984, had enabled SOS to root its claims in solid empirical research and had given the group's work prestige and visibility. These qualities, along with its track record of educational work in poor communities, made SOS an attractive partner for progressive forces within the state.[22] Collaboration with the Ministry of Health was followed by the selection of one of its founders as a candidate for the National Women's Rights Council. Despite some fears about the risks to their autonomy, SOS members accepted these challenges and plunged into the task of seeking to influence state policies from a feminist perspective.

The credibility earned through the NGO's relationship with the state no doubt in turn increased its cachet with international donors, who were eager to reinforce the democratization process and the role of civil society within it. As the decade of the 1980s wore on, SOS's grants multiplied. In 1985, with Ford phasing out its support, an SOS staff member made the first of a series of fundraising trips to expand the organization's contacts in Europe. The U.N. Women's Conference held in Nairobi that year had drawn 15,000 activists to a parallel NGO gathering, and development agencies were beginning to take notice. The SOS member found a receptive audience for her appeal. By 1987, the organization had funding from NOVIB, a Dutch nongovernmental donor organization, and from EZE, a Protestant development agency in Germany, as well as from UNIFEM, a women's fund within the U.N. system. A year later, SOS landed a three-year grant for several hundred thousand dollars from the private U.S.-based MacArthur Foundation, and one of its staff members won three years of funding from another U.S. non-profit organization, Ashoka.

Like other social movement NGOs around Brazil, SOS embraced the opportunities offered by the new flow of resources. As a result, its members saw their powers enhanced: As their budgets grew, their projects multiplied, their audiences diversified, and their infrastructure expanded. Feminist voices were beginning to be heard in the corridors of power as well as in the *bairros* and the *sertão*. But, as the next two sections will show, there was a price to pay. While its members were highly critical of the effects of the market on Brazilian society, SOS was itself increasingly immersed in market discourses and practices promoted or required by donors. The NGO's participation in a kind of transnational social movement market required structural changes and encouraged strategic ones, extending its reach while simultaneously posing challenges to its core political values.

From Collective to Professionalized Organization

In the first two years of its existence, SOS had a collective structure and functioned with what one staff member called "spontaneous horizontality." There were neither defined lines of authority nor paid staff. All responsibilities, from administrative tasks to cleaning the bathroom, were rotated within the group. "In the beginning, we did it all," remembered one founder. But the transition from a largely self-sufficient low-budget operation to a professionalized organization with an overhead paid for by external sources entailed fundamental structural changes.[23]

The second phase began in 1982, with the grant from the Ford Foundation, and lasted until the end of the decade. During this period SOS made a number of important internal structural shifts: from voluntarism to professionalization, from shared responsibilities to the beginnings of specialization, and from egalitarianism to the creation of a hierarchy of salary and authority. The process of professionalization was incremental but definitive: Ford funded one full-time salary for the sterilization study; later, another member was paid to direct a feminist street theater group; further grants provided additional salaries for researchers, and so on. Until 1985, the majority of SOS affiliates were still volunteers, but by 1987 the organization had ten and a half paid staff positions.

As SOS's projects multiplied and the organization became increasingly involved with the state, staff members grew harried and internal relations became strained, leading to what one insider described as "pure chaos." Internal tensions rose to such an intolerable level that at one point a psychoanalyst was brought in to help the group work through its differences. The Ford Foundation terminated funding in 1986 in part, according to an SOS member, because its representative feared the organization was too "institutionally unstable." Finally, in 1989, representatives of EZE, which was providing significant funding, laid down the law, demanding reorganization and financial accountability. The SOS staff member who traveled to Europe to meet with the agency described her experience:

> It was very clear. I went to Germany in '89 and they told me. They made a huge request about accounting.... They demanded...a full report for the three years of projects and this was real conditionality. It was, either you do it, [or] you won't have the money. When I got back, I came to Rio and I called [SOS]...and for three days I kept hearing screaming on the phone that I had submitted myself to the Germans, to the men, to whoever,...and I said, "Okay, it is up to you. You decide. If you want to say no, for me that is okay. Just remember that seven people from this organization are getting their salaries from that [grant]."

This incident produced fierce debates inside the organization about whether to accede to the agency's demands. In the end, an administrator was hired to handle financial matters, marking the first step in a process of formal specialization.

Though some saw it as an outcome of foreign imposition, others within the group welcomed the change, including the person on whose shoulders administrative tasks had increasingly fallen. She remembered this earlier period as:

> "the worst moment of my life. When I woke up and thought about it, I wanted to die, because if I died, someone [else] had to take on that task—that was the only solution I thought of. Because...[having the financial responsibility] was a horror!" When EZE insisted on changes, "It wasn't [just] my complaint any more, it wasn't just my whining. It was someone who was saying, 'Either you do this or I don't give [you] any more money.' So it meant survival."

Another SOS activist described this as a necessary step in the organization's development, which might have been delayed had sexism not led the agency to express itself more forcefully than it would have with other male-dominated NGOs. By overcoming its internal anarchy fairly early on, she argued, SOS was able to survive and institutionalize faster and more effectively than their non-feminist mixed-gender counterparts.

The move to create a formal hierarchy in the organization met resistance but also had support within SOS, given the increasing demands brought on by its relationship to the state. One founder described the situation in the mid-1980s this way:

> You know that even within a collective...there is a structure of different people who have different powers—who speaks, who argues, who has more experience, who has more forceful oratory....This idea of feminism, that we are all equal, that's a lie....We are great and all sisters, all good, perfect. No. All the same things exist [among women] that exist in any space. Intrigues...who worked with whom, with whom one got together and worked against the other, all those stories and those exercises of power. Where things were defined, who was the one to decide. That always existed. So [this idea] was a fiction and a true camouflage of power.[24]

Over time, people gravitated toward certain responsibilities according to their interests and experiences. In 1987, when a new staff person who had not been part of the original collective was hired, she questioned the practice of equal pay that had been established early on:

> When I was hired, I discovered that I was going to come in earning the same as they were. I thought that was absurd. [My saying so] ended up creating a topic for debate because they began to discuss if it really was [absurd] or not.

Ultimately, it was decided to create a system of differential remuneration. The change was accomplished through an internal vote that ranked each person according to the monetary value of their contribution.[25] The creation of formal lines of authority followed. In essence, SOS became what Bordt calls a "professional feminist organization." No longer a true "collective," but also not entirely bureaucratized, it was a non-profit dominated by professionals who shared political beliefs and functioned with a moderate division of labor.[26]

For some, the process of differentiation—having one's peers judge one's efforts as more or less than those of another—was extremely painful. Others justified it as essential to organizational development. "To guarantee this horizontal democracy, you have to create mechanisms, distribute responsibilities, allow for spaces of power," argued one founding member. As the organization increasingly incorporated professional and often younger staff less familiar with the earlier feminist cultural project and its emphasis on egalitarian processes, fewer questions were raised about the new direction.

At the end of the 1980s, shifts in the international funding world reflected the broader subjection of the social sector to the performance requirements of the market. If the 1970s were the "decade of solidarity" and the 1980s the "decade of partnership," the 1990s were the "decade of the domination of professionalism, impact and results," according to the representative of one Brazilian NGO.[27] European and U.S.-based development agencies faced increasing scrutiny of their spending from donors at home, more concerned with domestic problems than distant, and seemingly intractable, ones.[28] Women's funding units, newly institutionalized within many donor agencies, were perhaps particularly vulnerable to these pressures.[29] To justify their grants to doubters at home, agency officials imposed a growing array of conditions on money sent abroad.

The new decade brought further structural changes to SOS. Both the nature of staff responsibilities and the nature of staff themselves were transformed. Given the scope of the organization's work, it was no longer possible for everyone to do everything, and tasks became increasingly specialized in the interests of efficiency. At the same time, SOS members, once "*militantes*," became "*técnicos*," with new employees hired as much for their professional credentials as for their feminist commitments.[30] Despite initial resistance to conceiving themselves as an NGO, the unfamiliar identity began to take hold.

The explosion of new NGOs in Brazil in the 1980s meant increased competition among them for donor dollars in the 1990s.[31] For SOS, with its growing infrastructure, this required a new focus on institutional sustainability. Staff members spent more and more of their time writing proposals and reports to financial backers.[32] No longer could projects simply grow out of political concerns and individual interests as they had in the early years. While they continued to incorporate feminist principles in their work, a project's capacity to generate funds also had to become a criterion.

SOS's participation in what some critics called the "gender industry" was a case in point. Feminists had discovered and incorporated discourses of gender in the late 1980s, and, responding to their pressure, by the mid-1990s development agencies had also seized on the concept as a new category for funding. This created an immediate demand from non-feminist Brazilian NGOs, eager to gain access to donor funding, for training sessions on "gender relations." Given SOS's theoretical and practical expertise in the area, as well as their political commitments, they were soon drawn in to spreading the gender gospel, an activity that paid the bills, but absorbed more and more of their time. Staff complained that they were giving the same basic workshop over and over, with no opportunity to explore such issues as the connections of gender with other social relations.

As part of the push toward greater efficiency and independent sustainability in the 1990s, agencies increasingly demanded that SOS complement their contributions with locally generated funds. The feminist NGO turned to peddling its wares; videos, publications, workshops, and consulting time all became commodities that it marketed to the state as well as to other NGOs and movements.[33] Whereas, earlier, grant seekers had usually received enough funds to fully cover their projects, the new model offered only partial compensation. The expenses for a 1998 course on pedagogies for gender training, for example, were paid in part by international agencies; the rest of the funds SOS was required to raise itself. As with the workshop on rural women described in Chapter 5, the decision was made to ask participants, who came from NGOs and social movement organizations throughout the Northeast region, to pay $200 apiece to cover their housing, food, and conference materials, a significant amount in local terms.[34]

In part this was based on a familiar concept—that people value only what they pay for. SOS staff in charge of the gender course argued that the attendance and participation of NGO members taking the course were vastly improved over earlier workshops, which had been offered for free. But the agencies' idea, as one SOS staff member explained it, was more sophisticated. They hoped to introduce an element of marketplace choice into workshop offerings. Presumably, each NGO in search of training opportunities would apply for and receive funding with which they could shop around for the appropriate workshop. The effects of supply and demand would distribute resources effectively and guarantee a voice to the NGO "consumer." The problem, of course, was that the social movement marketplace was less than democratic. Not everyone had equal access to funds to cover the cost of a "vote." Beyond that, the effect of the changes on relations between those now designated as "buyers" and "sellers," as we'll see, threatened their status as feminist allies.

Ironically, as SOS struggled to sustain itself in the context of the 1990s, the structure of the organization came more and more to resemble the sleek new profile of globalized corporations.[35] In an effort to cut costs and respond to donor demands for efficiency, what was now referred to in planning documents as "human resources"—the permanent staff—saw a significant reduction, while the institution contracted out a growing number of services.[36] With a proliferation of increasingly complex projects aimed at both grassroots audiences and national political leaders, the NGO's employees, like the new industrial workforce, were expected to be flexible, highly trained, and able to deploy a wide variety of skills. Teams working on a given project had a degree of autonomy, but functioned within and answered to an overall organizational plan. Strategic planning and management became increasingly central, as did efficient use of resources and the use of information technology to coordinate activities. There was increasing concern with "branding" the NGO, giving it a distinctive image for marketing purposes, and with the production of tangible "products." Finally, while SOS maintained the local foothold that both rooted it in a constituency and provided its trademark Northeast Brazilian identity, the NGO also increasingly "went global," expanding the scope of its operations beyond the nation-state. All of these processes of "flexible specialization" were mirrored by other feminist—and non-feminist—NGOs around the world, also facing the financial pressures and conditionalities of the New World Order.

From Local Organizing to Global Influence

Along with the structural changes that accompanied SOS's insertion into a transnational social movement market, the last two decades of the twentieth century also saw the feminist organization make significant changes to both its primary objectives and the means used to pursue them. While SOS representatives insisted that their policies were never directly dictated by development agencies, their shifting focus was not entirely unrelated to their growing entanglement with international funding circuits and with the state.

In the early years of self-sufficiency, 1980–82, the collective's activism reflected a radical feminist politics of identity. As described in Chapter 3,

Table 6.1 SOS Corpo—Three Phases

	1980–82	1983–89	1990–98
Relation to agencies	Self-sufficiency	Growing dependence	Global insertion
Structure			
Work	Voluntarism	Remuneration	Specialization
Authority	Collective	Incipient hierarchy	Moderate hierarchy
Politics			
Goals	Identity Empowerment Autonomy	Empowerment Gender-sensitive social policy	Survival Citizenship Democracy
Themes	Sexuality	Health	Development
Targets	Women	Women and men Grassroots organizations	Institutions Leaders
Strategy	Educate/organize working-class women	Train state workers Support women's organizations Enter the state	Occupy sites of power Influence decision-makers Create transnational networks
Arenas	Local	Local and national	Regional, national, international

SOS founders aimed to empower women by helping them achieve a better informed, less inhibited relation to their bodies and their sexuality. After an initial focus inward on their own bodies, they turned to the impoverished *bairros* surrounding Recife, hoping to help educate and organize working-class women.

Between 1983 and 1989, as SOS established relations with international funders and the state and began to formalize its structure, its political approach shifted. From a focus on creating an identity embodied in the individual, there was a turn toward the broader goal of effecting structural transformation, including changes in government policy. From working exclusively with women, SOS began to address both women and their male co-workers, partners, and political allies. From direct grassroots organizing, its members moved into a support role for already existing community-based organizations, and into a deepening relationship with a democratizing state. The needs of the working-class communities with whom they engaged and the priorities of the state combined to lead them away from sexuality and further into the realm of women's health. From an exclusively local focus, SOS Corpo began to move onto the national stage, its expanding scope and rising ambitions underwritten by both its growing funding base and its access to the state.

In the third phase of its development, from the late 1980s to the late 1990s, SOS's goals shifted again. During this period, the global dominion of the market deepened and Brazilian state policies took a neoliberal turn. While SOS continued to "promote gender equality with social justice," its aims moved beyond seeking changes in policy to equipping civil society for active intervention in the democratization process.[37] It increasingly also battled for the physical survival of the marginalized populations in and beyond its geographic region, launching educational campaigns against cholera, cervical cancer, and AIDS, in cooperation with health authorities.

Responding to the effects of economic crisis, the staff chose to move beyond an exclusive focus on health and social policy toward addressing broader development issues and economic policy. They advocated with Northeast regional institutions for development that "produces gender equality," rather than simply "including women." Beyond their immediate benefits, health projects became a vehicle to help those left out of the development process articulate struggles for citizenship.

From its initial local focus SOS expanded its political arena to the nine Northeastern states, using its expertise in regional affairs to ground its continued participation at a national and, increasingly, international level. After an early foray into transnational feminist politics around the U.N. Conference on Women in Nairobi in 1985, the NGO's involvement in international networks and gatherings accelerated in the 1990s.[38]

While SOS Corpo continued to view poor and marginalized populations as the ultimate beneficiaries of its work, in the 1990s the immediate targets of its action shifted upward, and its own identity underwent a transformation. From projects that addressed the women (and, later, men) who were the foot soldiers of local community organizations and state health services, the NGO moved into activities aimed at "strategic actors" in key institutions—international development agencies, government ministries, regional development bodies, and state governments, as well as social movements.

Community-based campaigns, once vehicles for feminist organizing, were reoriented to become demonstration projects directed at public officials and development agencies. The new objective of one local anti-cancer campaign, for example, was to provide a model for public health campaigns that took gender into account, a model that could be taken on by state or other agencies, thereby multiplying its effects. Rather than offering gender classes to the rank-and-file health workers of the state, SOS gave seminars to policymakers. Rather than presenting workshops for the members of women's organizations, they offered courses for their leaders. Whereas, earlier, SOS responded to demands from the *bairros*, now they insisted on setting their own agenda. "We're finished with giving talks for whoever happens to call us," said one senior staff member.[39]

In fact, the relationship with grassroots women's organizations was undergoing a fundamental shift. Speaking about the organizational plan then being drawn up, one staff member explained:

> SOS will cease having its center in the women's movement and will begin to be centered in feminist theory and in the mentality of women and men. We were moving at the rhythm of the women's movement. But we are *feminists*; we are not going to go so slowly.... We are going to construct feminism, not the women's movement.

The NGO would no longer be at the beck and call of particular organizations, she asserted. Instead, SOS would offer courses of their own design and the leaders of these groups could attend. "We will not be subject to the logic of people from the grassroots," she said. Feminist ideology and strategic vision, rather than the immediate needs of women's movements, would guide the NGO's actions.

The strategy implied by these moves was to seek change by becoming an influential "player" among powerful decision-makers, rather than by participating directly in mobilizing pressure from below. Once merely an advisor to popular movements and the health ministry, SOS was reborn as what one leader called a "third-level NGO"—a kind of think tank, capable of producing knowledge, training decision-makers, creating networks among key social actors, and fomenting national and international political debate around gender, development, and social justice.[40]

The change from movement-building to policy-making was made possible in an immediate sense by SOS's formalization and professionalization, processes in turn both facilitated and demanded by its relation to international funding agencies. But the discursive shift from women to gender discussed in Chapter 3 had already laid the groundwork for both structural and strategic change. The discourse of gender was double-edged. Though it offered transformative possibilities, "gender" also allowed SOS to distance itself from accountability to a particular group of claimants—i.e., women—and underwrote its move toward the arena of social policy.

For some, at least, the organization's trajectory led toward the state. In the late 1990s, SOS's General Coordinator, Maria Betânia Ávila, argued that women should go beyond efforts to influence government officials from the outside to claim the public sphere for themselves. Historically, she said, feminists had been resisting this strategy. "Feminism is the heir of the insurrectionary perspective, the non-negotiated confrontation."

But, in her view, democratization had brought new demands and the uncompromising approach was no longer the best course of action. To achieve their social agenda, feminists must address their "denial about negotiating with the public sphere."[41]

The transformations in this period were clearly embodied in the organization's five-year Strategic Action Plan for the years 1999–2003. The Plan listed three objectives: "Strengthening the quality of women's action in the public sphere for the construction of Brazilian democracy"; "creating alternatives for regional development with gender equity"; and "promoting reproductive and sexual rights as an arena for the construction, defense and enjoyment of citizenship."[42] These broad objectives were then translated into program areas and specific projects, an organizational structure delineated, and dollar amounts budgeted.

After a months-long process of consultations with staff, leadership, and external advisors, including a paid consultant, a rough draft was presented to the NGO's personnel in a general meeting in March 1998. The discussion elucidated the gains, but also the losses, of the new strategic approach: Though it would achieve wider influence, SOS would have to shed some of its historic programs and restructure its relations with working-class women's organizations.

One of the casualties was a holdover from the first phase of SOS's work: the one-on-one counseling on women's health issues that SOS had always offered at its headquarters. Initially stimulated by a weekly radio call-in program with SOS members as guests, long after the program's demise there was a steady trickle of women, often of humble origins, who came to discuss "female problems," ask about abortion, and bare their souls. In the heated debate on the issue, core questions were raised about SOS's changing identity:

Leader A: The counseling in the office has a low level of impact, compared with community work. There isn't a lot of social pressure for it.

Leader B: It's not fundable. There is no strategic justification for it. SOS is a center for the dissemination of information. It…legitimates its action by producing products.…We work more on collective impact than individual impact. [The counseling] gives attention to a small elite.

Staff A: [But] if we don't do it, no one will.

Leader A: It has an impact on small numbers [of people].

Staff B: The tendency is growing. Students are asking for it more.

[Several people talking at once, noisy debate.]

Leader B: There will be materials available [for them].

Staff A: None of us is trained [to do counseling].…

Staff C: It's part of the trajectory of the institution. Individual counseling had an impact on the institution's work. Many people who came through here were influenced [by it].

[Silence.]

Leader B: [We leaders] don't have answers for all the questions.…[The person who does the counseling] is leaving in June! We don't have anyone available. It's not because of the Strategic Plan! Who disagrees?

Staff C: I disagree. There should be counseling. Since I've known SOS we've had this. Is it only about earning money?

Staff A: I think it's an issue, but I don't see how we can do it. I feel bad about it, but [counseling] doesn't fit in the plan.

Leader B: Who would prepare themselves…[to do counseling]? Would we hire someone else? It's impossible to contract this out. And we can't increase staff.…It's an area of tension for many of us.…It's very painful.

Leader A: We could look back at some points of the plan.

Staff A: Sentiment is not enough to go back over everything. The plan has logic.

Staff C: Sentiment has to do with the trajectory of the institution, of feminism. It was a hallmark of rebellion.

Another round of controversy surfaced in the meeting around the implications of the Strategic Plan for SOS's participation in the Women's Forum. The Forum was a coalition of Pernambucan NGOs, women's organizations, and individual feminists, formed in 1988 to promote women's interests in debates around the new constitution. Ten years later, it was struggling to sustain itself, relying heavily on the resources of the staff-based organizations among its members to carry out tasks and maintain internal communication. SOS's discussion of its future role in the Forum was initiated by a query from the woman who had been SOS's liaison to the group. One of the leaders responded:

Leader A: Some activities are not strategic. The Forum doesn't have the support to follow through. Our objective is not to strengthen the Forum for its own sake, to do things as if it was the Forum doing them. It's less of a priority. We can train leaders for the Forum.

Staff A: It's a delicate issue. There are a lot of expectations of us. Our role is different from that of others.

Leader A: These are very difficult choices. Instead of making feminism, we have been making a women's movement. We have been doing something artificial—it gives the impression that it's much stronger than it is. If [the Forum] dies because we leave, we have been creating something artificial.

Staff C: It's going to be a shock [for the other Forum members].

Staff D: The movement is going to be strengthened by our actions as a whole.

Staff C: Except that the actor is going to be SOS.

Leader B:...The Forum doesn't want to move into the public sphere.... The electoral road is the route to power in the public area.

Staff D: Training leaders makes movements more autonomous.

Leader A: Being inside [the local Forum] takes time away from organizing courses for all the forums of the Northeast. It's an affirmation of SOS as a subject....

Leader B: Having autonomy in relation to others.

These two debates illustrate the fundamental strategic-political changes the NGO went through in this period, as well as the painful dilemmas and internal tensions the process produced. Neither direct counseling nor full participation in the local Women's Forum met the new criteria for SOS projects, which one leader described as their level of impact, relation to organizational capacity, and possibility of receiving funding. Though critics within the institution raised questions about the nature of political impact, the reality of organizational capacity, and the morality of fundability as criteria, these voices did not prevail.

Not only were these projects not seen as "strategic" in the sense that they did not generate and make efficient use of resources to move SOS closer to its now-expanded political goals, but in some way each was seen as a "sentimental" legacy, holding the institution back from being able to articulate its vision as an "autonomous" social actor. Ironically, autonomy, once understood as independence from male political and social domination, had come to be redefined as independence from the very social sectors whose interests SOS hoped to serve. This, leaders argued, would strengthen the movement in the long run, though they recognized that there might be short-term casualties.

In response to demands placed on it by both the Brazilian state and international development agencies, and in hopes of widening its influence, SOS Corpo professionalized, expanded, and created a hierarchical and specialized structure. In the process, as it struggled to guarantee its own sustainability, the NGO found itself taking on more and more characteristics of a streamlined "flexible" corporate model. The new structure, and the increased access to Northern resources that fostered it, in turn made possible a much broader and more ambitious set of goals and strategies. Meanwhile, the social havoc being wreaked by trends in the global political economy created new needs to which members of SOS felt compelled to respond. As they confronted a health crisis increasingly exacerbated by global economic dislocations and neoliberal response, SOS staff sought to enhance the organization's impact by aiming up, rather than down. They aimed to influence those with power, rather than concentrating their efforts on helping to organize those without it. These were difficult political choices, made in the context of both new opportunities and the deteriorating conditions of the majority of Brazilian women.

Transnational Balancing Acts

In its early years, as it was first venturing onto the minefield of international development, SOS openly challenged its Northern benefactors. In 1984, the Reagan administration imposed what became known as the "gag rule," which eliminated all U.S. government funding to private organizations overseas that promoted abortion.[43] Several years later, SOS received a grant from the Pathfinder Foundation, which relied on USAID for 90 percent of its funds.[44] Disbursement of the funds was conditioned on a promise not to endorse abortion in any of its activities, even those not covered by the grant. SOS representatives refused to sign such a pledge, thereby forfeiting the money at a time when Ford was phasing out its support and they were hard pressed to make ends meet. The NGO's members were clearly proud of this story; nearly everyone I spoke to recounted the tale and it was used in their workshops as an example of women's empowerment. The organization's principled stance earned the NGO a certain notoriety in the non-profit world.

But, as SOS's reliance on international resources grew, and as it became an increasingly qualified player in the social movement market, its relationship with its Northern "partners" also began to change. Like other NGOs in Brazil that initially took an outsider stance, over time SOS became more of an insider, even as it held on to fundamental principles. The staff engaged in dialogue with funding agency representatives, facilitated their relations with other grant recipients, and even distributed funds to local groups on behalf of certain agencies.[45]

In the 1990s, as SOS's structure, mechanisms of accountability, and focus on efficient production grew more akin to those of a business enterprise, the organization also came to resemble its "partners" in the international funding world, who faced similar pressures. One staff member, sent to a meeting of NOVIB grant recipients, noted "similarities in the issues being confronted by a European development agency and an NGO like ours: the need for internal reformulation, competition for resources, the need to raise our 'own' funds etc."[46] The organization was becoming an increasingly reliable and productive partner for agencies in search of local Brazilian counterparts. In addition to its structure, SOS also had the appeal of its contacts with multiple grassroots organizations and leadership role in the NGO community, as well as its influence in certain branches of the state. A NOVIB document referred to SOS as a "strategic partner" and "a national reference point for NOVIB's gender trajectory.... SOS Corpo has an excellent network of contacts in the women's movement, among NGOs in general and with governmental organizations."[47]

Closer interaction with feminists in development agencies fit into SOS's new orientation toward seeking to change policies by influencing those at the top. Dialogue with the organization's Northern allies was a vehicle to influence both agency procedures and, indirectly, development policies in Europe and the United States. SOS's participation in the *Red Entre Mujeres* (Network Between Women) illustrated this evolving relationship. The Network was an unusual attempt to democratize South-North relations between a funding agency and its grantees in the context of looking critically at the larger questions of gender and development aid.[48] It initially included women program officers from NOVIB, a Dutch nongovernmental development agency, and its Latin American grantee organizations working on gender issues. *Entre Mujeres* was launched as a response to pressure from Latin American feminists for greater involvement in NOVIB's educational and lobbying activities in the Netherlands.[49]

Most of the Latin American participants were NGOs, both those exclusively dedicated to women's issues and "mixed" institutions that addressed a variety of themes; very few were grassroots membership organizations. After beginning in 1987 with five Latin American NGOs, it expanded to thirty-six NOVIB grantees the following year. By 1994, there were eighty participating organizations in thirteen countries, along with NOVIB representatives and women from other Dutch organizations. SOS was one of three Latin American organizations on the Network's coordinating committee.

The goals of *Entre Mujeres* and its activities spanned two arenas: South-North relations and the links among like-minded NGOs in the South.[50] Its members organized seminars—such as the one described at the beginning of this chapter—that brought together Southern NGOs and representatives of Northern funding agencies, produced reports directed toward European donor agencies and political decision-makers on the impacts of funding patterns on women in Latin American countries, and generated proposals for new kinds of collaborative North-South aid relationships. Within Latin America, members offered "gender training" to NGOs less savvy on the issue, sponsored debates and published texts on gender and development aid, and lobbied their governments for policies to benefit women.

Organizational documents hint at the delicate balancing act implicit in the effort to construct a trans-hemispheric dialogue between funders and grantees. On the one hand, there were tensions between the two parties. Most obviously, the dependence of Latin American NGOs on international funding created inequalities and divergent interests.[51] While donor agency representatives—NOVIB program officers, in this case—pursued their own agendas and sought to get the "most bang for their buck," the Southern NGOs asserted their right to autonomy from outside interference. They used the Network as a forum to share critiques and to hone alternative proposals. Documents repeatedly criticized the structure of funding, including many of the same issues raised by the representative of the rural women's movement at the seminar on gender and development: agencies' insistence on funding short-term projects rather than ongoing institutional needs, the pressure on NGOs to promise exaggerated results within unreasonably short timelines, the lack of economic support for planning or reflection, and the requirement to produce seemingly endless, time-consuming reports.

The central axis of tension between agencies and grant recipients, where the asymmetries of power were most keenly felt, revolved around the process of evaluation. As Dutch agency staff faced growing pressure from government and civil society at home to justify overseas outlays, their demands on grantees for immediate outcomes measurable in quantitative terms became increasingly insistent. Their Southern counterparts in the Network objected both to the nature of the indicators that were being imposed and to the lack of participation by grant recipients in the determination of these criteria. Just as the MMTR leader had done, NGO staff asserted that, while economic advances might be measured in these terms, the kind of qualitative changes they were striving for could not be reduced to a statistic. They also argued that the specificity of particular organizing situations was often overlooked and non-traditional work methods were devalued in the drive for universal markers of "efficiency" and "effectiveness."

At the same time that these conflicts divided Latin American NGOs like SOS Corpo from the funding agencies that supported them, the two parties were also drawn together as allies. In the first instance, their shared feminist politics created a convergence of interests. Both feminists within funding agencies and the staff of their Southern NGO counterparts were allied vis-à-vis certain states, elements of the funding world, and other non-feminist Southern NGOs. Though resistant in general to NOVIB's impositions of evaluation criteria, for example, Latin American feminist NGOs welcomed the agency's call to its grantees to adopt a "gender perspective" in their work. Not only did *Entre Mujeres* feminists support this policy, but they constructed their own role as a channel for dissemination of methodologies and as a vehicle for pressure on those "mixed" NGOs reluctant to incorporate gender into their programs.[52] They argued that discourses of gender should not be seen as an imposition, but rather as a hard-fought victory in a long struggle by women involved in development, North and South. Latin American members of *Entre Mujeres* also worked together with feminists in development agencies to educate Northern civil societies and lobby European governments for an increase in funds for women's projects in the global South.[53]

In the second instance, the tensions between donors and their beneficiaries were attenuated not only by shared politics, but also by more instrumental interests. Clearly, the NGOs in the South gained both funding and political support from their partners with more clout in the North. But feminists in funding agencies also benefited from the relationship. Their links to women's movements in the South brought legitimacy to the "Women (or Gender) in Development" programs with which they were affiliated, belying opponents' claims that gender concerns were an imperial imposition on reluctant Southern cultures.[54] The successful fulfillment of evaluation criteria by Southern NGOs also helped prove the effectiveness of the international funding programs administered by feminists in Europe. Beyond these less tangible and more indirect forms of support for European feminism, Latin American Network members also actively advocated for the greater incorporation of women into decision-making roles in development agencies and pressed for the expansion of programs aimed at supporting women's empowerment abroad. In the case of NOVIB, for example, the critical interventions of Latin American feminists contributed to the development of an internal gender policy in the agency.[55] In effect, the job security and political authority of feminists in funding agencies depended to a large degree on the advocacy of allies like SOS Corpo in the South. Without their backing, the claims of Northern feminism to be of service to Latin American women's movements would have lacked credibility.

In this context of conflicts and collaboration, the Latin American members of the Network, including SOS, used a variety of strategies to defend their interests and extend their influence. First, they insisted on strengthening links among grant recipients from the South in a "platform of counterparts" that could both strengthen Latin American women's movements and serve as a vehicle for collective dialogue with donor agencies around the terms of their aid.

At the same time, the feminists among these Latin American NGOs rejected a purely confrontational stance in North-South negotiations. Instead, they sought to educate the other non-feminist NGOs about the possibilities of making alliances with certain forces within the international funding world and urged them to "assume responsibility for their own role in this negotiation." Agencies were mutable and internally heterogeneous entities that included advocates of change as well as those that resisted it, they argued.[56]

Though conciliatory, SOS and its fellow NGOs also claimed a right to relations of equality with Northern donors by asserting their identity as producers of knowledge rather than as needy victims. According to the concluding document of an early meeting in Uruguay, "Being recipients of international cooperation identifies us, but so does being creators of knowledge and action, not only for Latin America, but, within a broad perspective of change for the First World as well."[57] Rather than being perceived as passive recipients of aid, the Latin American NGOs stressed their role as educators of agency officials and, through them, of European civil societies on "gender and the reality of Latin American and Caribbean women."[58] Language itself became a means of refusing the position of powerless Other. Whether or not it represented a conscious strategy, the egalitarian discourse of "cooperation" and "counterparts" helped obscure power relations between donors and grant recipients and constructed their ties as an equal partnership.

A document co-authored by the assistant coordinator of SOS described the ambitions of the Network's Southern members: "We propose to develop our own models of development and institutional strengthening, of effectiveness and efficiency, of indicators to measure impact and sustainability based on our own needs and interests."[59] They critiqued depoliticized versions of "gender" and seized the initiative to offer alternative approaches that linked gender to citizenship. And they put forward a view of the relations of donor and beneficiary that challenged paternalism:

> What kind of development cooperation…generates real citizenship [for women]?…[I]t is cooperation that considers them as subjects, that favors and supports their articulation around their democratically sustainable projects, and does not only see them as vulnerable subjects, victims of exclusion, in need of aid to have access to basic social services.[60]

Sustaining the Network and fulfilling this vision was not easy. The translation of meanings among the differently situated members faced a variety of obstacles. There were sometimes conflicting interests among Northern and Southern members, divisions between feminist and "mixed"

NGOs, national differences, tensions between weaker and more established institutions, and partial perspectives based on immersion in distinct issues and relations with different agencies. Money for international meetings was in short supply and there were complaints that NOVIB had too much control over the rhythm of negotiations.[61] The end of the 1990s saw the Network's demise, but efforts at dialogue between NGO feminists and their supporters in development agencies in the global North—and the balancing act that it represented—continued in other venues.

MMTR: NEGOTIATING AUTONOMY

Crumbs from the Global Table

In the last two decades of the twentieth century, in contrast to SOS Corpo, the MMTR was located on the margins of international funding circuits. Initially, the rural organization financed its meetings and events with small donations primarily from local unions and churches, as well as from its own members. Relying on their own resources was a means of maintaining financial independence and claiming ownership of their movement. One collaborator described how limited amounts of external funding were complemented with in-kind contributions:

> [Y]ou'd go to a meeting and the funding was for the meat [to be served during the event]. The workers would bring the rest.... There was squash from Flores, corn from I-don't-know-where. The money covered the things they didn't have, but the workers always brought the food [that they grew].

By 1985, however, the organization had reached the limits of local sources of funding and leaders went in search of others. The first organizational contact with the international funding world came through Oxfam UK, a British development agency that was financing projects in the *sertão*.[62] The request for support in the mid-1980s from the union organizer who had founded the MMTR dovetailed with the agency's own growing interest in women's issues and, for a time, Oxfam provided small amounts of project-oriented funding. Links to other international agencies were subsequently established, bringing intermittent support, primarily from European nongovernmental sources.

In the MMTR, development agencies found an organization whose substantial social base and minimal administrative expenses offered the chance to multiply the effect of modest levels of funding and the opportunity to support women's struggles among a broad new constituency. Despite this appeal, competition for funding was fierce, and the rural women struggled to get the attention of agencies overwhelmed with requests. No matter how supportive the agency, the relationship was fundamentally one in which the MMTR was forced to maneuver within its economic dependence, while contesting the conditionalities imposed by donors.

Though the amounts were limited, and dedicated to projects rather than institutional support, agency funding had multiple positive effects. By covering the costs of transportation, food, and lodging at meetings and workshops, it made possible the gathering of women with few resources of their own from isolated communities scattered across the *sertão*'s vast open spaces. The posters and reports whose design and publication were underwritten by donors played an important role in helping the movement assert its legitimacy with the unions and other institutions, and reach other women throughout the state.

The invitations and funding from agencies to attend national and international feminist events exposed rural women to unfamiliar kinds of gender politics and facilitated links between the MMTR and its counterparts in other states and countries. In 1985, the Oxfam liaison with the rural women's movement proposed that the group attend the *Encontro Feminista Latinoamericano e do Caribe* (Latin American and Caribbean Feminist Encounter) being held in Southern Brazil in July of that year, and provided funding for several rural women from the Northeast, as well as from other countries in the region, to go. The MMTR members returned home with astonished reports of stuck-up middle-class feminists, of women dancing nude and sociodramas about sex, and of meetings with women agricultural workers like themselves from beyond the borders of their state. It was at this *Encontro* that women from the *sertão* first met members of a rural women's movement based in Paraíba, the next state to the north of Pernambuco, and began discussing the formation of a regional network. As one MMTR organizer described it, the role of the funding agency "...was very important. Because here, at this distance, without communication, we were never going to participate in anything. How were we going to know about [events]? What financial means did we have to participate?"

While their support was much needed, however, decision-makers in international agencies often suffered from ignorance of local realities, operated on political assumptions based on conditions in the United States and Europe, and imposed bureaucratic requirements that made little sense in the *sertão*. This produced pressures and tensions but, perhaps in part because of the minimal funds involved, appeared to have little effect on the MMTR's internal structure or political strategy. The rural organization insisted on preserving its identity as a social movement, rather than becoming a formalized institution inserted into the webs of the market and the state.

MMTR: Defiance from the Margins

With far less access to international funding than SOS Corpo and fewer opportunities to engage in transnational dialogue, the MMTR developed distinctive means of asserting its independence in relation to the funding establishment. The small grants that the working-class organization received played a key role in helping the rural women maintain basic internal communication, sponsor gatherings of members, and establish their legitimacy with other social actors in and beyond the *sertão*. Nevertheless, as we have seen, the organization's spokeswomen did not hesitate to confront their feminist allies within funding agencies on what they saw as arrogant behavior. From the margins of the international development system, MMTR leaders launched a trenchant critique of its impositions on them as working-class grant recipients.

MMTR members were suffering the consequences of the uneven penetration of global capital and extension of "free trade" into their region, as well as the loss of protections from a shrinking state. Together, these developments fomented large-scale export agriculture and threatened the livelihood of subsistence farmers. The arrival of the aid industry accompanied the opening of the economy and the deterioration of their position as a social class. Development agencies held out the possibility of relief, but also the continuation of humiliating forms of dependency. Almeida's critique of the donor agencies reflected the anti-imperialist sensibilities of the left, as well as the rural pride of a region long scorned by the more developed parts of Brazil. Rather than taking a pragmatic and accommodationist approach, she chose a strategy of overt confrontation. But biting the hand that might someday be persuaded to feed the rural movement appeared to be a risky, if not ill-fated, strategy.

Some might claim that the MMTR's militant stance was based on the fact that an organization with little external funding had little to lose. But the significance, however small, of the contribution made by international agencies and the fact that MMTR staff and leaders were constantly bemoaning their difficulties in attracting more sizeable grants would seem to undermine that explanation. And, though the rural organization was less enmeshed in transnational funding relations and, therefore, perhaps less subject to the hegemony of its discourses and practices, leaders did maintain strong personal ties to individual program officers. One might assume that there would be a reluctance to compromise these relationships via public censure.

I argue that the MMTR's bold stance toward funding agency representatives, like its willingness to confront SOS Corpo as described in the last chapter, was made possible by a kind of local power based on its broad-based constituency. Almeida had both personal prestige as a long-time organizer from the *sertão*, and considerable political capital as representative of one of the few organizations present with a membership of hundreds of rural working-class women organized around gender politics. Whether consciously or not, in her speech at the seminar described above Almeida drew on and was protected by these discursive resources. The legitimacy and authenticity represented in the MMTR's leadership and its sizeable membership base gave the organization an appeal to funders—and therefore a certain autonomy for critique—not available to groups with a less secure footing in a working-class constituency. And, in some quarters, by underlining MMTR autonomy, Almeida's tirade may have even enhanced the value of the legitimacy the rural movement could provide to those who chose to become associated with it.

After the presentation that day, though most other potential grantees noticeably avoided Almeida, her outspoken critique did not appear to provoke a negative response from the agency representatives present. In the long run, though there was no great influx of funding, neither did the organization lose opportunities as a result.

Other moments of tension revolved around the organizing of the first *Encontro Latinoamericano e do Caribe da Mulher Trabalhadora Rural* (Latin American and Caribbean Rural Women Workers' Encounter) in 1996. MMTR representatives recounted how one donor agency representative, previously quite sympathetic to the group, responded to an appeal for money by saying that she did not feel they were ready to take on such an ambitious event, which would involve some two hundred people from more than twenty countries. They called her to a meeting to express their anger at what they considered a paternalistic attitude and to defend their capacities and the importance of the gathering. She came away chastened and convinced that that their plans would bear fruit. Her organization subsequently became one of the backers of the event. Another long-time supporter insisted that the event should be organized by the national agricultural union confederation, CONTAG, rather than by the autonomous Northeast regional rural women's organization, the MMTR-NE, but the women stood firm in their decision to organize the event outside the framework of the male-dominated union movement. As Almeida put it, "We always felt that we were worth a lot and that we wouldn't sell out like that. We never accepted impositions."

Beyond direct confrontations such as these, MMTR activists employed a wide variety of means to negotiate their relations with First World development institutions. The organization took pains to educate its members about how to maneuver in seemingly impenetrable international funding circuits. At one regional meeting in May 1998, a representative of a German funding agency was asked to speak on the history of development aid from rich to poor countries, on the different kinds of agencies, and these agencies' current priorities and criteria. The group then conducted a role-play of a negotiation between the MMTR-NE and an international funding institution, to help members conquer their fears of "speaking with doctors," as one woman put it.

In the discussion that followed, the organization's staffperson described her difficulties navigating agency expectations. When grants were written in the language of the rural workers, they were judged by international funders as lacking sophistication. When proposals were composed in the discourse of the educated middle class, members were unable to explain or defend them, and staff or advisors were accused of manipulation. Other MMTR-NE members raised the difficulty of convincing agency representatives, accustomed to developed country procedures, of the futility of demanding receipts from vendors in the market or from drivers of the precarious vehicles that served as transport for women traveling to organization meetings. To make the reality of the *sertão* more tangible for funding institutions in developed countries, the rural women invited representatives to the MMTR's own terrain and planned to re-enact their improvised negotiation session so that funders could see themselves as small farmers see them.

With this approach, the MMTR and its regional umbrella group claimed their autonomy in relation to often well-intentioned but disproportionately powerful funding sources that underwrote the influence of feminisms from their home countries in the North. The rural women insisted on their capacity and rights to define goals and carry out projects, to specify criteria and methods for evaluation, to maintain internal democracy, to make political judgments, and to speak in their own language. On the one hand, in this conflict, they used skills honed in their struggles as women within a male-dominated, class-based institution—the rural unions. With the agencies, on the other hand, MMTR members confronted representatives of a certain kind of feminism and here it was class, rather than gender, that was at issue. Their status as members of a rural sector increasingly marginalized by global flows of capital made MMTR members vulnerable to demands from the financial representatives of transnational feminism, whose support they needed for survival. The rural women contested this power by relying on the legitimacy of their local working-class constituency, even as they faced continuing economic limitations.

RISKS OF THE SOCIAL MOVEMENT MARKETPLACE

SOS's strategy of embracing the models offered by the development industry and using them to advance its feminist and social justice agendas had successes on a number of fronts. Not only did SOS give workshops to state health workers at the bottom of the pyramid, but it also gained entrée to the medical school to offer training on reproductive rights from a gender perspective. Thanks, in large part, to SOS's lobbying efforts, Recife became the first city in the country to provide legal abortions in a public hospital. The cervical cancer prevention campaign that SOS designed and carried out in Pernambuco was subsequently adopted by the Health Ministry as a model for a national anti-cancer program. There is no doubt that these and other achievements made a real difference in the lives of low-income Brazilian women.[63] However, there were losses as well as "profits" from SOS's ventures into the social movement market. In the process of the structural and strategic changes that made these accomplishments possible, tensions were generated between SOS and its grassroots allies.

In 1997, the year before SOS launched its five-year Strategic Action Plan, a staff member described the relation the NGO maintained with the rural women's movement:

> We respond to the specific…demands of the MMTR. So, for example, [if] they need someone to go give a talk on violence against women on [International Women's Day], we go. If it's about health, we speak; if it's about public policies, we speak; if they need someone to go to an assembly to do a workshop on identity, a day-long workshop, we go; if they need someone to help with the coordination of a meeting, we go and help; if they need someone to be secretary for whatever, we go and do it; they need a booklet or some educational material, we do it.…
>
> We respond to what they ask because we consider [the MMTR] to be a very important movement in the rural area. It has very great political significance here in this country as well as in Latin America and we think that it's SOS's role to strengthen this kind of thing and contribute in the sense that we can give a feminist character to their activities.

In this earlier period, SOS staff put themselves at the disposal of the rural organization hoping only for political recompense. But, as NGOs like SOS Corpo grew more entwined with international feminist agencies and the state and more subject to their requirements, shifts began to occur in their relations with long-time allies among working-class women's movements. On the one hand, there was growing polarization in terms of access to resources; on the other, there were growing risks of commodification in the connections between NGOs and grassroots movements.[64]

Though the "new world order" conferred broader influence on some social movement organizations, as we have seen, others remained on the margins. In less than ten years, SOS evolved from a small, informal, volunteer-based organization with no infrastructure and with an outsider status vis-à-vis the institutions of power to a large professionalized institution with strong ties to the state and to the world of development funding. The MMTR extended out into regional, national, and Latin American networks and acquired some international aid, but retained both its penury and its social movement character. For the most part, it continued to lobby for policy changes from outside the boundaries of the state and the development establishment.[65]

Lebon has argued that inequalities among Brazilian feminist organizations were exacerbated because of donor preferences for "stronger" organizations that could absorb larger quantities of funding, had a track record of successful projects, and required less time from overworked program officials.[66] Camurça and Cisneros also note that these kinds of organizations "offer 'less investment risk'" for development agencies.[67] One agency staff member told me that she would have liked to support the MMTR, but that she could not give funds to a group that could not make use of at least $40,000 at one fell swoop, a sum far beyond the organization's capacity to absorb, given its infrastructure at the time. In addition to these factors, as mentioned earlier, the cultural capital that middle- or upper-class NGO staff members could deploy made writing successful grants a much less difficult proposition than for those unfamiliar with the ways of Northern donors.

Perhaps even more than the unequal quantities of funding enjoyed by different kinds of organizations, however, it was the structural requirements and strategic effects of receiving it that threatened to drive a wedge between working-class women's movements and NGOs. The new premium placed on organizational efficiency by development agencies often led to a de-emphasis by NGOs on long-term training and support for grassroots movements, in favor of short-term projects with quick visible results.[68] Funds were rarely granted to institutions like SOS for planning or follow-up with project beneficiaries, limiting the time NGOs could spend facilitating the participation of working-class women in project design and evaluation.[69]

SOS's growing financial base intersected with new opportunities to address increasing social needs. Together, these developments led to changes in strategy that made intensive relations with groups like the MMTR less of a priority, and perhaps even an obstacle to larger aims. According to its Strategic Action Plan, SOS required "autonomy vis-à-vis its beneficiary public so that its action does not become prisoner of the particular interests of sectors of civil society to the detriment of broader public action…for broad groups of beneficiaries."[70] In the 1970s, Latin American feminists had asserted the validity of their "specific" demands as women and sought autonomy within the context of "general" struggles against dictatorial states. In the 1990s, they inverted the terms, assuming the mantle of the general and, ironically, defending the autonomy of a broadly defined feminism against what were viewed as the particularistic claims of working-class and other women. In the process, they grew closer to the donor agencies—and faced the risk of ceding their independence to another kind of ally.

At the same time as feminist NGOs and grassroots women's organizations were separated by a widening gulf of power and resources, they were also increasingly connected in ways that reflected their different locations in what was rapidly assuming the characteristics of a social movement market. First, as funders demanded a new self-sufficiency, based on the marketing of NGO products, professionalized institutions like SOS Corpo found themselves forced to purvey their educational materials, training workshops, and consulting time. Social movement organizations like the MMTR, in turn, were converted into consumers of these feminist goods and services. In the process, the locus and nature of NGO decision-making changed. Rather than responding to needs as the MMTR defined them, for example, SOS would now offer courses its staff deemed strategic and the rural organization could choose—or not—to pay the cost of attendance. One SOS leader said, "If [the MMTR doesn't] want to discuss agricultural policy, they don't have to; the course will be ours." The results were visible in the NGO's decision, described in the previous chapter, to offer a seminar on rural women without including the MMTR.

At this early moment, the transition toward commodified relations was far from smooth, and tensions flared between SOS and the MMTR on a number of occasions. Though the overlapping goals and longstanding ties between women in the urban NGO and the rural women's movement offered hope for a different outcome, the workings of the market threatened to push the two organizations toward a relationship of broker and client or, at times, vendor and consumer.

Second, as agencies increasingly drew NGOs into an intermediary role, SOS became a liaison to donors for movements of working-class women. The NGO served on the facilitating group that advised NOVIB on its relations with beneficiaries, and was viewed, as we have seen, as a key contact by the Dutch development agency. SOS was also the convener for meetings among recipients of funds from a consortium of European Protestant agencies.[71] In some cases, working-class movements actually became SOS grantees. In 1996, with funding of $10,000 per year from the German agency EZE, the urban NGO launched the Fund for the Support of Women's Initiatives in the Recife Metropolitan Region. Through the fund, two representatives of SOS, along with leaders of two grassroots organizations, distributed small grants to working-class activists.

Through its role as a kind of "proxy donor," as well as through its own success at fundraising, the urban organization gained insider knowledge about international funding circuits. This knowledge allowed SOS to serve as consultant to movements in search of funds, a function it served for the MMTR-NE, the regional organization of rural women, among others.

Finally, there was a paradox. The shift in SOS strategy—made possible by its access to funding—from supporting local organizing efforts to influencing regional, national, and even international decision-makers, from outsider to insider approach, distanced the NGO from grassroots constituencies. Yet its own politics, and its legitimacy with both funders and the state, continued to depend on its links to these same working-class women. While SOS was careful not to claim to "represent" a constituency, its staff members' knowledge of the lives of women from the *sertão* or from the urban periphery was fundamental to their value in the eyes of the state and the funding establishment.[72]

This "catch-22" created the temptation for the NGO to lean toward the instrumental in its relations with grassroots movements. Given the external pressures, as well as the opportunities, it became more and more difficult to separate SOS's institutional interests from its political commitments. For example, the SOS research project on the reproductive and sexual experiences of rural women had dual outcomes. The results of the research could serve as the basis for further organizing towards the empowerment of its subjects and more responsive state policies; it could also provide raw material for products and activities that enhanced SOS's reputation and clout as an institution.

In this period of conflicting pressures, decisions about priorities and how to spend time were increasingly framed in the language of the market. In a discussion about organizational priorities, for example, one SOS staffperson commented on the period of time the organization had spent working on a project with working-class women, "It was an investment that was greater than the result."

Overall, I argue, the relations between SOS Corpo and the MMTR were threatened with commodification by their insertion into a new world financial order, posing risks for relations of solidarity in the transnational feminist counterpublic. As SOS and other NGOs ventured onto the terrain of international development in search of support for feminist projects, the discourses and practices of the market invaded social movement relationships in an increasingly insidious manner. Ironically, as tensions rose and solidarity was undermined, one of SOS's key attractions to funders—its links to "authentic" grassroots movements—was also placed in jeopardy. If the institution no longer maintained close ties to groups like the MMTR, its own legitimacy might ultimately suffer. Given SOS's identity as of and for the Northeast, its relationship with the MMTR—the representative of one of the most marginalized and emblematic groups of women in the region—was particularly significant.

But the organizations studied here did not simply acquiesce to the intrusions of the market into their relationships as allies. In some instances, the two organizations worked together to contest the impositions of development funders. SOS, as insider, helped organize the meeting described at the beginning of this chapter and define the parameters of debate. Its staff members were part of the planning body that invited Vanete Almeida to make her presentation. The MMTR representative, as outsider, vigorously defended the autonomy of grantees vis-à-vis the power of the agencies, expressing her organization's local perspective with no apologies. Given SOS's own history with the MMTR, it cannot have been a surprise for its staff that Almeida would take a militant stance. In fact, she touched on many of the same issues raised in more muted form in the documents of the Network, reinforcing a message that more well-endowed institutions had tried to convey, but doing so in a manner that they, perhaps, could not. The MMTR's radical "bad cop" stance put issues on the table that SOS and the other "good cops" could then use their favored position to negotiate.[73]

When conflicts arose between the two Brazilian organizations, the MMTR, as described in Chapter 5, carefully patrolled the boundaries of its relations with the urban institution, monitoring the levels of respect and instrumentality between them. When, in the view of the rural women, SOS transgressed the bounds of solidarity, they levied moral sanctions and demanded redress.

For its part, SOS responded quickly to these initiatives, making concessions to maintain the relationship. The Recife feminists also made consistent efforts to share their knowledge and contacts in the international development world with grassroots organizations. While increased involvement with circuits of funding raised the possibility that market-like relations would then spread into new social arenas, economic realities often led working-class organizations to seek external support. By democratizing access to funding, SOS helped, in a small but significant way, to undermine its power as intermediary, allowing working-class movements to make their own choices and create their own relations with the Northern feminists in development agencies.

The processes of professionalization and their consequences described in this chapter bear some resemblance to what DiMaggio and Powell called "coercive isomorphism," the tendency to institutional conformity in response to inexorable pressures from more powerful institutions.[74] But the difference lies in the contested nature of structures and strategies in an oppositional counterpublic. Social movement organizations like SOS Corpo, with their hybrid identities and sometimes contradictory goals, depend on a variety of resources accessed through different relationships. While the links with funding agencies and insertion in market-like inter-actions pulled SOS toward one institutional form and set of behaviors, their political commitments and ties to allies like the MMTR pulled them in a very different direction. The outcome is not predetermined, but rather reflects both historically changing environmental pressures and political choices.

Counterpublics are porous spaces, at times vulnerable to the incur-sions of discourses and practices that violate fundamental sets of shared values within them. Development aid has clearly been indispensable for women's movements in the global South and has played a key role in the diffusion of feminist perspectives within the state and other dominant institutions. It is a condition that few organizations can or would choose to do without. The question posed by this study is, simply: How can feminists, North and South, sustain equitable political alliances in the face of forces that threaten to remake their relationships? How can they work together to resist the transformation of their social space from a counterpublic with its characteristics of horizontality and collaboration to a competitive, hierarchical social movement market?

7

MOVEMENT OR MARKET?

Defending the Endangered Counterpublic

The chapters of this book have traced the links between feminists in the global North and their counterparts in the South, across the barriers of class and gender in Brazil, and between women's movements there and their feminist allies in international development agencies in Europe and the United States. The narrative has moved from the arena of culture to the space of politics and on to economic ebbs and flows, finding increasingly greater obstacles to the construction of collaborative social movement relationships. We have seen women's movements draw on transnational discourses, exchange political resources, and navigate the shoals of international funding. Through their struggles and appropriations, alliances and negotiations, movements like SOS Corpo and the MMTR helped constitute and sustain a transnational feminist counterpublic in the late twentieth century.

Feminist philosophers have often imagined the counterpublic as a potentially idealized, democratic political space, where participants share a commitment to negotiate their differences, transforming those differences from acrimonious divisions into sources of collective power.[1] A look at the "actually existing" feminist counterpublic finds many examples of mutually sustaining, cooperative relationships, achieved through perseverance in the face of an enduring array of economic, political, cultural, and other divides. Though translations have not always come easily, discourses have sometimes traveled against the current, moving from South to North where feminist activists have used them to reinvent their practices in novel ways.[2] In many places, NGOs and grassroots organizations like SOS and the MMTR continue, with growing urgency, to negotiate conflicts and collaborate across class and other divides. And, in recent years, new transnational initiatives—successors to the Network Among Women—have emerged, bringing together politically committed donors and feminist movements across the global South to construct more horizontal relationships in the struggle to redefine development policies.[3]

These are hopeful signs of the resilience of the counterpublic and the alliances that give it life. But, as we have seen in the course of this narrative, feminist relations are also sometimes fraught with conflict and the workings of institutional interests, competition, and the commodification of social movement relationships. The counterpublic, as we know it, is a hybrid space, where mutuality and relations of power are intimately entwined. This heterogeneous scenario reflects neither the eternities of human nature nor the idiosyncrasies of individuals. It is instead the product of a particular moment in time, one in which structures of social solidarity stretched across the world exist in tension with systems organized around the mobilizing of instrumental interests. The hybrid counterpublic is a historical phenomenon whose own internal solidarities are increasingly at risk.

Racist, colonial, and heterosexist imaginaries have long shadowed transnational feminist relations.[4] The newer danger comes from the discourses and practices of neoliberal capitalism, which have extended relations of contractual exchange into ever wider arenas of social life. More than simply an economic system, neoliberalism has cultural and political effects, valuing the market relation as "an ethic in itself, capable of acting as a guide to all human action, and substituting for all previously held ethical beliefs."[5] This ethic poses a fundamental challenge to the values of collaboration and alliance so painstakingly cultivated by social movements like those of the feminists described in this book. Neoliberalism promotes unfettered individualism in the pursuit of economic profit, and produces self-managing, self-interested, and competitive citizens.[6] Its ethic values quantifiable "results," rather than processes of empowerment or the construction of alternative social forms. Though markets work through and construct some forms of diversity, their more significant accomplishment is the erasure of autonomous and uncontrollable difference. In this vision, democratic collaborations fall victim to hierarchical relations, and the marketization of relationships trumps the articulation of collective identities based on human solidarities.

The late twentieth century saw the extension of neoliberalism from Chicago School experiments in Chile in the mid-1970s, to Chinese economic liberalization and shifts in U.S. monetary policy later in the decade, through Reaganism and its British counterpart in the Thatcher administration in the 1980s, to its extension across the global South via foreign investment, coercive structural adjustment plans, and the privatization of public sectors from Brasilia to Bangkok.[7] Neoliberal conceptions and modes of operation spread beyond these macrostructural expressions as trade and investment broke out of regulated spaces, and markets were created in arenas until then only marginally integrated into relations of exchange.[8] Micro-enterprise formations spread through the developing world, and new business practices, such as "social marketing," gave rise to the unexpected appearance of "calculative agencies" on the terrain of non-profit activity.[9] International aid agencies, wittingly or not, circulated market-oriented discourses and practices through their net of grantees by means of their funding criteria, implementing procedures, and evaluation processes. As social movements increasingly entered international funding circuits, they confronted practices and worldviews antithetical to their own systems of value and forms of solidarity.[10]

The feminist counterpublic, like other oppositional spaces, found itself increasingly grappling with incursions by instrumental modalities. In effect, globally circulating discourses and practices were pushing the counterpublic toward what I have called a "social movement market," characterized not by overlapping values, common interests, and partially shared identities, but by competition, calculation, and the lure of institutional power.

Marx long ago warned of what he called "commodity fetishism," the alienation of products from the labor that produces them and their conversion into objects with an apparently independent life. Under capitalism, he argued, social relations between actual human producers are reduced to relations between their products in the form of their relative exchange values; the arena of market circulation obscures the sphere of production where real value is generated.[11]

Something similar occurs in the context of a social movement market. Relations among members of a counterpublic once grounded by values or ideals are congealed into products—whether forms of local knowledge or professional expertise, activist pedagogies, or representations of class authenticity. In the shadow of the market, these products then become objects of struggle as organizations seek to appropriate them from one another for their own agendas. In the purest expression of a social movement market, political alliances would be reduced to relations of contractual exchange where each party would draw on its cultural and economic assets to assert leverage in the transaction.

What risks being hidden in this process is not only the labor involved in producing theories, tactics, or forms of legitimacy, but the fact that social movement "commodities" are produced in and through social relations among members of a counterpublic. The feminist pedagogies of an NGO, like SOS, were produced in encounters with working-class women's movements, such as the MMTR; the local knowledge of rural women was articulated and made explicit through dialogue with urban feminists. In a social movement market, social relationships themselves become objects. The relations between social movement organizations or individuals are commodified and exchanged, while the history of collective labor and possibilities of solidarity between them lose their salience. In the worst case scenario, the parties become alien to one another, opponents in a struggle for advantage within a competitive market.

The social movement market, like the capitalist variant, threatens to reorganize social—and political—life, distorting the relationships that constitute counterpublics. Indeed, some might argue that feminist movements have already been subsumed in an inexorable capitalist logic, but my research leads me to think otherwise.[12] The cash nexus, and all that it implies, has not yet won hegemony among feminist and other social movements. Though more powerful in some quarters than others, market-like relations are still only a variable dimension of movement alliances, a set of tensions to be negotiated, a foreboding presence on the horizon.

Markets, in fact, are contingent constructions.[13] Rather than disembodied self-reproducing global forces, they are products of the links among social actors and institutions embedded in local social and physical geographies.[14] Once in place, commodified relations take on—apparently—a life of their own. But, in fact, they depend on the specificities of locale, on engagement with local discourses and populations, and on particular states, transnational corporations, and multilateral institutions.[15] Similarly, the social movement market is fostered by specific institutional structures within states and international donor agencies, and relies on political relationships to extend its reach.

This understanding of markets reveals their vulnerabilities and helps to eviscerate their discursive power. As feminist scholars have argued, the set of economic relations that have become known as "globalization" are not the irresistible "tidal wave" of neoliberal fantasy and critical left nightmare. In the provocative view of Gibson-Graham, contact between capitalist markets and alternative kinds of social formations may as easily lead to the undermining of the former as to the commodification of the latter. Discursive "contamination" can move in either direction, extending—or undoing—capitalist relations.[16]

Their insight gives cause for hope but, I would argue, more is needed to effectively confront the dangers markets pose for social movements, and for human life more broadly. Resisting the pull toward commodified relations within counterpublics demands constant vigilance and collective commitment. It begins with efforts to critique and resist the incursions of neoliberal discourse and practice into relations among allies. The struggles of SOS Corpo and the MMTR to sustain their relationship in spite of the inequalities between them is a case in point.

Two years after my fieldwork ended, in 2000, SOS Corpo and the MMTR launched a new collaborative action-research project on gender relations in family agriculture. The goals of the project were to develop knowledge about rural women's subordination, but also, in the process, to strengthen the capacity of the rural movement to analyze the experiences of its members and devise political strategies.

Over a period of four years, the two organizations worked together to plan, design, and carry out the project. SOS assumed the technical coordination of the project and members of the MMTR-NE were trained to do ethnographic and survey research in their own communities. The participants from both organizations met regularly to discuss theoretical frameworks, analyze data, and interpret results.[17] In the final report, Portella and her SOS co-authors described the relationship between the two organizations as not just a research collaboration, but also a "political interaction." As such, it brought inherent tensions and conflicts, but also benefits for both sides.[18]

Joint projects like this one, in which activists work together across borders of class, education, and life experience to create mutually sustaining and egalitarian relationships, represent struggles against commodification. But these battles, of necessity, are defensive and specific in their effects. In the long run, contesting the toxic effects of market discourse on social movements means taking the offensive against its economic and political structures.[19] This, in turn, requires conceptualizing the goals of feminism more broadly than has often been the case.

Feminism in North America and Europe in the latter part of the twentieth century initially engaged gender issues mainly of concern to white middle-class women. In the 1970s and 1980s, feminists in these regions, most of them women of color, broke open the narrow focus by articulating the links between the oppressions of race, sexuality, and gender. But the injustices of class and of global economic inequalities were less central to Northern feminist political projects. In contrast, in Latin America, and elsewhere in the global South, these latter issues have been fundamental for movements against gender subordination.[20]

In the last several decades, Latin American and Caribbean feminists like the ones described in this book have exposed the effects of neoliberalism on marginalized populations across the region and challenged its extension into the realm of values and politics. They have also waged struggles against the Free Trade Area of the Americas, and the structural adjustment and the commodification of health, as well as for the renegotiation of the international debt. Simultaneously, women's movements have developed within or parallel to mixed-gender organizations, such as those of the homeless in Brazil, unemployed workers in Argentina, and Afro-descended and indigenous populations across the continent.[21] In each of these cases, struggles around gender, race, and ethnicity are articulated with issues of class and marginality, and with opposition to neoliberal discourses and practices.

As these cases illustrate, resistance to the extension of capitalist markets necessitates linking publics organized around distinctive issues and social experiences, including class, race, ethnicity, and land and health rights, as well as gender. Within the feminist counterpublic itself, these efforts have also brought together differently situated political actors. Though awareness of the dangers of neoliberalism both for gender-based politics and for human well-being more generally has spread slowly in North America and Western Europe, in recent years struggles against the market have increasingly included feminist organizations from those regions as well.[22] Whether within or across publics, building coalitions has demanded discursive translations across difference and difficult negotiations of inequality.

Counterpublics are at risk. Capitalist markets threaten to invade their inner spaces, commodifying their relationships and undermining their very capacity to mount challenges to dominant social relations. As we face a global financial crisis at the end of the first decade of the new century, the prognosis for the counterpublic seems mixed. On the one hand, as banks fail, stock markets plunge, and funds evaporate, impoverished constituencies across the world will pay the price and resources for social movements are sure to shrink. On the other hand, the crisis has also made the failings of unregulated markets abundantly clear, perhaps creating an opening for the anti-neoliberal—or anti-capitalist—critiques being made by feminists and their allies. If this is indeed the case, we may see the emergence of stronger counterpublics, which could offer us a glimpse of politics and social relations beyond the market.

METHODOLOGICAL APPENDIX
Transnational Feminism as Field

If the intensification of transnational links has drawn diverse women's movements, North and South, into closer contact with one another, it has also had significant effects on the relationship between researchers who study these movements and their subjects. No longer are academics from the North the only ones who travel; our subjects are more likely than ever before to have entrée into our worlds, just as we have long had into theirs. Our struggles have become more intertwined and the stakes involved in transnational alliances higher. As a result, we no longer write with impunity. Not only are our research subjects more likely to have access to our work, but they are also more likely to care about what we say because of their dependence on international funding and insertion into global networks of allies.

The contrapuntal dance of power and alliance with the women's movements we study may not be entirely new, particularly to those who have long suffered our inquisitive attentions. But the intensification of the dynamics over the past several decades have made them more evident to academics from the global North, as the volume of writing on the subject attests.[1] Scholars engaged in ethnography are perhaps even more acutely aware of the growing tensions in transnational research relationships than those using methods that create more distance between themselves and their subjects.

In my own case, despite my familiarity with the subject of cross-border social movement relationships, awareness of the complexities as they affected my work crept in gradually. If the literature emphasized the relations of power involved in research, my background as an activist who had spent years living in Latin America, as well as my identification with the struggles of the movements I had chosen to study, produced a certain selective blindness. Though I had no illusions that the research process would be entirely mutual and egalitarian, I had hopes that I could produce a study that would serve in some way to further the feminist goals of my subjects.[2] In the process, I naively assumed, my political sympathies and experience would insulate me from the contaminations of power.

This assumption was given substance by the feelings of difference and impotence that I experienced in the field. Like others who do research outside of their zones of familiarity, I was always mindful of being on someone else's turf—immersed in a language, culture, and set of social customs, climate, physical setting, and political scenario that were not my own. I was acutely aware of my dependence on the goodwill of those I was studying for daily material and psychic survival, as well as for the success of my project, and frequently felt apologetic for imposing on their time, fearing (accurately, I think) that I had little in the immediate sense to offer in return. I could not, I thought, have been farther from being an agent of power/knowledge à la Foucault.[3]

Over time, however, I became increasingly aware of the often uncomfortable parallels between the subject of my research and my own relationships with my research subjects. As might be expected, the very tensions between power and solidarity that I was studying in social movement relations across borders were reproduced in the encounter between me as a U.S.-based scholar and the movements in Brazil that I was studying. On the one hand, there were strong elements of alliance in my links to these movements. I was inspired by the work of both SOS Corpo and the MMTR, and identified with their goals of social transformation and gender justice. During and after my fieldwork, I did what I could to support their efforts—from translating documents to helping prepare meeting sites, from passing on information about funding opportunities to sharing, when asked, the insights of a supportive observer. On the other hand, in the field and after I had left it, my subjects and I also engaged in struggles for control over knowledge about and representations of their work.

My initial forays into the field involved a series of interviews with activists, designed to "map" the arena of women's movements in Brazil and in the state of Pernambuco, my chosen site. At this stage, my interviewees shared their experiences and insights on feminisms in Brazil freely with this rather tentative and relatively ignorant *americana*. There seemed to be no complications in the relations between us.

It wasn't until my third visit to the country, when I undertook a five-week ethnographic pilot study of SOS Corpo, that strains surfaced. I was working in the office, conducting interviews, attending meetings, and translating organizational documents. Staff members were friendly and generous with their time, and my presence seemed generally accepted, until the disappearance of my laptop computer from its usual storage space in the office uncovered a chasm between us. Tensions erupted as we searched and sought explanations. My privileged status abruptly came into focus as it became clear how my ownership of a valuable commodity, not accessible to most middle-class Brazilians—and the awkward fact of its unexplained loss—had fostered internal turmoil and resentment at an unwanted intrusion. Global material inequalities had made their presence felt.

When I returned a year later to continue my research and expanded it to participant observation with the MMTR, other kinds of asymmetries became evident. Not only did I have access to economic resources not available to the women of the *sertão*, but I had an envious privilege: the freedom, as a woman, to come and go as I pleased. Beyond that, from the point of view of the organization, my entrée into the world of funding sources and academic networks, as well as my access to feminist knowledge and analysis, marked another kind of difference, one that made me, in some ways, a potential asset.

I was also a potential, though unwitting, threat. As a researcher, I was often privy to personal and political information whose delicacy was not always clear to someone not well versed in the complexities of local institutional relations. On several occasions, as I moved in the circles of women's movements, I narrowly escaped making blunders that could have inflamed tensions between the MMTR and other organizations. My access to conferences and publishing opportunities in the United States, meanwhile, amplified the risk that I could, unintentionally, portray the MMTR in a negative light to allies, enemies, or funding sources.[4]

Despite my initial feelings of powerlessness, in fact, the inequalities between myself as researcher and the organizations I had chosen to study gave me important advantages in these relationships that complicated a connection as allies with common goals and values. Though this was true for my relations with both SOS and the MMTR, here I will focus on my relations with the rural organization with whom the differences in access to resources were far more significant.

Throughout my fieldwork with the rural women's movement, recurring incidents of tension repeatedly intruded on the straightforwardly amicable relations I had hoped for. It was only much later that I recognized these as the same kind of negotiations around power and the control of access to local knowledge that I had observed in the transnational relationships among women's movements.[5] The first round of negotiations occurred when I first approached Vanete Almeida, the organization's founder, at the conference described in Chapter 6. Like the funding agency representatives in attendance, I had been impressed with her independence vis-à-vis potential benefactors, as well as with the impressive work that the organization had carried out among rural women, and I asked if I could come out and visit them in the *sertão*. Almeida immediately said yes, but also made her own strongly worded request. "If you plan to study us," she said, "we would like to see what you write." That would mean, of course, translating any material into Portuguese before delivering it to them. I was a bit surprised that she would bring this up so early on, but quickly agreed. Though I had not yet decided what role the organization might play in my dissertation, it was clear that it was a lead worth following.

Months later, after many visits to the *sertão* and participation in multiple MMTR activities, I was again made aware of my difference, as members of the organization perceived it. At a Northeast regional meeting that I was attending, the subject of researchers came up. The group launched into an embittered discussion of the ways they had been used by a series of academics, mostly Brazilian, who had taken their time and knowledge and then disappeared from the scene, never to be heard from again. No one mentioned or even looked at me during this interchange, but it was clear that, in some way, it was intended to serve as a warning, lest I might harbor the intention of doing the same.

The final round of negotiations occurred around the organization's archives. In the last week before I was to leave the *sertão*, I discovered several file drawers at the local rural union office filled with documents from the early history of the MMTR in the Central *Sertão* region. It had been difficult interviewing members from that period as many were older and few were able to dredge up specific memories of their early activities. I was hopeful that the minutes from meetings and other materials in the files might help fill some gaps in my understanding of the organization's beginnings, but I had little time left to spend reading and taking notes. Instead, I went through and identified documents that looked like they could be of use, thinking I would ask permission to photocopy them and read them later. They did not appear to be confidential and, in any case, I had no intention of publishing anything that might do the organization harm. But, when MMTR leaders heard my proposal, they were horrified. "Our archives are our history, our power," Almeida said to me. "You may read them here, but you may not take them with you." Once again, a line was drawn—and I, as researcher, was placed firmly on the other side of it.

Viewing all three of these incidents in retrospect, it was clear that, in the eyes of MMTR leaders, I might be a sympathetic ally who had good personal relations with the group, but my interests were not identical to theirs. I could not entirely be trusted to behave in a way that would not endanger them or tax their limited resources without return. As was the case in their relations with both funding agencies and feminist NGOs like SOS Corpo, access to the "wealth" of the MMTR—their constituency, history, and local knowledge—had to be negotiated carefully with this transnational visitor. While MMTR representatives were unfailingly warm, magnanimous with their time, and open to my participation in all their activities, they were also careful to protect the organization by asserting their rights in the relationship.

For my part, though I had material advantages, like SOS and the development agencies, I too needed access to the MMTR. Not only did I find inspiration in its unique form of gender politics, but the argument of my dissertation would be stronger for the inclusion of this rural working-class organization from a region ostensibly marginal to global flows. The MMTR's local leverage worked as well with me as with its other transnational allies.

The process of negotiations continued as I began writing, back in the San Francisco Bay Area. I had agreed to provide the MMTR copies of what I wrote, but I also wanted to give them a chance to comment on my work so that I could make revisions before publication. At a minimum, I wanted to avoid inaccuracies; at best, I hoped for a conversation in which we both might learn from one another.

Launching this dialogue was difficult because it meant acknowledging differences that I had been trying to suppress, unpacking tensions that I had been refusing to name. It also held the frightening possibility of opening the door to criticisms that might call into question fundamental aspects of my interpretation. It was with much trepidation, then, that I had my first article on the MMTR translated and sent it off to Almeida, my original contact and the only one with access to email. A year later I sent her another.[6]

The first article was to be published in the proceedings of a conference on Latin American feminisms; the second was to appear simultaneously in both a Brazilian and an English-language academic journal.[7] In both cases there was a narrow window of time between when the translation was ready and when the publishers needed my final revisions. Vanete was busy, as always, with a variety of political responsibilities, but she graciously agreed to respond within the time frame I gave her.

Her initial response was to list offensive sentences and phrases that she felt I should cut, without elaborating on the reasons. Since a number of them were fairly important to my argument, I wrote back and asked for further explanation, aware that this would impose an added burden she might not consider worthwhile. She responded in vivid detail, noting, in the case of the second article, that it was *only* because of our friendship that she had taken the time to do so.

Almeida's substantive criticisms focused on the way that I portrayed her organization's relations with more powerful others. Below, I excerpt selections from the drafts I had sent her along with her response to each point to give a sense of the nature of her critique and the tone of the negotiations. First, Almeida's comments on my version of the MMTR's relationship to transnational feminism:

MT: *The discursive field in the early 1980s when the MMTR was born was already shot through with both home-grown and international influences.*

VA: It's not true that the MMTR's field was shot through with influences. I didn't know anything about feminism. I had rarely left this region and had not yet suffered any influence. That's the truth.

MT: *From the MMTR's early years, the organization had both direct and indirect links to feminisms from beyond Brazil.*

VA: The MMTR didn't have the influence of feminism from the early years. It was after we had already carried out our first meeting, where we defined our organizational mission as WOMEN and as WORKERS, that we went to the…Latin American and Caribbean Feminist Meeting.… [It] was important for our Network at the Northeast regional level, since we met the women from Paraíba there, but not for our organizational policy. It was our first contact with feminism.

MT: *Materials provided and provocative questions raised in discussions by agency staff sensitive to MMTR concerns prompted new thinking in the organization.*

VA: I don't know what you are talking about here. The only idea that came from the agencies was GENDER. New ideas come from the women and from our discussions, participation and needs which were being brought up and discussed.… At the beginning we had to argue strongly with [one agency representative] who did not believe that the [MMTR] had the capacity to carry out a Latin American meeting. So I don't agree with your comments since you would have to talk about the disagreements and about our courageous confrontations with the agencies, which often did not want to recognize our knowledge.

On my portrayal of the MMTR's links to the urban Brazilian feminists who provided the initial links to transnational feminisms:

MT: *Throughout the 1980s and early 1990s, these two kinds of institutions—international funders with local offices in Brazil, and feminist NGOs in Northeast Brazilian cities—gave the rural women's movement access to transnational feminist resources and discourses.*

VA: SOS never brought resources to the Central Sertão and our first contact with feminism wasn't through them. They helped…[later] with ideas and feminist techniques. What I don't like is that you give a weight to SOS vis-à-vis [the MMTR in the] Central Sertão that isn't real.…And the movement in the Central Sertão neither came from within feminism, nor was fed by it.…The greatest desire of the rural workers was organization and better living conditions. Feminism came within this package but never as their guiding perspective, or as the outstanding one. That's how it happened.

MT: *Brazilian feminist NGOs located in nearby cities were the other significant point of entry into the sertão for transnational feminisms. These local institutions became both intermediate links to international funders and powerful vectors for the discourses circulating in global feminist networks.*

VA: I don't know where you get this idea that SOS is the one who brought resources, that SOS is the one who opened doors for us. Excuse me, Millie, but I think that is a prejudiced way of thinking, as if, because we live in the *sertão*, and are a movement from the country and not from the city, we don't have this capacity. We always established our own relations, from the beginning. It wasn't SOS or any other urban organization.

I replied to her email, accepting some points, and debating others. Rather than responding to her comments here, I will let my readers judge for themselves the ways I have—or have not—incorporated them in writing this book. It was not always easy to know what to do when we differed in our analyses. It seemed to me that, in addition to errors of fact or lacks of clarity on my part, or misunderstanding on hers, the distances between us reflected a combination of our distinct political histories, social locations, and angles of vision. We also spoke to different constituencies in the context of dissimilar political and professional arenas. Just as she could not renounce her role as union and political activist, I could not, with any integrity, abandon my perspective as sociological observer, no matter how sympathetic. There was also the not-so-small matter of the pressures exerted by the academy to produce a certain kind of study as the price of admission to the field. But Almeida demanded of me, and I accepted, a certain accountability to my research subjects and their perspective on the world.

Our transnational dialogue, which had begun in the field and continued over email, was an imperfect approximation of a truly participatory project.[8] After all, under my own set of pressures from the academy, I had maintained control over the design of the project, much of its execution, and the final product. Though I engaged in discussions of the issues I was writing about with MMTR members and leaders throughout my research, and their insights had great influence on my thinking, the conclusions here are ultimately my own.[9]

Though not exactly antagonists, my subjects and I were, nonetheless, engaged in a struggle over the representation of the rural women's movement, a discursive struggle with potential material effects for both of us. Our perspectives were not only situated, they were *unequally* situated. I had the power to develop and disseminate my version of the MMTR far beyond the range of its participants' voices. They could not, at that point, contest my views in the same Northern academic forums.[10] But the rural women had other means to negotiate this global relationship: by controlling access to their constituency, their activities, and their archives, and by making moral appeals based on our shared political commitments.

In an unequal world, there is no way to easily erase the power between us as feminist researchers based in the global North, and those whose movements we study in the global South. But acknowledging both the power and the stakes in collaboration on both sides may allow us to navigate the obstacles and construct dialogues among our partial and situated perspectives. The intensification of global connections not only makes this kind of collaboration possible, but makes it all the more necessary, as the fates of our geographically scattered movements are ever more closely entwined.

POSTSCRIPT

After I had sent Vanete the changes I had made in the text of the second article, she sent me this parting comment:

> Concerning your communication of June 5, I agree that SOS has more access to resources and contacts although that isn't everything. You wrote: "[T]hey [don't] deserve credit for having organized the movement of rural women workers." They NEVER WILL HAVE this credit because it wasn't they who organized. I don't think that the support of SOS was fundamental. It was important, but without it, the movement would [still] exist.

> Thank you very much for sending the corrections. I hope that you come in October and we will talk personally about many things.

NOTES

1 INTRODUCTION: RE-READING GLOBALIZATION FROM NORTHEAST BRAZIL

1 On the historical construction of the Brazilian Northeast, see Albuquerque, 2004.

2 As others have pointed out, all the terminologies for referring to structural differences among regions or nations are flawed in one way or another. Many of them take the form of hierarchical binaries—developed/underdeveloped or developing, core or center/periphery, First World/Third World—in which the economically dominant are the standard against which the "Rest" are measured. Some authors critical of the hierarchical approach have proposed the use of "early industrialized" and "late industrialized" as a partial remedy. Many feminists prefer the apparently more neutral distinctions of geography, referring to "Western feminism" as a dominant discursive unity rooted in colonial relations. Movements struggling for alternative forms of globalization in recent years have adopted the terms "global North" and "global South." From the perspective of Brazil, located in the Western hemisphere, but not of the "West," this choice makes more sense, and here I use global North to refer to the economically dominant countries in North America, Europe and Asia, and global South to refer to those countries considered part of the so-called Third World. Like the others, these categories too have their inadequacies, erasing the growing diversity within each pole and ignoring the presence of "the South" in "the North" and vice versa. As well, they obscure the important political and economic differences among states in the North as well as among those in the South. Nevertheless, the labels do serve to mark, however roughly, the historical differences between winners and losers, advantaged and disadvantaged, in the global economy, while bracketing the tremendous complexities and interrelationships within and among them. For other reflections on geo-political terminologies see Bello 2004; Dirlik 1997; Grewal and Kaplan 1994a; Naples 2002.

3 Following the lead of other scholars I refer to feminisms as "transnational" rather than "global" or "international" in an effort to locate movements in their local and national contexts while simultaneously acknowledging the ways they transcend borders to construct relations with one another (Alexander and Mohanty 1997; Grewal and Kaplan 1994a; Hannerz 1996; Smith 2001). As will be argued in this chapter, the preference

reflects a vision of globalization as historically specific links between local sites, rather than as nameless omnipotent forces disconnected from the local and immune from history. While "international" affirms a false discreteness of nations, the term "global" errs too much in the opposite direction, obliterating local meanings and mystifying the origins and interests of forces that reach across borders. As Shiva (1993) points out, those institutions labeled—or self-appointed—as "global" take on a power and representative status that they do not necessarily deserve. Here I use "global" to describe phenomena that characterize many regions of the world or whose local roots have lost meaning or become obscured, "international" to refer to institutions that assume clear national distinctions, and "transnational" to describe phenomena that link one part of the world with another.

4   Castells 1996a; 1996b. Harvey (1990) argues that, ironically, place does appear to matter as competing localities seek to market their ostensibly unique properties in a desperate effort to attract investment. But, in fact, the outcome of their efforts is communities that are more and more the same.

5   Castells 1996b, p. 474.

6   Bauman 1998; Castells 1989; 1996a; 1997; Harvey 1990. Their accounts evoke the ethnically-based conflicts in parts of Africa and the former Soviet Union.

7   Gibson-Graham 2006. See also Bergeron 2001; Grewal 2005a.

8   Tsing 2005.

9   See, e.g., Barnet and Cavanagh 1994; Brecher et al. 2002; Harvey 1990; Loker 1999; Mander and Goldsmith 1996.

10   For a more optimistic perspective, see Evans 2000, p. 235.

11   Benería and Roldán 1987; Kabeer 2000; Lim 1983.

12   Ferree and Mueller (2004) make the useful distinction between "women's movements" and "feminism." The former are organized around a gendered *constituency*, but do not necessarily challenge power relations between men and women. Feminist movements, in contrast, are defined, not by their membership, but by their *goal* of eradicating gender subordination, a goal that may be articulated with struggles against other forms of inequality. Participants in self-defined "women's movements" take diverse stances toward "feminism" as a label, ranging from identification to rejection (Basu 1995). While respecting the terms activists have chosen to describe their *organizations*, this study describes them as feminist and locates them in a larger transnational feminist arena if their *practices* challenge dominant forms of gender relations.

13   Vargas 2003.

14   Brennan 2004; Freeman 2001; Sassen 1998; 2002.

15   For a similar perspective, see Hannerz 1991.

16   See Bandy and Smith 2005; della Porta et al. 1999; della Porta and Tarrow 2005; Desai 2002; Edwards and Gaventa 2001; Eschle and Maiguashca 2005; Ferree and Tripp 2006; Guidry et al. 2000; Keck and Sikkink 1998; Moghadam 2005; Risse-Kappen 1995; Smith et al. 1997; Tarrow 2005; Wapner 1996.

17   Ferree 2006.

18   della Porta and Tarrow 2005; Tarrow 2005.

19   These cultural processes are elaborated by Melucci 1985; 1988; 1989.

20   See, for example, the literature on framing: Gamson et al. 1982; Snow and Benford 1988; 2000; Snow et al. 1986. My own understanding of the relation between culture and politics draws on the work of Alvarez et al. 1998b and of Poletta 2004.

21   Khasnabish 2008.

22   Massey 1994. Others who take a similar theoretical approach include Freeman 2001; Hannerz 1996; Tsing 2005.

23   Grewal (2005a) refers to these kinds of discursive connections as "transnational connectivities."

24   Mohanty 1991b. See also Grewal and Kaplan 1994a.

25 See Benhabib 1999; Dean 1996; Ferguson 1998; hooks 1984; Mohanty 1991a; Shih 2005; Yuval-Davis 2006.

26 I use the term "movement" to encompass a variety of forms, from formalized organizations to loose collections of social actors linked through informal networks around shared values. I also use it to denominate organizations, like the MMTR (Rural Women Workers' Movement), whose members refer to them as "movements."

27 See Waterman (1998) for a useful critique of the range of pre-existing notions of "solidarity." Like him, I understand solidarity, in part, as "an active process of negotiating differences" rather than as an assumption of already-existing identity (p. 235).

28 The use of the plural reflects a recognition that contemporary feminist movements have emerged in a wide variety of social locations and define their historical trajectories, collective identities, goals, strategies, and tactics in diverse and not always congruous ways.

29 Alvarez 1990; Hahner 1990; Lobo 1987; Teles 1993.

30 Hahner 1990; Miller 1991; Teles 1993. In response to feminist pressure, the vote was decreed in 1932 and incorporated into the constitution two years later.

31 Alves 1985.

32 Alvarez 1990.

33 The percentage of women in the workforce rose from 13.5 percent in 1950 to 27.4 percent in 1980 (Bruschini 1985, p. 92; Bruschini and Rosemberg 1982; Humphrey 1984).

34 Alvarez 1990. See Alvarez, Chapter 3, for a discussion of the ways new currents within the Church after the Second Vatican Council (1962–65) opened space for women's organizing while maintaining socially conservative positions on issues of morality, the family, and sexuality. Alvarez argues that women's movements were able to continue mobilizing, while other forms of opposition were not permitted, because, for sexist reasons, the regime did not take them seriously. What women did was not considered "politics."

35 For one of the earliest writings on Brazilian women, see Saffioti 1976.

36 There is no verifiable record of the number of women involved in the armed opposition. Nevertheless, Teles (1993, p. 64) reports that of the names of the dead or disappeared in this period collected by the Comitê Brasileiro de Anistia—Brazilian Amnesty Committee, 11.7 percent were women.

37 Alves 1985; Skidmore 1989.

38 Alvarez and Dagnino 1995.

39 *Brasil Mulher* was launched in October 1975, followed by *Nós Mulheres* in June 1976, and *Mulherío* in 1981.

40 These conflicts culminated in 1980 when the *III Congresso da Mulher Paulista* (Third São Paulo Women's Congress) split into two events, one organized by left party members and the other by autonomous feminists (Alvarez 1990; Teles 1993).

41 Alvarez's (1990, p. 96) feminist interviewees described this early feminism as "essentially economistic." See also Lobo 1987.

42 Alvarez 1990; Caldeira 1984; Gohn 1985; Sardenberg and Costa 1993; Teles 1993.

43 Jelin 1990; Radcliffe and Westwood 1993; Stephen 1997.

44 Alvarez 1990; Castro 1999; Stephen 1997. As noted above, not all of these women called themselves "feminists."

45 Caldwell 2007; Carneiro 1999; Fernandes 1994; 2002; Gonzalez 1982.

46 Andrews 2004; Caldwell 2007; Twine 1997. For an overview of the effects of racial stratification in Brazil, see Reichmann 1999.

47 During my fieldwork, I observed two exceptions. One was a group of rural activists from a town linked historically to a *quilombo*—a community founded by escaped or freed slaves; the other was a group of young women in an urban bairro outside Recife who had been organized by members of the *Movimento Negro Unificado* (MNU [Black Unified Movement]).

48 The concept spread quickly. One year later, there were 6 such stations in Saõ Paulo and 36 around the country. By 2003, there were 339 throughout Brazil (Santos 2005, p. 41).

49 The CNDM was made up of women legislators from a variety of political parties and representatives of civil society, including academics and activists from the autonomous women's movement. It was modeled on a similar initiative—the *Conselho Estadual da Condição Feminina* (State Council on the Feminine Condition)—founded in the opposition-governed state of São Paulo in 1983. The CNDM's early proponents saw it as a step toward the creation of a women's ministry, a development which did not, however, occur (Alvarez 1990).

50 Massey 1994, p. 149.

51 While these are based on actual organizations, they are also, in some sense, ideal types. In real life, feminist actors exist on a continuum that allows for all kinds of overlap among the distinctive categories described here.

52 Though mainstream liberal feminism had greater access to resources, radical feminist discourses and practices also occupied a place within this dominant configuration. It was this latter version of feminism, for reasons discussed in Chapter 2, that had the greatest resonance among women's movement activists in Northeast Brazil.

53 Grugel 1999; Hulme and Edwards 1997b. The number of European development agencies, for example, grew from 1,600 in 1980 to 2,970 in 1993, and their spending rose from $2.8 billion to $5.7 billion in current dollars (Hulme and Edwards 1997b, p. 4). In the mid-1990s, the World Bank estimated that about 30 percent of agency funding came from donor states; the five largest development agencies in the U.K. depended on the state for between 20 and 55 percent of their funding (Hulme and Edwards 1997b, pp. 6–7). This trend reflected what was called the "New Policy Agenda," which advocated replacing government—North as well as South—with private initiative and the workings of the market. The reliance on nongovernmental actors was also seen as a vehicle to strengthening political democratization (Hulme and Edwards 1997b; Pearce 1997).

54 On the one hand, those with less access to resources had more autonomy to define their politics; on the other, their voices were less likely to be heard.

55 NGOs have "functionally specialized, paid, professional staff and, sometimes, a limited set of volunteers, receive funding from bilateral or multilateral agencies and (usually foreign) private foundations, and engage in pragmatic, strategic planning to develop reports or projects aimed at influencing public policies and/or providing advice…to the…grassroots women's movement and varied services to low-income women" (Alvarez 1999, pp. 185–186). In contrast, grassroots movements are organized by groups around the defense of particular identities. They operate largely (though not necessarily entirely) with volunteer labor, have less formal structures and, if they receive any international funding, receive significantly smaller amounts than their NGO counterparts.

56 Lebon 1996. By 1986, a survey found 196 feminist NGOs in Brazil, out of a universe of 1,208, focused on issues of race, gender, and social justice (Landim 1988b). Several years later, the same author estimated there to be 3,000 NGOs in Brazil (Landim 1993). A 1995 survey by the Inter-American Foundation (1995) found more than 20,000 NGOs in Latin America; over half were devoted to women's issues. Globally, the UNDP estimated that 13 percent of official aid disbursements were destined for NGOs (Pearce 1997, p. 268).

57 According to Landim, "For the entities composed of women and directed to women—therefore, with a common thread linking the identities of 'agents' and 'beneficiaries' (*destinatárias*), even when they are from different social sectors—the tension between 'being an institution or being a movement' is much greater than in a universe like that of the [NGOs that serve the poor], where the action is 'from the intellectuals for the people'" (Landim 1988a, p. 57). See also Alvarez 1999.

58 Alvarez 1999.

59 Hulme and Edwards 1997b; Pearce 1997. Hulme and Edwards (1997a, p. 270) describe an evolutionary process in which NGOs may come more and more to resemble their Northern benefactors: "It commences with the agreement to use aid monies: progresses with the adoption of donor techniques for programming, implementing, monitoring

and accounting for performance…subsequently it moves on to shaping the nature of appointments and the internal structures of NGOs with the recruitment of English speaking, logical framework experts and information departments which function as public relations units; eventually, the organizational culture is attuned to donors—and the local, indigenous and informal features…are lost." Others also noted the influence of foreign donors on the activities and discursive frameworks of feminist NGOs (Bickham Mendez 2005; Lebon 1996; Lind 2000; Ready 2000).

60 Lebon 1996, p. 604.

61 Many of these advisors came out of church-based popular education movements influenced by liberation theology.

62 Smith 1987.

63 Wallerstein 1974.

64 IBGE; Rocha 2001, both cited in Font 2003, p. 221. In 2003, the poorest half of the population received only 14.8 percent of the country's income, while the wealthiest 1 percent received 13.3 percent (IBGE 2003).

65 The Northeast region includes nine states: Bahia, Sergipe, Alagoas, Pernambuco, Paraiba, Rio Grande do Norte, Ceará, Maranhão, and Piaui. Social indicators paint a grim picture. Here, in 1999, the poverty rate was 51 percent. (Rocha 2001, cited in Font 2003, p. 221). In 2002, infant mortality in the region was 43 per 1,000, compared with 29 per 1,000 for the country as a whole; illiteracy was double that of the national figure and more than three times that of the more prosperous regions of the South and Southeast (IBGE 2003). The situation in rural areas was particularly acute. The Northeast had 46 percent of Brazil's rural population, but 63 percent of the rural poor (Araújo 2004, p. 17).

66 Following the practice of the agricultural unions with which it was affiliated, the MMTR used the term "rural workers" to refer to people with a wide range of relationships to the land, including small producers, as well as wage workers, sharecroppers, and others. For studies of the MMTR in Southern Brazil, see Rubin and Sokoloff-Rubin forthcoming; under review; Schaff 2001; Stephen 1997.

67 In this study, I focus on North-South relations for reasons to be explained later in this chapter. However, women's movements in Brazil also sustained relations with movements in other parts of the global South (as well as with marginalized groups in the global North) that were often more "horizontal" and less shaped by inequalities than the ones described here.

68 Burawoy 1998; Burawoy et al. 1991.

69 The outcome of this process was the book Global Ethnography, coedited by Burawoy and nine of his graduate students (Burawoy et al. 2000).

70 Melucci 1985; 1988; 1989.

71 From a similar perspective, but with a distinctive approach, the contributors to the volume edited by Diani and McAdam (2003) seek to bring together network and social movement theory.

72 Felski (1989) was the first to use the term "counter-public spheres." The concept has since been elaborated by others, including Fraser (1997, p. 81), who describes counterpublics as spaces whose members "invent and circulate counter-discourses, which, in turn, permit them to formulate oppositional interpretations of their identities, interests and needs."

73 Asen 2000; Calhoun 2002; Felski 1989.

74 Calhoun 2002; Fraser 1997. Alvarez (1999) has a similar conception of what she calls "fields."

75 Asen 2000; Calhoun 1992; Felski 1989; Mackie 2001.

76 For that reason, I have chosen not to use Fraser's (1997) term "subaltern counterpublics," which runs the risk of eliding intersectional identities and appears to imply that members are subordinate on all dimensions. I find compelling Asen's (2000) argument that defining a counterpublic by its political stance vis-à-vis dominant publics is more useful than identifying it by the nature of its members.

77 George et al. 2000.

78 Bickham Mendez and Wolf 2001; Thayer 2001b.

79 Fraser (1997), for example, describes feminist conflicts as being over conceptions of women's needs, while Warner (2002) defines publics through attention to the circulation of texts. See also Asen 2000; Calhoun 1992.

80 Vargas 2003.

81 Calhoun 2002.

82 It is important to note that market relations themselves are the outcome of the interactions of particular social actors in specific circumstances. For the sake of brevity, here I bracket the multiple relations through which the "global market" is constructed.

83 Though my primary fieldwork came to an end in the late 1990s, subsequent trips suggest that many of the patterns described here have continued into the twenty-first century.

84 This is not meant to imply that discourses exist disconnected from the material world. On the contrary, as this study will show, they had important material effects, just as material resources were not separable from their discursive incarnations. Nevertheless, there were historical moments when the relations among feminists were predominantly organized around meanings rather than the exchange or transfer of material resources.

85 It is important not to romanticize the early connections among women's movements. Certainly there were elements of paternalism and dependency in their relationships, but the kind of explicit commodification that developed later did not exist at this earlier stage.

2 UNEASY ALLIES: THE MAKING OF A TRANSNATIONAL FEMINIST COUNTERPUBLIC

1 Cited in Miller 1990, p. 20.

2 Cited in Miller 1990, p. 14.

3 Cited in Ehrick 1999, p. 77.

4 Miller 1991.

5 Cited in Ibid., p. 69

6 Ibid.

7 Ehrick 1999.

8 Miller 1991.

9 Guy 1999. Though maternalist feminism may have also existed in the United States, Guy argues that it was a more common phenomenon in Latin America.

10 Ehrick 1999. The differences in timing of movement emergence, their access to resources or success in building a constituency created hierarchies among them. Ehrick notes that the leader of the movement in Uruguay, while grateful for help from her counterparts in more established movements in Argentina, was also wary of their influence.

11 Miller 1990; 1991. These congresses, first sponsored by the *Sociedad Científica Argentina* (Argentine Scientific Society), took place in Buenos Aires (1898), Montevideo (1901), Rio de Janeiro (1905), and Santiago (1908).

12 The Congress was organized by the University Women of Argentina. Sponsors included the National Argentine Association against the White Slave Trade, the Socialist Women's Center, the Association of Normal School Teachers, the Women's Union and Labor Group, and the National League of Women Freethinkers. Attendees ranged from anarchists to members of traditional opposition parties and from factory workers to charitable aristocrats. They included delegates from Argentina, Chile, Peru, and Uruguay, as well as from Italy and the United States (Little 1978; Miller 1991).

13 These included support for universal suffrage, the right to divorce, and an eight-hour day.

14 Little 1978; Miller 1990; 1991.

15   It was the exclusion of women from the World Anti-Slavery Conference in 1840 that inspired Elizabeth Cady Stanton and Lucrecia Mott to organize the first Women's Rights Convention in Seneca Falls, New York, in 1848. Activism for suffrage in the United States went on to adopt many of the tactics of temperance and antislavery campaigns and drew members from the ranks of these earlier movements (Keck and Sikkink 1998).

16   These included the International Council of Women, founded in 1888 in Washington, DC; the International Women's Suffrage Alliance, founded in 1904 in Berlin; and the Women's International League for Peace and Freedom, founded in 1915 in The Hague (Rupp 1997).

17   Representatives of the World Women's Christian Temperance Union established eighty-six organizations in twelve years. After a 1913 tour by the International Women's Suffrage Association, national organizations throughout Asia and the Middle East signed on; by 1926, the IWSA had member organizations in forty-two countries (Keck and Sikkink 1998, pp. 54, 57, 53).

18   Rupp 1997.

19   Ibid.

20   Members formed study groups, supported the establishment of schools for women in Africa, and pressured U.S. school superintendents to include materials about African literature and history in their curricula. They also participated in other organizations, such as the International Council of Women (ICW), but racism often divided feminist ranks. In 1925, for example, the group walked out when their members were asked to sit in a segregated gallery of the ICW's chosen meeting hall (Neverdon-Morton 1989). On the International Council of Women of the Darker Races, see also Barnett 1978.

21   Evans 1977, p. 166. The countries represented were limited to the global North.

22   Burton 1991. See also Grewal and Kaplan 1994a; Ware 1992. Ehrick (1999) reported similar discursive practices in the U.S. feminist movement at the beginning of the century. These accounts of the international politics of feminism parallel those of the American suffrage movement's domestic politics of race (Davis 1983; Dubois 1978).

23   Barnett 1978.

24   Rupp 1997, p. 75.

25   Cited in Miller 1990, pp. 14, n.11. Held in Washington, DC in the midst of World War I, the second Pan American Scientific Congress was seized on by the United States as an opportunity for promoting its foreign policy agenda. Women were considered irrelevant to this kind of diplomatic gathering and excluded. Instead, they organized their own parallel conference at which they founded the Pan American Union of Women (Miller 1990).

26   The IACW later served as a model for the Commission of Women for the League of Nations, as well as for the United Nations Commission on the Status of Women, launched in the post-World War II period (Miller 1991). On the IACW, see also Meyer 1999.

27   Miller 1990; 1991.

28   Letters of Carrie Chapman Catt, Reel 2, Container 2, 12–13, cited in Ehrick 1999, p. 75.

29   Caulfield 2000. Williams wrote a widely used text on Latin America: Williams 1945.

30   Ehrick 1999.

31   Ibid.

32   Ibid.

33   Taylor 1989.

34   Miller 1991.

35   Suffrage was won in successive Latin American countries between 1929 (Ecuador) and 1961 (Paraguay). Even when political rights had been legally won, universal suffrage was often far from reality. Though Brazilian women won the right to vote in 1932, for example, literacy and property requirements effectively restricted the vote to only 5 percent of

the population, male and female, until 1946. Universal suffrage did not exist anywhere in Latin America until the post-World War II period (Ibid., pp. 96, 101).

36   The Congress, organized by the Women's International League for Peace and Freedom, also included members from the United States and Canada (Miller 1991).

37   Miller 1991.

38   Grewal and Kaplan 1994b. This is similar to Mohanty's (1991a) concept of "common contexts of struggle."

39   Antrobus 2004; Galey 1995; Snyder 2006.

40   The decade also saw the establishment of a series of institutions within the U.N. system, such as UNIFEM (U.N. Development Fund for Women) and INSTRAW (International Research and Training Institute for the Advancement of Women), designed to serve women's interests, as well as the passage of CEDAW (Convention on the Elimination of All Forms of Discrimination against Women) in 1979.

41   The International Women's Year Tribunal in Mexico was attended by 6,000 NGO representatives; ten years later in Nairobi, there were 15,000; and over 30,000 attended the parallel women's gathering in Beijing (here "NGO" includes a wide range of movements, from grassroots to highly professionalized) (Desai 2002, p. 28). While only thirty Brazilians participated in the events at the conference in Nairobi, there were three hundred in Beijing (Alvarez 1998, p. 309).

42   Basu 2003; Desai 2002; Tripp 2006.

43   Desai 2002; Petchesky 2003; Pettman 2004; Tripp 2006.

44   Tripp 2006, p. 62.

45   This period was dubbed the "Lost Decade" by CEPAL (Camisión Económica para América Latina [the Economic Commission for Latin America]) because of its devastating impact on the well-being of the populations of the global South (CEPAL 1990).

46   Desai 2002. Incipient alliances during this period between women of color in the United States and women of what was then called the "Third World" may have also contributed to the breaking down of North-South divides. For an account of these cross-border relations, see: Blackwell under review.

47   Desai 2002.

48   Feminist NGOs involved in organizing around U.N. conferences included: Alt-WID (Women's Alliance for Development Alternatives), AWID (originally Association for Women in Development, now Association for Women's Rights in Development), CFFC (Catholics for a Free Choice), CWGL (Center for Global Women's Leadership), DAWN (Development Alternatives with Women for a New Era), IWRAW (International Women's Rights Action Watch), IWTC (International Women's Tribune Center), WAND (Women and Development Unit), WEDO (Women's Environment and Development Organization), WGNRR (Women's Global Network for Reproductive Rights),WICEJ (Women's International Coalition for Economic Justice),WILDAF (Women in Law and Development in Africa), WILPF (Women's International League for Peace and Freedom), and WIN (Women's International Network).

49   These events included the 1992 U.N. Conference on Environment and Development (UNCED) in Rio de Janeiro, the 1993 World Conference on Human Rights in Vienna, the 1994 International Conference on Population and Development (ICPD) in Cairo, and the 1995 World Summit for Social Development in Copenhagen.

50   On interpretive struggles at U.N. meetings and other international institutions around the discourse of reproductive rights, see Hartmann 1995; Higer 1999; Petchesky 2003. On struggles around understandings of violence against women and human rights, see Bunch et al. 2001; Joachim 1999; Keck and Sikkink 1998; Peters and Wolper 1995. For discussions of feminist participation in organizing around U.N. conferences from the perspective of activists from the global South, see Antrobus 2004; Vargas 2003.

51   Friedman's (1999) research in Venezuela, for example, suggests that when local movements were weak and incipient, U.N. conferences could play a galvanizing role; when

movements were more developed, the redirection of feminist attention to institutional politics could have less salutary effects. In some countries, opposition to the imposition of global norms led activists to engage in a complex process of "translating" discourses of rights in local contexts (Wing 2002).

52   For debates on the use of human rights discourse by feminists, see Bunch 1995; Grewal 2005b; Petchesky and Judd 1998; Yuval-Davis 2006. On their use of development discourse, see: Harcourt 2005. On their engagement with population discourse, see Higer 1999. For an insider's reflections on Latin American feminist organizing for the Beijing conference, see Vargas 1996. For a more cynical perspective, see Spivak 1996. For further discussion of these debates, see Moghadam 2005.

53   Petchesky 2003, pp. 22, 26–27; Petchesky 2000, cited in Moghadam 2005, p. 129. Harcourt (2005), who chairs WIDE, a European-based NGO that played an early and important role in organizing feminist participation in the U.N. arena, also articulates an ambivalent stance. She warns against the dominant "bio-prescriptions" produced by feminist interactions with U.N. discourses of "women and development" but also finds a kind of counter-biopower in women's "place-based" organizing. Like Petchesky, she advocates for multilayered strategies that can respond to the fluid nature of modern forms of power.

54   Alvarez 1999; Bickham Mendez 2005; Ford-Smith 1997; Friedman 1999; Lebon 1996; Murdock 2008.

55   Antrobus 2004; Desai 2002; Tripp 2006.

56   Alvarez 1999.

57   "Femocrat" was originally an Australian term for professionalized feminist politicians and state employees (Eisenstein 1991).

58   Tripp 2006.

59   On feminist struggles at Beijing over the inclusion of the word "gender," see Franco 1998; 2001. On conflicts at Cairo and Beijing with the population establishment and with fundamentalists, see Higer 1999; Petchesky and Judd 1998.

60   Slatter 2001, p. 4, cited in Pettman 2004, p. 57. See also: Antrobus 2004.

61   It is important to note that conventional advocacy work and grassroots organizing were often intimately connected. In Brazil, for example, for two years before Beijing more than 800 national, state, and local feminist and women's organizations mobilized to educate the population about gender-based discrimination and to generate input from women's movements around the country to the official governmental delegation. Post-Beijing, the effort to "bring Beijing home to Brazil" continued (Alvarez 1998, p. 309). In Recife, feminists used a variety of tactics, from workshops to street theater, to spread the word about the rights contained in the conference platform and to create pressure for their implementation.

62   These latter included DAWN, 1984; Women Living Under Muslim Laws (WLUML), 1984; WILDAF, 1990; and the *Articulación Feminista Marcosur* (Feminist "Marcosur" Network), 2000. For a discussion of transnational networks whose strategies expanded beyond lobbying international institutions, see Moghadam 2005.

63   Higer 1999.

64   Ibid. For a description of the incremental process of diversification, see Estrada-Claudio 2006. The International Women and Health Meetings have continued, with the tenth held in New Delhi in 2005. AWID has also sponsored a series of International Forums among feminist organizations in the global South, with a focus on issues such as development, social change, and feminist movements. The tenth such Forum, held in South Africa in 2008, attracted some 1,500 participants.

65   In Brazil, an important coordinating role was played by the MMTR-NE, the Northeast regional umbrella organization of which the MMTR was a part. The headquarters of the *Rede de Mulheres Rurais da América Latina e Caribe* (Latin American and Caribbean Rural Women's Network) was located in Recife.

66 The *Primeiro Encontro Latino Americano e do Caribe da Mulher Trabalhadora Rural* (First Latin American and Caribbean Meeting of Rural Women) was attended by 230 women from 25 countries (Romero 2007).

67 Alvarez et al. 2002; Sternbach et al. 1992. The Encuentros have been held in Bogotá, Colombia (1981); Lima, Peru (1983); Bertioga, Brazil (1985); Taxco, Mexico (1987); San Bernardo, Argentina (1990); Costa del Sol, El Salvador (1993); Cartagena, Chile (1996); Juan Dolio, Dominican Republic (1999); Playa Tambor, Costa Rica (2002); and Serra Negra, Brazil (2005). The next *Encuentro* was originally planned for 2008 in Mexico. Ironically, it was rescheduled for the following year because of a conflict with two other international feminist meetings and the inadequacy of funding to support broad attendance at all three events. Whereas once the *Encuentro* was one of the few such meetings, almost three decades after its founding, the very density of transnational feminist relationships had outrun the logistical and financial capacities to pull them off simultaneously (Romero 2007). "*Encuentro*" is the Spanish term; the Portuguese translation is "*Encontro*."

68 Alvarez et al. 2002, p. 539.

69 Ibid.

70 Ibid., p. 546.

71 Cited in Ibid., p. 555.

3 TRANSLATING FEMINISMS: FROM EMBODIED WOMEN TO GENDERED CITIZENSHIP

1 Unless otherwise noted, all quotes in this and succeeding chapters are from the interviews I conducted in March and April, 1997, and between February and December, 1998. For reasons of confidentiality I have chosen not to use the names of my interviewees. Names appear only when they refer to authors of published works or to those making public presentations in the name of an organization. All quotes or textual citations originally in Portuguese are translated by the author.

2 For a discussion of the body politics of early U.S. second-wave feminism, see Davis 2007; Gerson 1996; Morgen 2002. On the women's movement in France and Switzerland, the two countries where some SOS founders had lived, see Budry and Ollagnier 1999; Dardel 2007; Duchen 1986; Stetson 1987.

3 The group, which began by offering an informal women's health class, was initially known as the Boston Women's Health Course Collective.

4 Boston Women's Health Course Collective 1971, p. 4. The initial printing in 1970 was entitled *Women and Their Bodies*, but the book was renamed the following year. In subsequent printings, "Our Selves" became "Ourselves."

5 By 2008, it had sold more than four million copies in over twenty languages, including Braille (*Our Bodies Ourselves* 2009).

6 Ryan and Cross 1943. Early diffusion theory described the processes by which technical innovations spread, intact, from "diffusion agencies" to individual "acceptors," usually through face-to-face relationships. The theory had some parallels to modernization theory, assuming that the innovations were necessarily beneficial, and that populations would progress as they increasingly adopted them. For reviews of this literature, see Chabot 2002; Rogers 1995; Strang and Soule 1998. In more recent years, the theory has been elaborated to incorporate the transnational spread of social movement tactics and "frames," to explore the interpretive work involved in diffusion, and to recognize that process does not always occur in a linear manner, nor only by means of face-to-face relationships. See Chabot 2002; McAdam and Rucht 1993; Snow and Benford 1999; Strang and Soule 1998.

7 Tsing 1997. See also Sperling et al. 2001.

8 For fascinating accounts of the cultural adaptations involved in translating the book itself, see Davis 2007; Shapiro 2005. I elaborate further on the conception of feminist political

translation in Thayer forthcoming. My thinking about these issues developed through discussions with my *compañeras* in the "*Translocas*" working group on "Feminist Theories in the Latin/a Americas," initially sponsored by the Hemispheric Dialogues Project, at the University of California in Santa Cruz, 2000–2003. For the edited collection that grew out of this project, see Alvarez et al. under review.

9   For another perspective on meaning-making by social movements, which comes out of a quite different intellectual tradition, see the literature on "framing": Gamson et al. 1982; Snow and Benford 1988; 2000; Snow et al. 1986. The political discourses, described in this book, are less necessarily strategic and coherent, more dependent on practices and rooted in their social context than the concept of "frames" seems to suggest. For some provocative critiques of framing theory, see Ferree and Merrill 2003; Khasnabish 2008; Steinberg 1998. For a range of feminist perspectives on discursive politics, see Fraser 1989; Jenson 1987; Katzenstein 1998; Mansbridge 1995.

10 Said 1983. His lead was followed in succeeding decades by a growing body of work, much it by feminist scholars interested in untangling the complex and often disjunctive connections among feminisms in different geographical locations. See Amireh and Majaj 2000; Clifford 1989; Costa 2000; 2006; Grewal and Kaplan 1994a; John 1996; Mani 1989; Miller 1996.

11 John 1996, p. 3.

12 Snow and Benford 1992.

13 Thayer forthcoming; under review. In the context of this study, for example, liberal feminism—the dominant form of feminism in the U.S.—found little resonance in Brazil during this period. On the other hand, Brazilian feminists actively rejected discourses of the market disseminated by international funding agencies, a process described in Chapter 6.

14 Hannerz 1996.

15 In a critique of Bourdieu and Wacquant's work on the export of U.S. conceptions of race to Brazil, French (2003) makes the point that a simplistic model of Northern hegemony that overlooks the creative process of local appropriation runs the risk of giving unwarranted power to U.S. discursive influence.

16 Davis 2007. On the Latin American and Latina translation, see also Shapiro 2005.

17 Tsing 1997, p. 253.

18 Costa 2006; Miller 1996.

19 For a similar understanding of translations, see Costa 2006; Tsing 1997. "Discourse" is a broad term that includes both *theories*—coherent and explicit systems of thought—and what I refer to as *political discourses*—ways of representing social experience that are often fragmentary, sometimes contradictory, and frequently founded on only partially conscious assumptions. As I show here, while movements draw on both of these sources, the latter are a much more flexible and easily assimilated weapon for tactical maneuver and improvisation. When movements do call on more formal theories, they often dismantle and reconstruct them as political discourses, which can be linked, not only to other discourses, but to a variety of practices.

20 Costa (2006, p. 3) makes the interesting analogy between translation and ethnographic interpretation, arguing that "any process of description, interpretation, and dissemination of ideas and worldviews is always already caught up in relations of power and asymmetries between languages, regions, and peoples."

21 In the case of the BWHBC, for example, founding members of the organization worked together with those seeking to do cultural adaptations of their text, providing resources and other kinds of assistance (Davis 2007).

22 The term "discourse" is often understood to include both particular forms of language and the practices that express them. Here, I am separating language from enactment to explore the relationship between the two in the making of meaning.

23 Scott 1991. The Portuguese version was a translation of Scott 1988.

24　It should be said that discursive battles are not always won, and victories are not always decisive. Dominant discourses can shape the political terrain, shifting the way social movements conceive issues and limiting their range of responses. Chapter 6 will explore one example—the ways SOS Corpo and the MMTR grappled with the discourses disseminated by international funding agencies. Also, see Katzenstein 1998.

25　They were a doctor, a body movement teacher, a sociologist, an architect, a photographer, two social workers, and a student; Maria Betânia Ávila, cited in Aquino and Costa 1983.

26　Ação Mulher/Brasil Mulher 1980, p. 4.

27　The group made the decision not to translate *Our Bodies Ourselves*, preferring to produce their own material.

28　SOS Corpo 1982, p. 7.

29　Though feminism in the cities of Southeastern Brazil also had an influence in Recife, in the interview I conducted with her, this woman argued that, to some degree, feminists in Northeast Brazil looked abroad for inspiration as a means to assert the independence and innovative capacity of a region often disparaged by those in the more industrialized intellectual hubs around São Paulo and Rio de Janeiro.

30　This approach, which focused on women in production, rather than on reproductive or social welfare issues, sought equality for women without questioning larger paradigms of development. It was reflected in USAID programs as well as in U.N. conferences and projects during the U.N. Decade for Women (Rathgeber 1990; Razavi and Miller 1995).

31　Already, in 1974 and 1976, the opposition had made increasing gains in circumscribed electoral processes. In 1978, the Geisel government had relaxed some of the earlier repressive policies, while leaving the security apparatus in place. In 1979, Figueiredo declared an amnesty for political prisoners and exiles (Skidmore 1989).

32　Corrêa 1984/1989a; 1984/1989b.

33　From 1952 to 1983, the Ford Foundation spent $260 million on these efforts (Hartmann 1995, p. 120).

34　Corrêa 1994b; Petchesky 2003.

35　Hartmann 1995.

36　Ação Mulher/Brasil Mulher 1980 (translated into English by the author from the original French version).

37　Ávila, cited in Aquino and Costa 1983, p. 16.

38　Alvarez 1990.

39　The "private" programs were often largely funded by foreign government agencies such as USAID, which thereby avoided accusations of imperialist interference. In the 1970s, for example, half of the budget of the International Planned Parenthood Federation (IPPF) came from USAID (Hartmann 1995). Bemfam, the Brazilian IPPF affiliate, was one of the largest family planning agencies operating in the Northeast.

40　BEMFAM/DHS 1997,cited in Diniz et al. 1998, p. 31.

41　Corrêa 1989a, p. 6. According to BEMFAM/DHS (1991), in 1986, 47 percent of all women using contraceptives had been sterilized. Roland (1999) points out that the higher rates of sterilization in the Northeast meant that, because of the demographics of the population, it was disproportionately black women whose fertility was being curtailed.

42　Ávila 1995, p. 7.

43　Though a campaign for direct elections, supported by 90 percent of the population, was not successful, the vote that installed José Sarney as president—after the death of the elected candidate, Tancredo Neves—is considered to mark the end of the military regime in place since 1964 (Alvarez 1990; Skidmore 1989).

44　Brazil's largely progressive priesthood and some sectors of the Church hierarchy played an important role in the opposition to the military regime and the defense of the economic rights of poor Brazilians (Della Cava 1989). However, while women were invited to play an equal role in the local organizing work of the *comunidades eclesiais de base* (CEBs)—Christian base communities, Church leaders opposed even the discussion of issues such as contraception, abortion, sexuality, and divorce (Alvarez 1990).

45   Universities in the region suffered from lack of resources and experienced a "brain drain" to more prestigious and better-endowed universities in Rio de Janeiro and São Paulo, especially by those academics who had had opportunities for study abroad. In the Northeast, NGOs produced as much, if not more, theory than the local academy. Staff members were often intellectuals whose political commitments, developed in the opposition to dictatorship, had led them into community-oriented work. They frequently had greater resources and more international contacts than did their counterparts in local universities.

46   Castro and Lavinas 1992. The first women's studies program was founded in Rio de Janeiro in 1980. After 1990, when gender "arrived" in local theorizing, there was a dramatic increase in the numbers of programs established, mainly in the Southern part of the country. Six were created in one year, all with "gender," rather than "women," in the title. Gender work groups were created in eight different professional organizations, and the Ford Foundation began funding scholarships for "gender studies" (Costa and Sardenberg 1994, p. 6).

47   Rubin 1975; Scott 1988.

48   SOS publications in the 1990s about the theory of gender and its applications included Camurça and Gouveia 1995b; Corrêa 1994a; Fernandez and Camurça 1995; Gouveia and Camurça 1997; Portella 1998. In 1998, SOS published a 250-odd-page manual of techniques for working with gender (Portella and Gouveia ND). That same year, a series of pamphlets summarizing the experience of SOS and three "mixed" NGOs with a three-year gender training program was produced (Pacheco and Camurça 1997).

49   See Baden and Goetz 1997. Costa (2006, p. 70) argues that, while gender was not inherently "sinister," the combination of theoretical trajectories that defined the term in the Brazilian academy did lend itself to a depoliticized understanding.

50   Fernandez and Camurça 1995, p. 41.

51   Moser 1993; see also Baden and Goetz 1997.

52   Costa and Sardenberg 1994. In "Being There and Writing Here," Costa (2000) discusses the factors that made it difficult for Brazilian feminist academics to develop a gender analysis with more radical implications, as well as citing references to those who did.

53   Cited in Fernandez and Camurça 1995, p. 41.

54   Moser 1993.

55   See, for example, Castro 1992; Saffioti 1992. Other authors cited by SOS members were: Teresa Barbieri (Mexico), Françoise Collin (France), Elizabeth Souza Lobo (Brazil), and Gayle Rubin (United States).

56   On the development of black women's movements at a national level, see Caldwell 2007; Carneiro 1999b; Gonzalez 1982. On Brazilian lesbian movements, see Fernandes 1994; 2002.

57   For a discussion of how the construction of feminists as "experts" by states, as well as funding agencies and other institutions, threatened to undermine their role as social critics and political advocates, see Alvarez 1999.

58   The United States, in this period, saw a flowering of feminist and other critiques of the concept of citizenship, but not its widespread use as a mobilizing banner. For examples of late twentieth-century feminist critiques, see James 1992; Jones 1990; Orloff 1993; Pateman 1988; 1992; Vogel 1991. For critiques that address citizenship in relation to race, ethnicity, and national origin in the United States, see Lowe 1996; Yuval-Davis 1991. For a discussion of gender and citizenship in the context of Eastern Europe, see Einhorn 1993. For a feminist perspective from Britain, see Lister 1993.

59   Collor held office for two years, from 1990–92, before resigning to avoid being impeached for corruption. He was replaced by his vice president, Itamar Franco.

60   SOS Corpo 1997a.
61   The *Articulação* was founded in 1994 during the preparations for the U.N. Women's Conference in Beijing. In an effort to generate awareness of gender inequality and women's rights, as well as to mobilize for Beijing, the *Articulação* and its members helped to organize or revive local women's forums in twenty-five of twenty-six states, and the Federal District (Alvarez 1998, p. 309).
62   Ávila 1993, p. 392.
63   Camurça and Gouveia 1995a, p. 7.
64   Ávila 1993, p. 391.
65   Ibid., p. 387.
66   The Brazilian regime, hoping to defuse tensions that threatened to undermine the national security state, itself initiated a process of "decompression" beginning in the mid-1970s. In counterpoint with the protests and other forms of pressure from the opposition, the political opening led to a gradual process of democratization that ultimately slipped out of the hands of the military regime (Alves 1985; Skidmore 1989; Stepan 1989).
67   Corrêa 1994a. The Women's Global Network on Reproductive Rights was founded at this meeting.
68   Ibid., p. 383.
69   Ávila 1995; Corrêa 1993.
70   BEMFAM/DHS 1991.
71   "Demographic transition" refers to the decrease in both fertility and mortality levels between so-called pre-modern and industrialized societies (Coale 1989). For a Brazilian feminist perspective from a founding member of SOS Corpo, see Corrêa 1989c.
72   Though my fieldwork ended in 1998, "gender"—and its companion, "citizenship," discussed in the next section—did not disappear from SOS discourse. By the mid-2000s, however, the organization had once again changed its name. *SOS Corpo: Gênero e Cidadania* (SOS Corpo: Gender and Citizenship) became *SOS Corpo: Instituto Feminista para a Democracia* (SOS Corpo: Feminist Institute for Democracy). There is another story to be told someday about the changes that underlay this new discursive shift.
73   Davis 2007; Shapiro 2005.
74   For other examples of BWHBC's difficulties in assimilating innovations from Latin American and Latina feminists into its outreach efforts, see Shapiro 2005.
75   The fact that these trends were not reflected among feminist activists in the United States was testimony to the gap in this country between the academy and women's movements, a gap that was, for historical reasons, far less significant in Brazil and elsewhere in Latin America.
76   Unlike in the United States, "gendered citizenship" *was* a part of the discursive landscape among activists in much of Europe. But it seems likely that this was inspired less by the example of the global South than by political developments closer to home: in the case of "citizenship," the movements around democratization in the countries of Eastern Europe, and, in the case of "gender," the academy and development agencies, which promoted a "gender perspective." In other words, the discourses had their own separate genealogies and developed in tandem with those in Brazil, rather than as a result of their influence.
77   As in the case of "citizenship," European feminist discourses of class have local antecedents, rather than reflecting the influence of activists in countries like Brazil.
78   Costa 2000.

4 NEGOTIATING CLASS AND GENDER: DEVALUED WOMEN IN A LOCAL COUNTERPUBLIC

1   Sindicato de Trabalhadores Rurais do Sertão Central 1985.
2   In her study in Rio Grande do Sul, Stephen (1997) too notes the ways rural women workers' movements linked class and gender issues.

3   The literature on coalition-building offers insights into some of the factors that constrain or facilitate this process. See Hathaway and Meyer 1997; Roth 2003; Staggenborg 1986.

4   Over the last century or more, social movement theories have seesawed from an emphasis on the internal mental states of participants (the collective behavior school) to the availability of resources and political opportunities (the resource mobilization and political process models) as key explanatory factors for the emergence of social movements. For the former, see, among others, Kornhauser 1959; Le Bon 1960; Smelser 1962; Turner and Killian 1957. For the latter, see, among others: Gamson 1975; Gamson et al. 1982; Jenkins and Perrow 1977; McAdam 1982; McCarthy and Zald 1977; Oberschall 1973; Tilly 1978. In the 1990s, scholars broke new ground by seeking to integrate social and political factors with cultural ones. See Johnston and Klandermans 1995; Morris and Mueller 1992. But the marriage is still rocky, with culture too often being reduced to an instrumental role as a tool for social movements to achieve concrete reform. Critics point to a lack of recognition of the ways that culture constrains as well as enables, shaping movements as well as providing them resources. For a review of these critiques, see Jasper 1997; Steinberg 1999. My own work takes inspiration from interdisciplinary approaches to cultural politics, in which social conflicts are seen as having both material and discursive dimensions: Movements struggle to shift dominant meanings as well as to win reforms. See Alvarez et al. 1998a; Hall 1992; Jordan and Weedon 1994; Poletta 2004; Steinberg 1999. I am concerned here with resources that are attached in some way to social movements, rather than the broader conditions, such as legal frameworks or political cultures, that may also serve to advance or impede their causes.

5   Jasper 1997; McAdam 1982; Steinberg 1999.

6   Oberschall 1973; Sperling et al. 2001.

7   For a discussion of how discourses of expertise, for example, served as a social movement resource for environmental justice movements, see Di Chiro 1998.

8   Here I differ from Steinberg (1997) and Jasper (1999), who emphasize the material character of resources, distinguishing them from the kinds of discourses that I categorize as symbolic assets. The problem with their definition, in my view, is that it overlooks both the cultural dimension of material resources, such as money or membership, and the material dimension of discursive forms of symbolic resources, such as legitimacy and authenticity.

9   My conception of political resources owes much to Bourdieu's (1998; and Wacquant 1992) understanding of the ways capital is constituted and accumulated in fields. The difference is that capital, in his view, appears inevitably to serve instrumental interests, while in my conception resources are more agnostic. They may serve selfish interests, but they may also produce a kind of "profit," to extend the entrepreneurial metaphor, that benefits a wider public. The MMTR, for example, deployed its resources to stimulate processes of change that would both benefit rural women and further the larger project of gendered social transformation.

10 These included the progressive wing of the Catholic Church, municipal governments, and Pernambuco's branch of the Workers' Party (PT).

11 In addition to my interviews, the following section on union history is based on material from Cerqueira 1986; Maybury-Lewis 1994; Morais 1988; Pereira 1997.

12 During this period, infant mortality in the region was five hundred for every one thousand babies born, and there were reports of people surviving only on a sugarcane product known as *rapadura* (Cerqueira 1986, p. 13). The Peasant Leagues were a decentralized set of local organizations that were founded in 1955 under middle-class leadership. They carried out land occupations and other kinds of protests until they were crushed by the military regime in 1964. On the phenomenon of "*coronelismo*" in the sertão, see Domingos 2004.

13 Between 1961 and 1964, fifty-nine new unions were founded in Pernambuco: twenty-nine in the zona da mata—the sugarcane region along the coast—twenty-three in the agreste—the transitional area just inland—and seven in the *sertão* (Cerqueira 1986, p. 25).

14 More than three hundred leaders in the historically more militant sugar cane workers' unions along the coast were purged after the coup (Pereira 1997, p. 39).

15 Pereira (Ibid.) offers a number of explanations for this development, including: the regime's relative independence from landowners, the lack of threat from a strong agrarian reform movement during the earlier populist period, and the relative "softness" of Brazilian authoritarianism and its greater degree of continuity with the previous regime than in other countries.

16 Unions were required to submit budgets to review, elections to regulation, and candidates, as well as their programs, to official approval.

17 Maybury-Lewis 1994, p. 40. The union leaders interviewed by Pereira (1997, p. 91) reported that medical assistance was the most important specific reason for affiliating with the union. The significance of this aid was underlined by Balbachevsky's finding that, between 1973 and 1975, FUNRURAL services accounted for up to 50 percent of the disposable income of rural inhabitants in the Northeastern state of Piaui. Cited in Maybury-Lewis 1994, p. 41.

18 Cerqueira 1986, pp. 29–30.

19 The state was organized into a series of ten such "poles," each a grouping of local unions from a particular geographical area. They included Araripe, Médio São Francisco, Sertão Central, Sub-Médio São Francisco, Vale do Pajeu, Agreste Meridional, Setentrional, Agreste Central, Mata Norte, and Mata Sul.

20 Cited in Pereira 1997, p. 93. Land reform may have also had less urgency in a region where land—by virtue of the difficult climatic conditions—was not in such short supply as in the fertile coastal regions.

21 Critics note that, unlike the pre-1964 mobilizations, these strikes did not challenge the structure of property relations and may have even benefited landowners who used labor's wage gains to justify price increases. Many of the more significant contract clauses were never enforced. Among workers, only the narrow sector with permanent employment on sugar plantations saw its position improved (Ibid.). Nevertheless, the annual mobilizations in the 1980s were testimony to the efforts of some within union leadership to sustain a movement based on the defense of workers' interests, rather than simply on acting as an extension of the government bureaucracy.

22 Facó 1980; Pessar 2004.

23 Diniz et al. (1998) found an average of eight pregnancies and 5.9 living children for each of their interviewees from the sertão.

24 Heredia 1979; Lima 1992; Spindel 1987.

25 See Deere 2003; Deere and León 2001. Even eight years after the Constitution established women's land rights under the agrarian reform, only 12.6 percent of beneficiaries were female. Though statistics on the broader picture of women's landownership are unreliable, observers agree that it is far less than the levels of participation in land reform (Deere 2003, p. 258).

26 As described later in the chapter, union membership policy changed after the MMTR brought a resolution to CONTAG's fourth national congress in 1985, urging the unionization of women workers and greater attention to their concerns (Deere 2003; CONTAG 1985).

27 In the 1988 Constitution, in addition to access to land, rural women won social security benefits (including unemployment benefits, disability insurance, retirement benefits, and maternity leave) and equality with men in terms of labor rights but, as noted earlier, implementation was uneven and often non-existent (Deere 2003; Deere and León 2001).

28 The drought lasted five years, from 1979 to 1984, and is reported to have killed more than seven hundred people (MMTR 1994, p. 11).

29 Though I interviewed both advisors and members of the MMTR, I have relied heavily on the accounts of advisors in the sections on organizational strategy since they were the ones most involved in making contacts with both unions and feminist NGOs. Given the difficult lives of most members, and their geographic dispersal, with a few exceptions, between meetings it was the advisors who were most often involved in strategic planning and evaluation.

30 Almeida and Parisius 1995, pp. 115–16.

31 Reports by my interviewees of the numbers of women in attendance at this first meeting ranged from eight to fifteen.

32 To preserve privacy, as elsewhere in this book, I made the decision to use names of MMTR organizers and members only when quoting from published material or public presentations. In discussions of the rural movement's history, that means that I refer to only Almeida by name, since she is the only one to have published a memoir and the information from the other participants comes from interviews or anonymous published material. Almeida has been and continues to be a central figure in the organization's history, but it is also true that this editorial practice may exaggerate her prominence and erase the names of others with less access to the world of publishing. In the absence of a better alternative, I insert this cautionary note.

33 These founders were joined later by other volunteers, both from Recife and from the local area, who offered different kinds of logistical support.

34 Freire 1970.

35 For social movement theorists writing on the construction of collective identity, see Buechler 2000; Johnston and Klandermans 1995; Johnston et al. 1994; Melucci 1988; 1989; Taylor and Whittier 1992.

36 Almeida and Parisius 1995, p. 117.

37 In some parts of the *sertão*, marijuana cultivation and drug trafficking have led to increased violence and highway robbery.

38 Almeida and Parisius 1995, p. 126.

39 MMTR 1994, p. 34.

40 Ibid., p. 10.

41 According to a movement advisor, wages at the time were so low in relation to prices that increases did not significantly affect landowners. For that reason, the battle was relatively easy to win.

42 MMTR 1994, p. 42.

43 Part of the conflict also lay in the distinct character of each of the state's three regions and the political differences linked to them. Most of the CEMTR leadership at the state level was from the *zona da mata* and the *agreste*, regions which had been earlier to unionize and were both geographically and politically closer to FETAPE's headquarters in the city of Recife on the coast. The sugar cane regions in particular, as the historical base of the unions' power, were a priority for the state leadership, which maintained close control over the local organizations there. Women's movements, seen as potentially divisive, were not encouraged to develop independently in the *zona da mata* and lacked the active membership built in the *sertão*, leaving open the possibility of clientelistic relationships with leaders.

44 Almeida and Parisius 1995, p. 121.

45 MMTR 1994, p. 12.

46 Of the five thousand delegates at the Congress, only sixty were women (Almeida and Parisius 1995, p. 121).

47 During this period, internal political divisions were beginning to appear within CONTAG, and the organization faced competition from a more left-leaning union federation, the Central Única dos Trabalhadores (CUT), formed in response to corrupt and welfarist unionism. In 1994, the rural section of the CUT merged with CONTAG (Deere 2003; Deere and León 2001).

48 The resolution passed at the Congress read as follows:
    6. ROLE OF THE UNION IN BROADENING WOMEN'S UNION PARTICIPATION
    CONSIDERING:
    — that women's participation is still not sufficient for the needs of the struggles of the
    Union Movement;
    — that women experience specific problems of general discrimination as women, as
    well as discrimination as workers participating, directly or indirectly, in production;
    — that a union program will activate the great potential for women's participation in
    strengthening the Union Movement and in social transformations in the country;
    RECOMMENDATIONS:
    66. that the unions conduct and coordinate programming specifically directed toward
    women;
    a) through meetings of rural women workers;
    b) through trainings for female leaders so that they may support the union in developing
    women's union participation;
    c) by taking up and promoting women's specific demands;
    67. that women's unionization be stimulated;
    68. that women's decision be respected in relation to monthly dues: to contribute on her
    own or to pay them in a form linked to that of her husband or father.
    (CONTAG 1985, pp. 53–54).
49 MMTR 1994, p. 35.

5 THE LEVERAGE OF THE LOCAL: "AUTHENTIC" RURAL WOMEN IN GLOBAL COUNTERPUBLICS

1   Diniz et al. 1998
2   SOS Corpo's knowledge of rural gender issues was not solely based on its MMTR focus
    groups. The NGO had, in fact, conducted other research projects in the rural zones
    in other parts of the country in the early 1990s and had served as a consultant for the
    newly-formed Women's Commission of the national agricultural workers' union fed-
    eration, CONTAG (Pacheco and Camurça 1997; Portella et al. 2004). Nevertheless, the
    relationship with the MMTR was its most longstanding with rural women.
3   It was in this period that SOS shifted from being simply a group of volunteers to become
    a staff-based organization.
4   In their study of U.S.-based feminists working with women's organizations in Russia,
    Sperling et al. (2001, p. 1180) also found local and transnational actors negotiating over
    a range of resources. The relationships between the two parties, as in my case, were
    "reciprocal, albeit unequal."
5   As discussed in Chapter 1, issues of race were largely occluded in feminist organizing
    during this period.
6   Almeida and Parisius 1995, p. 124.
7   Like the MMTR, SOS made use of popular education methodologies based, in part, on
    the approach of Paulo Freire. For an analysis by an SOS founder of how feminists pushed
    Freire's class-based pedagogy in new directions, see Corrêa 1994a.
8   MMTR 1992.
9   Camurça and Gouveia 1995b.
10 Almeida, cited in Ibid., p. 3
11 Ibid., p. 16; Gouveia and Camurça 1997, p. 18.
12 It was not clear what this speaker meant when she said that the MMTR "couldn't sell"
    the pamphlet. It may have been because the first pamphlet was funded with the stipula-
    tion that it was to be given away, or because the MMTR lacked the kind of distribution

network that established and better-funded NGOs like SOS had. In any case, the resentment felt by members of the rural organization is what came through most strongly.

13   MMTR 1994, p. 37. Grugel (1999) suggests that funding agencies use their connections to NGOs in the global South to strengthen their own commitments to "substantive democracy." Their participation in these "ethical networks" functions to create a model of transnational relations based on egalitarian values. I argue that the same can be said of urban middle-class movements in their relations with working-class organizations.

14   Whether or not the MMTR consciously and strategically deployed this resource is less important than the effect that it had.

15   A number of authors make reference to the key role played by the relationship to grassroots constituencies. For its importance to funders, see Grugel 1999. With regard to NGOs, see Alvarez 1999.

16   Centro Ecumênico de Documentação e Informação 1989.

17   On the effects of neoliberal "stabilization" in Brazil, see Font 2003.

18   In other unions that did not immediately institutionalize gender concerns within their structure, such as the telephone and the railroad workers' unions, activists nonetheless began to sponsor projects directed at women, such as workshops on women's health or activities to celebrate International Women's Day.

19   One example was an NGO called the *Centro de Educação Comunitária Rural* (CECOR [Center for Rural Community Education]), which had its office in Serra Talhada and was staffed by a number of former local union activists.

20   According to a study conducted by FETAPE (1997), out of twenty-three rural unions surveyed in the *sertão*, 54 percent of the members were men and 46 percent were women. (Interestingly, if only paid-up members were counted, 44.4 percent were men and 55.6 percent were women.) However, 85 percent of those in leadership at the local level were men and only 15 percent were women. The figures in the agreste were similar, but in the zona da mata, where sugar-cane fields dominated, still only 18 percent of the members and 7 percent of the leaders were women.

21   In 1997, after the CUT-CONTAG merger, CONTAG established a national commission on women.

22   Martin (2005) noted a similar practice in the United States among mainstream organizations which adopted innovations initially proposed by feminist rape crisis centers.

23   Her omission of "NE" from the regional organization's title may have been shorthand, but also bespoke a telling conflation, common among both women's movement and union activists, between the local women's organization in the central *sertão* and the nine-state umbrella organization. (In fact, it took me some months to sort out the relationship as well.) Despite its alliance with the unions, the MMTR, like the MMTR-NE was autonomous and took a stance far more independent than any of the other Pernambucan rural women's organizations represented in the state women's commission. This may explain why the MMTR and the MMTR-NE were often confused and referred to by the same name.

24   McAdam et al. (2001) and Tarrow (2005) propose the useful concept of "scale shift" to describe the changes in actors, targets, and the scope and meaning of claims that occur when a movement moves from a local to a global scale or vice versa. The unions' move into the global arena and the subsequent changes in the kinds of claims they began to make is an apt illustration of this concept, but the MMTR's story adds another dimension. The case of the rural women begins with a shift across counterpublics, rather than a conscious move to the global arena. The MMTR's change in scale, from local to global action, was not a cause, but a result, of the shift from issues of class to issues of gender (and class), as rural women found transnational allies concerned with gender injustice.

25   MMTR 1994, p. 39.

6 FEMINISTS AND FUNDING: PLAYS OF POWER
IN THE SOCIAL MOVEMENT MARKET

1 Lebon, who was also present at this meeting, describes Almeida's presentation as "the most outspoken, critical position" (Lebon 1998, p. 306).

2 Funding for particular projects, rather than general infrastructural support, was the preferred modality of development agencies because it was viewed as a means to produce easily demonstrable results with their funds. From the grantee's perspective, such funding constrained their activities and left them struggling to pay salaries, rent, and other ongoing expenses.

3 There is a rich and growing set of critical analyses of what Alvarez (1998; 1999) calls the "NGOization"—formalization and professionalization—of feminist movements around the world, as well as their multiplying links to the state and to international donors. Geographically, their cases are largely located in Eastern Europe and Latin America, both regions that have seen processes of democratization followed by neoliberal policies and the influx of donor funding. See, for example, Bagic 2006; Bickham Mendez 2005; Ewig 1999; Ford-Smith 1997; Hemment 2007; Lang 1997; Lebon 1996; 1998; Lind 2005; MacDonald 1997; Murdock 2008; Piscitelli 2005; Schild 1998; Silliman 1999; Sperling et al. 2001; Thayer 2001b. For a discussion of similar issues in the context of India, see Sangtin Writers and Nagar 2006. For analyses of how processes of professionalization played out among feminist organizations in the United States and other early industrializing countries, see Bordt 1997; Ferree and Martin 1995; Katzenstein 1998; Morgen 2002; Schmitt and Martin 1999; Staggenborg 1988; Thomas 1999. Though the literature on feminist organizations in the global North finds some drawbacks to professionalization, in general it is more sanguine about the phenomenon than most studies done in the South.

4 See note 53, Chapter 1.

5 Though some progress had been made, clearly, the amounts fell far short of the need. AWID researchers found that, in 2003, only 3.6 percent of the net disbursement of Official Development Assistance had gender equality "as a significant or principal objective." In that same year, only .04 percent of aid from the European Commission was allotted to women-specific projects and programs—$2.5 million out of a total of $6.8 billion. U.S. private foundations spent 7.3 percent of their total giving on initiatives to benefit women and girls, but only 8 percent of their funding was destined for locations outside the United States (Clark et al. Feb. 2006, p. 11).

6 On this point, see also Sperling et al. 2001.

7 For other discussions of the market-based relations that emerge in donor-recipient relations, see Bob 2005; Cooley and Ron 2002; Lebon 1998.

8 On the growing divide between feminists of different social classes in the contemporary conditions of neoliberalism in Latin America, see also Alvarez 1999; Bickham Mendez 2005; Lebon 1998; Lind 2005; Murdock 2008; Schild 1998; Thayer 2001b.

9 On this subject, also see Fowler 1992; MacDonald 1997.

10 See, e.g., Petras 1997; Roelofs 2003. For a more nuanced view of funding relations, see Bagic 2006; Bennesaieh forthcoming; Bickham Mendez 2005; Fisher 1997; Ford-Smith 1997; Hemment 2007; Lebon 1998; Pearce 1997; Pearce 2007; Silliman 1999; Sperling 2001; Piscitelli 2005; Murdock 2008.

11 Morgen (2002) and many of the contributors to Ferree and Martin (1995) make this point in regard to feminist organizations that take funding from the state in the United States and other countries of the global North. For a more critical perspective, see Incite! Women of Color Against Violence 2007. Kamat (2002) argues that cooptation of an NGO is measured by organizational praxis, rather than by whether or not it receives funding.

12 Araújo 1997; Pereira 1996.

13   Foreign debt rose from $64 billion to $123 billion between 1980 and 1990. Cited in Font 2003, pp. 214–15.

14   Annual inflation rose from 105 percent in 1981 to 2,938 percent in 1990, while per capita GDP declined 5.3 percent during this period. The real minimum wage fell 40 percent from 1980 to 1989 (Soares 1995, pp. 9–10).

15   Ibid..

16   SOS Corpo 1998. Most of SOS's funding came from nongovernmental sources.

17   Hartmann 1995; Petchesky 2003.

18   Ajamil 1995.

19   Ford, which had funded international population-control research and activities since the early 1950s, made a transition to supporting "reproductive health" programs in the mid-1980s (Coleman 1994; Hartmann 1995; Petchesky 2003). For an analysis of debates among feminists with different perspectives on how or if to collaborate with population control advocates, see Higer 1999.

20   SOS's success contrasted with the experience of feminist projects around other issues, such as violence and income generation, which reported greater difficulty acquiring funding. On this issue, see Santos 1998.

21   Corrêa 1983, p. 10.

22   In situations where states were overtly hostile to feminism, scholars have found that movements used international aid explicitly as a form of leverage to win concessions. See Bickham Mendez 2005; Hemment 2007.

23   Unlike women's organizations in Eastern Europe, many of which were actually brought into being by international aid, in Latin America the more common pattern was for pre-existing informal organizations to be transformed by infusions of funding (Hemment 2007).

24   For early U.S.-based analyses that reached similar conclusions, see Freeman 1970; Mansbridge 1973. For more recent analyses of similar tensions, see Acker 1995; Mueller 1995; Reinelt 1995; Staggenborg 1995.

25   By 1998, there were five steps on the salary scale, ranging from $4.90 to $11.70 per hour, not including additional payments for those with coordinating responsibilities. The scale was nowhere near as unequal as that of a typical business enterprise, nor did it take the form of a pyramid. There were nine people earning at the top two levels of the scale (including one at part-time), and only seven at the bottom three levels (including two at part-time) (SOS Corpo 1998).

26   Bordt 1997.

27   Cited in Fernandez and Camurça 1995, p. 13.

28   Donors to nongovernmental development agencies included states, corporations, foundations, and individuals. The pressures on agencies that supported projects in Latin America were exacerbated by the way that the fall of the Berlin Wall in 1989 and subsequent upheavals in Eastern Europe drew the reduced quantities of international aid away from projects in the late industrializing countries. Furthermore, though structural adjustment programs were creating greater disparities and shifting the burden to the poor across Latin America, overall economic indicators in countries like Brazil showed apparent signs of improvement, undermining the argument for aid (Ruiz Bravo 1994; Lebon 1998; Red Entre Mujeres 1993).

29   This was, of course, less true of foundations specifically directed toward supporting women's projects, such as the Global Fund for Women in the United States or Mama Cash in the Netherlands.

30   The former translates as "militants"—politicized volunteer activists without defined occupational identities. The latter translates literally as "technicians"—a term commonly used among NGOs for paid staff who coordinate and carry out projects, using a variety of skills. The increasing presence on the staff of educators, researchers, and communications specialists, many with college degrees in their fields, required a new

approach to compensation. Salaries were raised to appeal to professionals who might be attracted by more lucrative offers elsewhere, as well as to compensate for the heavy workload implied by the travel and night and weekend meetings that employment with a social movement NGO required. Higher salaries, in turn, required more fundraising. See also Bagic 2006; Bickham Mendez 2005; Ford-Smith 1997; Hemment 2007; Lang 1997; Lebon 1998; Murdock 2008; Schild 1998.

31   This was exacerbated by the trend among European donors studied by Biekart (2005) to concentrate their resources "strategically" on fewer, and generally larger, organizations.

32   Bickham Mendez (2005) found that relations with donors often led to internal centralization. Those with grantwriting skills and understanding of what might "sell" increasingly set organizational agendas.

33   The income earned from sale of services, educational resources and other items associated with particular projects rose from 13 percent in 1996 to 22 percent in 1997. SOS's 1998 Strategic Plan called for "the consolidation of an ongoing policy of sales of services and products" (SOS Corpo 1998).

34   Even so, SOS was forced to run the workshop at a loss. The agencies refused to make up the difference between income and expenses, saying that it was a result of poor planning. Bagic (2006) found a similar funding practice in the former Yugoslavia.

35   For a discussion of the changing structure of global production, see Harvey 1990.

36   While SOS had twenty-one permanent staff in 1995, by the end of 1998 they had only fourteen (SOS Corpo 1998).

37   Ibid.

38   SOS representatives participated in the U.N. International Conference on Population in Cairo (1994), and in the Fourth World Conference on Women in Beijing (1995), as well as in a transnational research network (IRRAAAG), a network of documentation centers that included the Boston Women's Health Book Collective, the Women's Global Network for Reproductive Rights (WGNRR), the *Red Entre Mujeres* (Network Among Women), the *Red de Salud de las Mujeres Latinoamericanas y del Caribe* (RSMLAC [Latin American and Caribbean Women's Health Network]), and others. The organization played a leadership role in a number of these networks.

39   In part this may have been a response to exhaustion in the face of constant requests; in part it represented a strategic choice about the perceived best use of organizational resources.

40   According to SOS members, a "first-level" NGO works entirely at the grassroots level, while one that acts at a "second level" functions as an advisor to popular movements and is influenced by those at the third. Interestingly, these levels roughly correspond to the three stages of development of SOS identified here. (See Table 6.1.)

41   Ávila 1998. Her approach bore a resemblance to the "politics of engagement" with state institutions practiced by the U.S.-based domestic violence shelter staff described by Reinelt (1995). See also Matthews 1994; Spalter-Roth and Schreiber 1995. However, while feminists in the United States and Western Europe turned to the state primarily as a defensive response to the hostile political climate of the 1980s, in Latin America in many cases the reasons had more to do with economic need and the opportunities offered by democratization and international funding.

42   SOS Corpo 1998.

43   The Clinton administration suspended the "gag rule" on January 22, 2001. George Bush Sr. left the suspension in place, but as one of his first acts as president, George W. Bush re-imposed the restrictions. The incoming Obama Administration once again eliminated the rule on January 23, 2009.

44   Hartmann 1995, p. 108.

45   In the case of some feminist NGOs, representatives were actually hired as agency staff, evaluators, trainers, or consultants, creating not just a similarity, but an identity, of interests.

46   SOS Corpo 1996, pp. 1–2.

47   Cited in SOS Corpo 1997b, p. 9.

48   Networks were also formed among NOVIB counterparts around other themes, but the one with a focus on gender was the first, and the only one to address North-South relations in the 1990s.

49   Papma and Sprenger 1994.

50   In the mid-1990s, the network's literature cited four goals: "To contribute to modifying the current terms of development and cooperation and its impact on women in Latin America and the Caribbean; to generate a space for dialogue and solidarity among women of South and North, creating common demands and emancipatory proposals; to strengthen the capacity of the Southern NGOs for institutional management and the development of proposals aimed at new social relations of gender for society as a whole; to conduct debates and reflection that create a basis for political pressure on governments, development agencies, and the institutions that direct the international development process" (Red Entre Mujeres ND).

51   Ruiz Bravo 1994.

52   Red Entre Mujeres 1989.

53   Ruiz Bravo 1994.

54   Centro de Investigación y Documentación 1993.

55   Papma and Sprenger 1994. The openness of agencies to this kind of lobbying from the South varied, with European donors generally being more responsive than their U.S. counterparts.

56   Ruiz Bravo 1994.

57   Red Entre Mujeres 1989.

58   It should be noted that the knowledge being produced and shared by Southern NGOs was, at least in part, knowledge about the lives of working-class women, and relied on their ongoing relations with organizations such as the MMTR, as we saw in the preceding chapter.

59   Camurça and Cisneros 1998, p. 33.

60   Ibid., p. 16.

61   Ibid.

62   By the early 1990s, Oxfam UK was the largest British development agency and the one that received the most government funding—some 24 percent of its income in 1992 (Grugel 1999, p. 127). Today, the trend is increasingly toward the privatization of governmental foreign aid.

63   To these kinds of concrete achievements should be added the less tangible effects of the organization's continuous production of research and publications on gender, feminism, and social policy, as well as its organization of or participation in innumerable conferences, seminars, forums, workshops, media interviews, and international tribunals. SOS staff acted as consultants, not only to local, regional, and national governments, but also to the United Nations and other international organizations.

64   Murdock (2008) argues that NGOs' growing involvement with the state and more technical-professional strategies required levels of education and cultural capital to which most working-class women did not have access. These new strategies took more and more NGO staff time away from collaborations with working-class women and undermined the capacity of middle-class women to understand or, much less, "represent" the interests of their working-class counterparts in state and development arenas, as they were increasingly called on to do.

65   The exception was the presence of MMTR leader Almeida on the National Council for Women's Rights. As Spalter-Roth and Schreiber (1995) point out, "insider" and "outsider" are not dichotomous categories, but endpoints on a continuum. Not all working-class women's movements took such a definitively outsider stance. There were two strands: On the one hand, those that sought funding and moved into a role as trainers and/or

service providers and whose development mirrored that of middle-class NGOs; on the other, those, like the MMTR, that continued to see themselves primarily as advocacy organizations. Even these latter, as we have seen, often worked in tandem with more professionalized organizations on specific campaigns.

66 Lebon 1998.
67 Camurça and Cisneros 1998, p. 23.
68 Ibid.
69 Ruiz Bravo 1994; Murdock 2008; Rew 1997.
70 SOS Corpo 1998.
71 The meetings were sponsored by the *Processo de Articulação e Diálogo—PAD* (Process of Networking and Dialogue). PAD was made up of eight European agencies and two hundred Brazilian grantee organizations around the country.
72 These issues of representation and accountability were being exacerbated in the context of shrinking states which relied increasingly on the so-called "Third Sector" of NGOs to meet basic needs that were formerly the responsibility of the state (Alvarez 1999).
73 Haines 1984.
74 DiMaggio and Powell 1983.

7 MOVEMENT OR MARKET? DEFENDING THE ENDANGERED COUNTERPUBLIC

1 See, e.g., Benhabib 1999; Dean 1996; Shih 2005.
2 Discourses from the global South have more often surfaced among immigrant women, women of color, or feminists with more internationalist practices—all constituencies more likely to sustain connections with movements in Asia, Africa, and Latin America. For a fascinating discussion of one case of cross-border work between Latinas in the United States and Mexican women, see Carrillo 1998. For evidence of the influence of feminist critiques of funding relations from the South on U.S. activists, see Incite! Women of Color Against Violence 2007.
3 One example is a 2006 international meeting on "Money and Movements," organized by the Association for Women's Rights in Development (AWID). The event, held in Queretaro, Mexico, brought together women's rights activists and donors from around the world to discuss the issue of funding for feminist work and to debate strategic approaches. In a number of countries, newly established women's funds have attempted both to direct funds to activism and to challenge the relations of power between donors and recipients. One of them, the Central American Women's Fund, for example, involves its applicants in the decision-making process about how grants should be distributed (Criquillion 2007).
4 Grewal and Kaplan 1994a; John 1996; Lazreg 2000; Mohanty 2003b; Narayan 1997; Spivak 1988; Tripp 2006.
5 Treanor, cited in Harvey 2005, p. 3.
6 Ong 2006.
7 Harvey 2005.
8 For a discussion of the ways the market has shaped international health policies, see Petchesky 2003.
9 Callon 1998, p. 27.
10 Bob (2005) illustrates some of the consequences of this clash of values, describing how, to receive funding, social movements must engage in a process of self-marketing, constrained to the limited range of terms understandable and acceptable to potential financial backers.
11 Marx 1972.

12   Grewal (2005), for example, is far more pessimistic than I, viewing social movements as already thoroughly "marketized." Feminist discourses, she argues, have become an extension of neoliberal technologies.

13   Gibson-Graham 2006; Tsing 2005.

14   Freeman 2001; Hannerz 1996; Massey 1994.

15   Sassen 1998; Tsing 2005.

16   Gibson-Graham 2006.

17   For a fascinating account of the research process and its findings written by SOS participants after collective discussion with MMTR-NE members, see Portella et al. 2004.

18   Ibid., p. 36.

19   Corrêa and Petchesky 2003; Marchand and Runyan 2000; Moghadam 2005; Mohanty 2003; Petchesky 2003; Pettman 2004; Sen and Grown 1988; Vargas 2006.

20   In turn, the incorporation of race and sexuality into feminist analysis and action has been slower to occur in many parts of Latin America. On race-based movements and feminism in Brazil, see Caldwell 2007; Carneiro 1999; Gonzalez 1982. On lesbian movements and feminism, see Fernandes 1994; 2002.

21   Asher 2007; Di Marco 2008; Domínguez and Garza 2006; Silva 2009; SOF 2009; Speed et al. 2006.

22   The Canadian, U.S., and European feminists working with AWID are one example.

METHODOLOGICAL APPENDIX: TRANSNATIONAL FEMINISM AS FIELD

1   Among others, see Brettell 1993; Clifford and Marcus 1986; Freeman and Murdock 2001; Grewal and Kaplan 1994a; Mohanty 1991b; Nagar 2002; Narayan 1997; Stacey 1991; Visweswaran 1994; Wolf 1996.

2   Relatively early in my graduate student career, I was informed by one professor that research motivated by sympathy for social movements "was *not* sociology." Never having had much faith in professions of "objectivity" among sociologists, I found this comment odd. In fact, I cannot imagine doing academic work that is not motivated by one's passions, as well as being guided by one's intellectual integrity and critical faculties. We cannot avoid having both a location and a stance on our subject matter, whether or not they are explicit; our angle of vision is, perforce, partial in both senses of the word. Following Haraway (1988), I would argue for the validity of "situated knowledges" that are cognizant of and humble about their own partialness/partiality.

3   Foucault 1980.

4   Program officers in development agencies are often drawn from the ranks of academe and most stay current with the latest scholarly writing on subjects related to the areas in which they work.

5   Was I able to "see" these negotiations in the relations between organizations because of my own personal experiences, however unconscious I was of the dynamics in the initial stages? It seems likely there was a connection. Does this "bias" my conclusions in some way? I believe that, if ethnographers give up claims to absolute truth and accept our partiality, our experiences and feelings in the field can be powerful tools to understanding.

6   While I also sent two of my papers to SOS Corpo staff and received comments on one of them from the coordinator, we did not have the same kind of sustained interaction around my work that I had with the MMTR.

7   Thayer 2000; 2001a; 2001b.

8   For a discussion of feminists' experiences with participatory research, see Wolf 1996.

9   There were other circumstances which had an impact on my analysis of the MMTR's political trajectory and were a symptom of its partial-ness. Within the MMTR of the

Central *Sertão*, I detected few substantive political differences, but there were certainly distinctions of class and education. The leaders, including Almeida, who provided me with much of my data, had more education and economic security than the vast majority of members. Most came from cities or towns, rather than the countryside, and had had more opportunities to travel. The democratic structure of the organization too ensured some accountability between the two groups, but the perspective of leaders on organizational strategy and priorities may have been distinct in some ways from that of the small farmers and landless peasants who made up the membership. Unfortunately, logistical factors and our greater social distance from one another, as well as the age issues noted earlier, created constraints on my ability to apprehend the full spectrum of views among members.

10   In 2009, however, during an appearance on a panel of the Latin American Studies Assocation, Almeida spoke warmly—but forthrightly—about the differences I have described here.

BIBLIOGRAPHY

Ação Mulher/Brasil Mulher. Dec. 23, 1980. "Letter requesting funds for women's health projects." Recife: SOS Corpo Archives.

Acker, Joan. 1995. "Feminist Goals and Organizational Processes." Pp. 137–44 in *Feminist Organizations: Harvest of the New Women's Movement*, edited by Myra Marx Ferree, and Patricia Yancey Martin. Philadelphia, PA: Temple University Press.

Ajamil, Menchu. 1995. "A visão de gênero na cooperação internacional: Trajetória histórica e perspectivas." Pp. 27–28 in *Gênero e desenvolvimento institucional em ONGs*, edited by Maria da Graça Ribeiro das Neves and Delaine Martins Costa. Rio de Janeiro, Brazil: IBAM/ENSUR/NEMPP.

Albuquerque, Jr., Durval Muniz de. 2004. "Weaving tradition: The Invention of the brazilian northeast," *Latin American Perspectives* 31(2)(March, Special Edition): 42–61.

Alexander, M. Jacqui, and Chandra Talpade Mohanty, eds. 1997. *Feminist Genealogies, Colonial Legacies, Democratic Futures*. New York: Routledge.

Almeida, Vanete, with Cornelia Parisius. 1995. *Ser mulher num mundo de homens*. Serra Talhada, Brazil: DED/SACTES, MMTR/NE, Gráfica Editora Papelaria Universal.

Alvarez, Sonia E. 1990. *Engendering Democracy in Brazil: Women's Movements in Transition Politics*. Princeton, NJ: Princeton University Press.

——. 1998. "Latin American Feminisms 'Go Global': Trends of the 1990s and Challenges for the New Millennium." Pp. 293–324 in *Cultures of Politics, Politics of Cultures: Re-Visioning Latin American Social Movements*, edited by Sonia Alvarez, Evelina Dagnino, and Arturo Escobar. Boulder, CO: Westview Press.

——. 1999. "Advocating Feminism: The Latin American Feminist NGO 'Boom.'" *International Feminist Journal of Politics* 1: 181–209.

Alvarez, Sonia E., and Evelina Dagnino. 1995. "Para além da 'democracia realmente existente': Movimentos sociais, a nova cidadania e a configuração de espaços públicos alternativos." Paper presented at the XIX Annual Encounter of the Associação Nacional de Pós-Graduação e Pesquisa em Ciências Soicias (ANPOCS [National Association of Graduate Study and Research]). Caxambú, Brazil.

Alvarez, Sonia E., Claudia de Lima Costa, Verónica Feliú, Rebecca Hester, Norma Klahn, and Millie Thayer, with Cruz C. Bueno, eds. Forthcoming. *Translocalities/Translocalidades: Feminist Politics of Translation in the Latin/a Americas*.

Alvarez, Sonia E., Elisabeth Jay Friedman, Ericka Beckman, Maylei Blackwell, Norma Stoltz Chinchilla, Nathalie Lebon, Marysa Navarro, and Marcela Ríos Tobar. 2002.

"Encountering Latin American and Caribbean Feminisms." *Signs: Journal of Women in Culture and Society* 28: 537–79.

Alvarez, Sonia E., Evelina Dagnino, and Arturo Escobar, eds. 1998a. *Cultures of Politics, Politics of Cultures: Re-Visioning Latin American Social Movements.* Boulder, CO: Westview Press.

———. 1998b. "Introduction: The Cultural and the Political in Latin American Social Movements." Pp. 1–29 in *Cultures of Politics, Politics of Cultures: Re-Visioning Latin American Social Movements*, edited by Sonia Alvarez, Evelina Dagnino, and Arturo Escobar. Boulder, CO: Westview Press.

Alves, Maria Helena Moreira. 1985. *State and Opposition in Military Brazil.* Austin: University of Texas Press.

Amireh, Amal, and Lisa Suhair Majaj, eds. 2000. *Going Global: The Transnational Reception of Third World Women Writers.* New York: Garland.

Andrews, George Reid. 2004. *Afro-Latin America.* New York: Oxford University Press.

Antrobus, Peggy. 2004. *The Global Women's Movement: Origins, Issues and Strategies.* New York: Zed Books.

Aquino, Estela de, and Dina C. Costa. 1983. "Entrevista realizada com Betânia, integrante de grupo SOS-Corpo, Recife." Unpublished interview conducted by two Masters' students in the Social Medicine program of the Institute of Social Medicine of the University of the State of Rio de Janeiro.

Araújo, Tania Bâcelar. 1997. "O Nordeste brasileiro face à globalização: Impactos iniciais, vantagens e desvantagens competitivas." *Revista Rumos de Desenvolvimento* 21.

———. 2004. "Northeast, Northeasts: What Northeast?" *Latin American Perspectives* 31: 16–41.

Asen, Robert. 2000. "Seeking the 'Counter' in Counterpublics." *Communication Theory* 10: 424–46.

Asher, Kiran. 2007. "*Ser y Tener*: Black Women's Activism, Development and Ethnicity in the Pacific Lowlands of Colombia." *Feminist Studies* 33: 11–37.

Ávila, Maria Betânia. 1993. "Modernidade e cidadania reproductiva." *Revista Estudos Feministas* 1(2): 382–93.

———. 1995. "PAISM: Um programa de saúde para o bem estar de gênero." edited by SOS Corpo. Recife, Brazil: SOS Corpo.

———. 1998. "Alianças e parcerias do movimento de mulheres." *Democracia Viva* 2: 25–31.

Baden, Sally, and Anne Marie Goetz. 1997. "Who Needs [Sex] When You Can Have [Gender]? Conflicting Discourses on Gender at Beijing." Pp. 37–58 in *Women, International Development and Politics: The Bureaucratic Mire*, edited by Kathleen Staudt. Philadelphia: Temple University Press.

Bagic, Aida. 2006. "Women's Organizing in Post-Yugoslav Countries: Talking about 'Donors.'" Pp. 141–65 in *Global Feminism: Transnational Women's Activism, Organizing, and Human Rights*, edited by Myra Marx Ferree and Aili Mari Tripp. New York: New York University Press.

Bandy, Joe, and Jackie Smith. 2005. *Coalitions across Borders: Transnational Protest and the Neoliberal Order.* Lanham, MD: Rowman & Littlefield.

Barnet, Richard J., and John Cavanagh. 1994. *Global Dreams: Imperial Corporations and the New World Order.* New York: Simon & Schuster.

Barnett, Evelyn Brooks. 1978. "Nannie Burroughs and the Education of Black Women." Pp. 97–108 in *Afro-American Woman: Struggles and Images*, edited by Sharon Harley and Rosalyn Terborg-Penn. Port Washington, NY: Kennikat Press.

Basu, Amrita, ed. 1995. *The Challenge of Local Feminisms: Women's Movements in Global Perspective.* Boulder, CO: Westview Press.

———. 2003. "Globalization of the Local/Localization of the Global: Mapping Transnational Women's Movements." Pp. 68–77 in *Feminist Theory Reader: Local and Global Perspectives*, edited by Carole R. McCann and Seung-Kyung Kim. New York: Routledge.

Bauman, Zygmunt. 1998. *Globalization: The Human Consequences.* New York: Columbia University Press.

Bello, Walden. 2004. "The Global South." Pp. 49–69 in *A Movement of Movements: Is Another World Really Possible?*, edited by Tom Mertes. New York: Verso.

BEMFAM/DHS. 1991. *Pesquisa sobre saúde familiar no nordeste Brazil.* Rio de Jeneiro: BEM-FAM/DHS.

Benería, Lourdes, and Martha Roldán. 1987. *The Crossroads of Class and Gender: Industrial Homework, Subcontracting, and Household Dynamics in Mexico City.* Chicago: University of Chicago Press.

Benessaieh, Afef. Forthcoming. "Global Civil Society: Speaking in Northern Tongues?" *Latin American Perspectives.*

Benhabib, Seyla. 1999. "Sexual Difference and Collective Identities: The New Global Constellation." *Signs: Journal of Women in Culture and Society* 24: 335–61.

Benqué, Elza. 1999. "Sterilization and Race in São Paulo." Pp. 207–16 in *Race in Contemporary Brazil*, edited by Rebecca Reichmann. University Park, PA: The Pennsylvania State University Press.

Bergeron, Suzanne. 2001. "Political Economy Discourse of Globalization and Feminist Politics." *Signs: Journal of Women in Culture and Society* 26: 983–1006.

Bickham Mendez, Jennifer. 2005. *From the Revolution to the Maquiladoras: Gender, Labor and Globalization in Nicaragua.* Durham, NC: Duke University Press.

Bickham Mendez, Jennifer, and Diane L. Wolf. 2001. "Where Feminist Theory Meets Feminist Practice: Border-Crossing in a Transnational Academic Feminist Organization." *Organization* 8: 723–50.

Biekart, Kees. 2005. "Políticas de las ONGs europeas para América Latina: Tendencias y perspectivas recientes." Utrecht: ICCO/ALOP.

Blackwell, Maylei. Forthcoming. "Translenguas: Mapping the Possibilities and Challenges of Transnational Women's Organizing across Geographies of Difference." In *Translocalities/ Translocalidades*, edited by Sonia E. Alvarez, Claudia de Lima Costa, Verónica Feliú, Rebecca Hester, Norma Klahn, and Millie Thayer, with Cruz C. Bueno.

Bob, Clifford. 2005. *The Marketing of Rebellion: Insurgents, Media, and International Activists.* New York: Cambridge University Press.

Bordt, Rebecca L. 1997. *The Structure of Women's Nonprofit Organizations.* Indianapolis: Indiana University Press.

Boston Women's Health Course Collective. 1971. *Our Bodies, Our Selves.* Boston: New England Free Press.

Bourdieu, Pierre. 1998. *Practical Reason.* Stanford, CA: Stanford University Press.

Bourdieu, Pierre, and Loïc J. D. Wacquant. 1992. "The Purpose of Reflexive Sociology (The Chicago Workshop)." Pp. 61–215 in *An Invitation to Reflexive Sociology*, edited by Pierre Bourdieu, and Loïc J. D. Wacquant. Chicago: University of Chicago Press.

Brecher, Jeremy, Tim Costello, and Brendan Smith. 2002. *Globalization from Below: The Power of Solidarity.* Cambridge, MA: South End Press.

Brennan, Denise. 2004. *What's Love Got to Do with It? Transnational Desires and Sex Tourism in the Dominican Republic.* Durham, NC: Duke University Press.

Brettell, Caroline B. 1993. *When They Read What We Write: The Politics of Ethnography.* Westport, CT: Bergin and Garvey.

Bruschini, Christina. 1985. *Mulher e trabalho: Uma avaliação da década da mulher.* São Paulo: Nobel and Conselho Estadual da Condição Feminina.

Bruschini, Cristina, and Fulvia Rosemberg. 1982. "A mulher e o trabalho." In *Trabalhadores do Brasil*, edited by Cristina Bruschini, and Fulvia Rosemberg. São Paulo: Brasiliense.

Budry, Maryelle, and Edmée Ollagnier. 1999. *"Mais qu'est-ce qu'elles voulaient?" Histoires de vie du MLF à Genève.* Lausanne: Editions d'en bas.

Buechler, Steven M. 2000. *Social Movements in Advanced Capitalism: The Political Economy and Cultural Construction of Social Activism.* New York: Oxford University Press.

Bunch, Charlotte. 1995. "Transforming Human Rights from a Feminist Perspective." Pp. 11–17 in *Women's Rights, Human Rights: International Feminist Perspectives*, edited by Julie Peters, and Andrea Wolper. New York: Routledge.

Bunch, Charlotte, Peggy Antrobus, Samantha Frost, and Niamh Reilly. 2001. "International Networking for Women's Human Rights." Pp. 217–29 in *Global Citizen Action*, edited by Michael Edwards, and John Gaventa. Boulder, CO: Lynne Reinner Publishers.

Burawoy, Michael. 1998. "The Extended Case Method." *Sociological Theory* 16: 4–33.

Burawoy, Michael, Alice Burton, Ann Arnett Ferguson, Kathryn J. Fox, Joshua Gamson, Nadine Gartrell, Leslie Hurst, Charles Kurzman, Leslie Salzinger, Josepha Schiffman, and Shiori Ui. 1991. *Ethnography Unbound: Power and Resistance in the Modern Metropolis.* Berkeley, CA: University of California Press.

Burawoy, Michael, Joseph A. Blum, Sheba George, Zsuzsa Gille, Teresa Gowan, Lynne Haney, Maren Klawiter, Steven Henry Lopez, Seán Ó Riain, and Millie Thayer. 2000. *Global Ethnography: Forces, Connections, and Imaginations in a Postmodern World.* Berkeley: University of California Press.

Burton, Antoinette. 1991. "The Feminist Quest for Identity: British Imperial Suffragism and 'Global Sisterhood,' 1900–1915." *The Journal of Women's History* 3: 46–81.

Caldeira, Teresa P.R. 1984. *A política dos outros: O cotidiano dos moradores da periferia e o que pensam do poder e dos poderosos.* São Paulo: Brasiliense.

Caldwell, Kia Lilly. 2007. *Negras in Brazil: Re-envisioning Black Women, Citizenship, and the Politics of Identity.* Chapel Hill, NC: Rutgers University Press.

Calhoun, Craig. 1992. "Introduction: Habermas and the Public Sphere." In *Habermas and the Public Sphere,* edited by Craig Calhoun. Cambridge, MA: MIT Press.

——. 2002. "Imagining Solidarity: Cosmopolitanism, Constitutional Patriotism and the Public Sphere." *Public Culture* 14: 147–71.

Callon, Michel. 1998. *The Laws of the Markets.* Oxford, UK: Blackwell Publishers.

Camurça, Silvia, and Margarita Argott Cisneros. 1998. "Feminismo y cooperación paral la democracia y el desarrollo en América Latina." Mexico: Red Entre Mujeres.

Camurça, Silvia, and Taciana Gouveia. 1995a. *Cidade, cidadania: Um olhar a partir das mulheres.* Recife, Brazil: SOS Corpo.

——. 1995b. "O que é gênero? Um novo desafio para a ação das mulheres trabalhadoras rurais." Recife, Brazil: MMTR/DED/SOS Corpo.

Carrillo, Teresa. 1998. "Cross-Border Talk: Transnational Perspectives on Labor, Race, and Sexuality." Pp. 391–411 in *Talking Visions: Multicultural Feminisms in a Transnational Age,* edited by Ella Shohat. New York: New Museum of Contemporary Art/MIT Press.

Carneiro, Sueli. 1999. "Black Women's Identity in Brazil." Pp. 218–28 in *Race in Contemporary Brazil,* edited by Rebecca Reichmann. University Park, PA: The Pennsylvania State University Press.

Castells, Manuel. 1989. *The Informational City: Economic Restructuring and Urban Development.* Cambridge, MA: Basil Blackwell.

——. 1996a. "The Net and the Self: Working Notes for a Critical Theory of the Informational Society." *Critique of Anthropology* 16: 9–38.

——. 1996b. *The Information Age: Economy, Society and Culture, Vol. 1 The Rise of the Network Society.* Malden, MA: Blackwell.

——. 1997. *The Information Age: Economy, Society and Culture, Vol. 2 The Power of Identity.* Malden, MA: Blackwell.

Castro, Mary Garcia. 1992. "A dinâmica entre classe e gênero na América Latina: Apontamentos para uma teoria regional sobre gênero." Pp. 39–69 in *Mulher e políticas públicas,* edited by Maria da Graça Neves, and Delaine Martins. Rio de Janeiro: Editora Rosa dos Tempos/ Fundação Carlos Chagas.

——. 1999. "The Rise of Working Class Feminism in Brazil." *NACLA Report on the Americas* January/February 1999: 28–41.

Castro, Mary Garcia, and Lena Lavinas. 1992. "Do feminino ao gênero: A construção de um objeto." Pp. 216–51 in *Uma questão de gênero,* edited by Albertina de Oliveira Costa, and Christina Bruschini. Rio de Janeiro: Editora Rosa dos Tempos/Fundação Carlos Chagas.

Caulfield, Sueann. 2000. "American National Biography: Mary Wilhelmine Williams." American Council of Learned Societies. Accessed Jan. 18, 2009 from http://home.surewest.net/bergerot/williams-anb.html.

Centro de Investigación y Documentación, Mujeres y Autonomía (VENA), Universidad Estatal de Leiden. 1990. "Estudio para el proyecto *Entre Mujeres*: Posibilidades para influir en políticas y hacer lobby en Holanda y la Comunidad Europea." Leiden.

Centro Ecumênico de Documentação e Informação. 1989. "Sindicalismo no campo. Entrevistas. Avaliação, perspectivas e desafios." São Paulo.

CEPAL. 1990. *Transformación productiva con equidad: La tarea prioritaria del desarrollo de América Latina y el Caribe en los años noventa.* Santiago, Chile: Comisión Económica para América Latina.

Cerqueira, Maria do Milagres Leite. 1986. *A ação sindical dos trabalhadores rurais de Pernambuco.* Recife, Brazil: Instituto de Desenvolvimento de Pernambuco (Condepe).

Chabot, Sean. 2002. "Transnational Diffusion and the African-American Reinvention of the Gandhian Repertoire." Pp. 97–114 in *Globalization and Resistance: Transnational Dimensions of Social Movements*, edited by Jackie Smith, and Hank Johnston. Lanham, MD: Rowman & Littlefield.

Clark, Cindy, Ellen Sprenger, and Lisa VeneKlasen, with Lydia Alpizar Durán, and Joanna Kerr. 2006. *Where is the Money for Women's Rights? Assessing Resources and the Role of Donors in the Promotion of Women's Rights and the Support of Women's Organizations.* Mexico: AWID/Just Associates.

Clifford, James. 1989. "Notes on Travel and Theory." Pp. 177–88 in *Inscriptions: Traveling Theories, Traveling Theorists*, edited by James Clifford, and Vivek Dhareshwar. Santa Cruz: University of California.

Clifford, James, and George E. Marcus, eds. 1986. *Writing Culture: The Poetics and Politics of Ethnography.* Berkeley: University of California Press.

Coale, Ansley. 1989. "Demographic Transition." Pp. 16–23 in *Social Economics: The New Palgrave*, edited by John Eatwell, Murray Milgate, and Peter Newman. New York: Norton.

Coleman, Elizabeth. 1994. "From Population Control to Reproductive Health." *Ford Foundation Report*, Summer 1994: 32.

CONTAG. 1985. *4º Congresso Nacional dos Trabalhadores Rurais: Anais 25 a 30 de maio de 1985.* Brasilia, Brazil: CONTAG.

Cooley, Alexander, and James Ron. 2002. "The NGO Scramble: Organizational Insecurity and the Political Economy of Transnational Action." *International Security* 27: 5–39.

Corrêa, Sonia. 1983. *Causas e condições da esterilização feminina voluntária na região metropolitana do Recife.* Recife, Brazil: SOS Corpo/Ford Foundation.

——. 1989a. "Direitos reprodutivos como direitos humanos." Pp. 26–38 in *Os direitos reprodutivos e a condição feminina*, edited by Ana Paula Portella. Recife, Brazil: SOS Corpo/Liber Gráfica e Editora Ltda.

——. 1989b. "Uma recusa da maternidade? Causas e condições da esterilização feminina voluntária na Rede Metropolitana do Recife." Pp. 26–38 in *Os direitos reprodutivos e a condição feminina*, edited by Ana Paula Portella. Recife: SOS Corpo/Liber Gráfica e Editora Ltda.

——. 1989c. "Os direitos da reprodução no contexto da transição demográfica brasileira." Pp. 9–16 in *Direitos reprodutivos como direitos humanos*, edited by Ana Paula Portella. Recife, Brazil: SOS Corpo/Liber Gráfica e Editora Ltda.

——. 1993. *PAISM: Uma história sem fim*, edited by SOS Corpo. Recife, Brazil: SOS Corpo.

——. 1994a. *Gênero: Reflexões conceituais, pedagógicas e estratégicas; Relações desiguais de gênero e pobreza.* Recife, Brazil: SOS Corpo.

——. 1994b. *Population and Reproductive Rights: Feminist Perspectives from the South.* London: Zed Books.

Corrêa, Sonia, and Rosalind P. Petchesky. 2003. "Reproduction and Sexual Rights: A Feminist Response." Pp. 88–102 in *Feminist Theory Reader: Local and Global Perspectives*, edited by Carole R. McCann, and Seung-Kyung Kim. New York: Routledge.

Costa, Ana Alice A., and Cecilia M.B. Sardenberg. 1994. "Teoria e praxis feministas na academia: Os núcleos de estudos sobre a mulher nas universidades brasileiras." *Revista Estudos Feministas*: 387–400.

Costa, Claudia Lima. 2000. "Being There and Writing Here: Gender and the Politics of Translation in a Brazilian Landscape." *Signs: Journal of Women in Culture and Society* 25: 727–60.

———. 2006. "Lost (and Found?) in Translation: Feminisms in Hemispheric Dialogue." *Latino Studies* 4: 62–78.

Criquillion, Ana. 2007. "The Central American Women's Fund: An Alternative Contribution to the Central American Women's Movement Sustainability and Autonomy." Paper presented at the XXVI International Congress of the Latin American Studies Association. Montreal.

Dardel, Julie de. 2007. *Révolution Sexuelle et Mouvement de Libération des Femmes à Genève (1970–1980)*. Lausanne: Editions Antipodes.

Davis, Angela Y. 1983. *Women, Race, and Class*. New York: Vintage Books.

Davis, Kathy. 2007. *The Making of Our Bodies, Ourselves: How Feminism Travels across Borders*. Durham, NC: Duke University Press.

Dean, Jodi. 1996. *Solidarity of Strangers: Feminism after Identity Politics*. Berkeley: University of California Press.

Deere, Carmen Diana. 2003. "Women's Land Rights and Rural Social Movements in the Brazilian Agrarian Reform." *Journal of Agrarian Change* 3: 257–88.

Deere, Carmen Diana, and Magdalena León. 2001. *Empowering Women: Land and Property Rights in Latin America*. Pittsburgh, PA: University of Pittsburgh Press.

Della Cava, Ralph. 1989. "The 'People's Church,' the Vatican, and *Abertura*." Pp. 143–67 in *Democratizing Brazil: Problems of Transition and Consolidation*, edited by Alfred Stepan. New York: Oxford University Press.

della Porta, Donatella, Hanspeter Kriesi, and Dieter Rucht, eds. 1999. *Social Movements in a Globalizing World*. New York: St. Martin's Press.

della Porta, Donatella, and Sidney Tarrow. 2005. *Transnational Protest and Global Activism*. Lanham, MD: Rowman & Littlefield.

Desai, Manisha. 2002. "Transnational Solidarity: Women's Agency, Structural Adjustment, and Globalization." Pp. 15–33 in *Women's Activism and Globalization: Linking Local Struggles and Transnational Politics*, edited by Nancy A. Naples, and Manisha Desai. New York: Routledge.

Diani, Mario, and Doug McAdam, eds. 2003. *Social Movements and Networks: Relational Approaches to Collective Action*. Oxford, UK: Oxford University Press.

Di Chiro, Giovanna. 1998. "Environmental Justice from the Grassroots: Reflections on History, Gender, and Expertise." Pp. 104–36 in *The Struggle for Ecological Democracy: Environmental Justice Movements in the United States*, edited by Daniel Faber. New York: The Guilford Press.

DiMaggio, Paul, and Walter W. Powell. 1983. "The Iron Cage Revisited: Insititutional Isomorphism and Collective Rationality in Organizational Fields." *American Sociological Review* 48: 147–60.

Di Marco, Graciela. 2008. "Social Movements' Demands: Beyond Civil Society Discourses?" Paper presented at Interrogating the Civil Society Agenda: Social Movements, Civil Society, and Democratic Innovation conference. Amherst, MA.

Diniz, Simone Grilo, Cecilia de Mello e Souza, and Ana Paula Portella. 1998. "'Not Like Our Mothers': Reproductive Choice and the Emergence of Citizenship among Brazilian Rural Workers, Domestic Workers and Housewives." Pp. 31–68 in *Negotiating Reproductive Rights: Women's Perspectives across Countries and Cultures*, edited by Rosalind P. Petchesky, and Karen Judd. New York: IRRRAG/Zed Books.

Dirlik, Arif. 1997. "The Local in the Global." in *The Postcolonial Aura: Third World Criticism in the Age of Global Capitalism*, edited by Arif Dirlik. Boulder, CO: Westview Press.

Domingos, Manuel. 2004. "The Powerful in the Outback of the Brazilian Northeast." *Latin American Perspectives* 31: 94–111.

Domínguez, Edmé R., and Rosalba Icaza Garza. 2006. "Women Organizing against Restructuring and Free Trade: From Mar del Plata to Quito via Beijing." Paper presented at the XXV International Congress of the Latin American Studies Association. San Juan, Puerto Rico.

Dubois, Ellen Carol. 1978. *Feminism and Suffrage: The Emergence of an Independent Women's Movement in America, 1848–1869*. Ithaca, NY: Cornell University Press.

Duchen, Claire. 1986. *Feminism in France: From May '68 to Mitterand*. London: Routledge & Kegan Paul.

Edwards, Michael, and John Gaventa, eds. 2001. *Global Citizen Action*. Boulder, CO: Lynne Rienner Publishers.

Ehrick, Christine. 1999. "*Madrinas* and Missionaries: Uruguay and the Pan-American Women's Movement." Pp. 62–80 in *Feminisms and Internationalism*, edited by Mrinalini Sinha, Donna J. Guy, and Angela Woollacott. Malden, MA: Blackwell.

Einhorn, Barbara. 1993. *Cinderella Goes to Market: Citizenship, Gender, and Women's Movements in East Central Europe*. London: Verso.

Eisenstein, Hester. 1991. *Gender Shock: Practising Feminism on Two Continents*. New South Wales, Australia: Allen & Unwin.

Eschle, Catherine, and Bice Maiguashca. 2005. *Critical Theories, International Relations and 'the Anti-Globalisation Movement': The Politics of Global Resistance*. New York: Routledge.

Estrada-Claudio, Sylvia. 2006. "The International Women and Health Meetings: Catalyst and End Product of the Global Feminist Health Movement." Paper presented at the Transnationalisation of Solidarities and Women Movements workshop. Political Science Department, Université de Montréal. April 27–28.

Evans, Peter. 2000. "Counter-Hegemonic Globalization: Transnational Networks as Political Tools for Fighting Marginalization." *Contemporary Sociology* 29: 230–41.

Evans, Richard J. 1977. *The Feminists: Women's Emancipation Movements in Europe, America and Australasia 1840–1920*. New York: Barnes & Noble Books.

Ewig, Christina. 1999. "The Strengths and Limits of the NGO Women's Movement Model." *Latin American Research Review* 34: 75–102.

Facó, Rui. 1980. *Cangaceiros e fanáticos: Gênese e lutas*. Rio de Janeiro: Editora Civilização Brasileira.

Felski, Rita. 1989. *Beyond Feminist Aesthetics: Feminist Literature and Social Change*. Cambridge: Harvard University Press.

Ferguson, Ann. 1998. "Resisting the Veil of Privilege: Building Bridge Identities as an Ethico-Politics of Global Feminisms." *Hypatia* 13: 95–113.

Fernandes, Marisa, ed. 1994. *Lésbicas no Brasil: Contribuição para avaliação da década da mulher, 1985–1995*. São Paulo: Coletivo de Feministas Lésbicas.

———. 2002. "Lesbianismo no Brasil." *Tempo e Presença* 24: 17–20.

Fernandez, Cida, and Silvia Camurça, eds. 1995. *Relações de cooperação ao desenvolvimento e a política de gênero: Experiêncas e perspectivas no Brasil*. Recife, Brazil: SOS Corpo: Gênero e Cidadania.

Ferree, Myra Marx. 2006. "Globalization and Feminism: Opportunities and Obstacles for Activism in the Global Arena." Pp. 3–23 in *Global Feminism: Transnational Women's Activism, Organizing, and Human Rights*, edited by Myra Marx Ferree, and Aili Mari Tripp. New York: New York University Press.

Ferree, Myra Marx, and Aili Mari Tripp, eds. 2006. *Global Feminism: Transnational Women's Activism, Organizing, and Human Rights*. New York: New York University Press.

Ferree, Myra Marx, and Carol McClurg Mueller. 2004. "Feminism and the Women's Movement: A Global Perspective." Pp. 576–607 in *The Blackwell Companion to Social Movements*, edited by David A. Snow, Sarah A. Soule, and Hanspeter Kriesi. Oxford, UK: Blackwell Publishing.

Ferree, Myra Marx, and David A. Merrill. 2003. "Hot Movements, Cold Cognition: Thinking about Social Movements in Gendered Frames." Pp. 247–261 in *Rethinking Social Movements: Structure, Meaning, Emotion*, edited by Jeff Goodwin, and James M. Jasper. New York: Rowman & Littlefield.

Ferree, Myra Marx, and Patricia Yancey Martin, eds. 1995. *Feminist Organizations: Harvest of the New Women's Movement*. Philadelphia, PA: Temple University Press.

FETAPE. 1997. "Participação dos trabalhadores e trabalhadoras rurais nos STRs." FETAPE. Recife, Brazil.

Fisher, William F. 1997. "Doing Good? The Politics and Antipolitics of NGO Practices." *Annual Review of Anthropology* 26: 439–464.

Font, Mauricio A. 2003. *Transforming Brazil: A Reform Era in Perspective*. Lanham, MD: Rowman & Littlefield.

Ford-Smith, Honor. 1997. "Ring Ding in a Tight Corner: Sistren, Collective Democracy, and the Organization of Cultural Production." Pp. 213–58 in *Feminist Genealogies, Colonial Legacies, Democratic Futures*, edited by M. Jacqui Alexander, and Chandra Talpade Mohanty. New York: Routledge.

Foucault, Michel. 1980. *Power/Knowledge: Selected Interviews and Other Writings*. New York: Pantheon Books.

Fowler, Alan. 1992. "Distant Obligations: Speculations on NGO Funding and the Global Market." *Review of African Political Economy* 19: 9–29.

Franco, Jean. 1998. "Defrocking the Vatican: Feminism's Secular Project." Pp. 278–89 in *Cultures of Politics, Politics of Cultures: Re-Visioning Latin American Social Movements*, edited by Sonia E. Alvarez, Evelina Dagnino, and Arturo Escobar. Boulder, CO: Westview Press.

——. 2001. "Bodies in Contention." *NACLA Report on the Americas* 34: 41–44.

Fraser, Nancy. 1989. *Unruly Practices: Power, Discourse and Gender in Contemporary Social Theory*. Minneapolis: University of Minnesota Press.

——. 1997. "Rethinking the Public Sphere: A Contribution to the Critique of Actually Existing Democracy." Pp. 69–98 in *Justice Interruptus: Critical Reflections on the "Post-Socialist" Condition*. New York: Routledge.

Freeman, Carla. 2001. "Is Local: Global as Feminine: Masculine? Rethinking the Gender of Globalization." *Signs: Journal of Women in Culture and Society* 26: 1007–37.

Freeman, Carla, and Donna F. Murdock. 2001. "Enduring Traditions and New Directions in Feminist Ethnography in the Caribbean and Latin America." *Feminist Studies* 27: 423–59.

Freeman, Jo. 1970. "The Tyranny of Structurelessness." *Berkeley Journal of Sociology* 17: 151–165.

Freire, Paulo. 1970. *Pedagogy of the Oppressed*. New York: Herder & Herder.

French, John D. 2003. "Translation, Diasporic Dialogue, and the Errors of Pierre Bourdieu and Loïc Wacquant." *Nepantla: Views from the South* 4: 375–89.

Friedman, Elisabeth. 1999. "The Effects of 'Transnationalism Reversed' in Venezuela: Assessing the Impact of U.N. Global Conferences on the Women's Movement." *International Feminist Journal of Politics* 1: 357–81.

Galey, Margaret E. 1995. "Women Find a Place." Pp. 11–27 in *Women, Politics, and the United Nations*, edited by Anne Winslow. Westport, CT: Greenwood Press.

Gamson, William A. 1975. *The Strategy of Social Protest*. Homewood, IL: Dorsey Press.

Gamson, William A., Bruce Fireman, and Steven Rytina. 1982. *Encounters with Unjust Authority*. Homewood, IL: Dorsey Press.

George, Sheba, Seán Ó Riain, and Millie Thayer. 2000. "Introduction to Part Two: Global Connections." Pp. 139–143 in *Global Ethnography: Forces, Connections, and Imaginations in a Postmodern World*, edited by Michael Burawoy, Joseph A. Blum, Sheba George, Zsuzsa Gille, Teresa Gowan, Lynne Haney, Maren Klawiter, Steven Henry Lopez, Seán Ó Riain, and Millie Thayer. Berkeley: University of California Press.

Gerson, Deborah A. 1996. "Practice from Pain: Building a Women's Movement through Consciousness Raising." Ph.D. thesis, Department of Sociology, University of California, Berkeley.

Gibson-Graham, J.K., ed. 2006. *The End of Capitalism (As We Knew It)*. Minneapolis: University of Minnesota Press.

Gohn, Maria da Glória Marcondes. 1985. *A força da periferia: A luta das mulheres por creches em São Paulo*. Petrópolis: Vozes.

Gonzalez, Lélia. 1982. "A mulher negra na sociedade brasileira." Pp. 87–104 in *O lugar da mulher*, edited by Madel T. Luz. Rio de Janeiro: Relume Dumará.

Gouveia, Taciana, and Silvia Camurça. 1997. *O que é gênero*. Recife, Brazil: SOS Corpo.

Grewal, Inderpal. 2005a. *Transnational America: Feminisms, Diasporas, Neoliberalisms*. Durham, NC: Duke University Press.

——. 2005b. "'Women's Rights as Human Rights': The Transnational Production of Global Feminist Subjects." Pp. 121–57 in *Transnational America: Feminisms, Diasporas, Neoliberalisms*, edited by Inderpal Grewal. Durham, NC: Duke.

Grewal, Inderpal, and Caren Kaplan. 1994a. "Introduction: Transnational Feminist Practices and Questions of Postmodernity." Pp. 1–33 in *Scattered Hegemonies: Postmodernity and Transnational Feminist Practices*, edited by Inderpal Grewal and Caren Kaplan. Minneapolis: University of Minnesota Press.

Grewal, Inderpal, and Caren Kaplan, eds. 1994b. *Scattered Hegemonies: Postmodernity and Transnational Feminist Practices*. Minneapolis: University of Minnesota Press.

Grugel, Jean. 1999. "European NGOs and Democratization in Latin America: Policy Networks and Transnational Ethical Networks." Pp. 120–37 in *Democracy without Borders: Transnationalization and Conditionality in New Democracies*, edited by Jean Grugel. New York: Routledge.

Guidry, John A., Michael D. Kennedy, and Mayer N. Zald. 2000. *Globalization and Social Movements: Culture, Power, and the Transnational Public Sphere*. Ann Arbor, MI: University of Michigan Press.

Guy, Donna J. 1999. "The Politics of Pan-American Cooperation: Maternalist Feminism and the Child Rights Movement, 1913–1960." Pp. 105–25 in *Feminisms and Internationalism*, edited by Mrinalini Sinha, Donna J. Guy, and Angela Woollacott. Oxford, UK: Blackwell Publishers.

Hahner, June Edith. 1990. *Emancipating the Female Sex: The Struggle for Women's Rights in Brazil, 1850–1940*. Durham, NC: Duke University Press.

Haines, Herbert H. 1984. "Black Radicalization and the Funding of Civil Rights: 1957–70." *Social Problems* 32: 31–43.

Hall, Stuart. 1992. "Cultural Studies and its Theoretical Legacies." Pp. 277–94 in *Cultural Studies*, edited by Lawrence Grossberg, Cary Nelson, and Paula A. Treichler. New York: Routledge.

Hannerz, Ulf. 1991. "Scenarios for Peripheral Cultures." Pp. 107–28 in *Culture, Globalization and the World-System: Contemporary Conditions for the Representation of Identity*, edited by Anthony D. King. Binghamton, NY: Department of Art and Art History, State University of New York at Binghamton.

——. 1996. *Transnational Connections: Culture, People, Places*. New York: Routledge.

Haraway, Donna. 1988. "Situated Knowledges: The Science Question in Feminism and the Privilege of Partial Perspective." *Feminist Studies* 14: 575–99.

Harcourt, Wendy. 2005. "The Body Politic in Global Development Discourse: A Women and the Politics of Place Perspective." Pp. 32–47 in *Women and the Politics of Place*, edited by Wendy Harcourt, and Arturo Escobar. Bloomfield, CT: Kumarian.

Hartmann, Betsy. 1995. *Reproductive Rights and Wrongs: The Global Politics of Population Control*. Boston: South End Press.

Harvey, David. 1990. *The Condition of Postmodernity*. Oxford, UK: Blackwell.

——. 2005. *A Brief History of Neoliberalism*. Oxford, UK: Oxford University Press.

Hathaway, Will, and David S. Meyer. 1997. "Competition and Cooperation in Movement Coalitions: Lobbying for Peace in the 1980s." Pp. 61–80 in *Coalitions and Political Movement: The Lessons of the Nuclear Freeze*, edited by Thomas R. Rochon, and David S. Meyer. Boulder, CO: Lynne Rienner Publishers.

Hemment, Julie. 2007. *Empowering Women in Russia: Activism, Aid and NGOs*. Bloomington: Indiana University Press.

Heredia, Beatriz Maria Alasia de. 1979. *A morada da vida: Trabalho familiar de pequenos produtores do Nordeste do Brasil*. Rio de Janeiro: Paz e Terra.

Higer, Amy J. 1999. "International Women's Activism and the 1994 Cairo Population Conference." Pp. 122–141 in *Gender Politics in Global Governance*, edited by Mary K. Meyer, and Elisabeth Prugl. Lanham, MD: Rowman & Littlefield.

hooks, bell. 1984. *Feminist Theory: From Margin to Center*. Boston: South End Press.

Hulme, David, and Michael Edwards. 1997a. "Conclusion: Too Close to the Powerful, Too Far from the Powerless?" Pp. 275–84 in *NGOs, States and Donors: Too Close for Comfort?*, edited by David Hulme, and Michael Edwards. New York: St. Martins Press.

——. 1997b. "NGOs, States and Donors: An Overview." Pp. 3–22 in *NGOs, States and Donors: Too Close for Comfort?*, edited by David Hulme, and Michael Edwards. New York: St. Martins Press.

Humphrey, John. 1984. *Trabalho feminino na grande industria paulista*. São Paulo: CEDEC.

IBGE. 2003. "Síntese de indicadores sociais 2002." *Estudos e pequisas: Informação demográfica e socioeconômica* 11.

Incite! Women of Color Against Violence. 2007. *The Revolution Will Not be Funded: Beyond the Non-profit Industrial Complex*. Cambridge, MA: South End Press.

Inter-American Foundation. 1995. *A Guide to NGO Directories: How to Find over 20,000 Nongovernmental Organizations in Latin America and the Caribbean*. Arlington, VA: Inter-American Foundation.

James, Susan. 1992. "The Good-Enough Citizen: Female Citizenship and Independence." Pp. 48–65 in *Beyond Equality and Difference: Citizenship, Feminist Politics and Female Subjectivity*, edited by Gisela Bock, and Susan James. New York: Routledge.

Jasper, James M. 1997. *The Art of Moral Protest: Culture, Biography, and Creativity in Social Movements*. Chicago: University of Chicago Press.

Jelin, Elizabeth, ed. 1990. *Women and Social Change in Latin America*. London: Zed Books.

Jenkins, J. Craig, and Charles Perrow. 1977. "Insurgency of the Powerless: Farm Worker Movements (1946–1972)." *American Sociological Review* 42: 249–68.

Jenson, Jane. 1987. "Changing Discourse, Changing Agendas: Political Rights and Reproductive Policies in France." Pp. 64–88 in *The Women's Movements of the United States and Western Europe: Consciousness, Political Opportunity, and Public Policy*, edited by Mary Fainsod Katzenstein, and Carol McClurg Mueller. Philadelphia: Temple University Press.

Joachim, Jutta. 1999. "Shaping the Human Rights Agenda: The Case of Violence against Women." Pp. 142–60 in *Gender Politics in Global Governance*, edited by Mary K. Meyer, and Elisabeth Prugl. Lanham, MD: Rowman & Littlefield.

John, Mary E. 1996. *Discrepant Dislocations: Feminism, Theory, and Postcolonial Histories*. Berkeley: University of California Press.

Johnston, Hank, and Bert Klandermans, eds. 1995. *Social Movements and Culture*. Minneapolis: University of Minnesota Press.

Johnston, Hank, Enrique Laraña, and Joseph R. Gusfield. 1994. "New Social Movements: Identities, Grievances and Ideologies of Everyday Life." Pp. 5–35 in *New Social Movements: From Ideology to Identity*, edited by Enrique Laraña, Hank Johnston, and Joseph R. Gusfield. Philadelphia: Temple University Press.

Jones, Kathleen B. 1990. "Citizenship in a Woman-Friendly Polity." *Signs: Journal of Women in Culture and Society* 15: 781–812.

Jordan, Glenn, and Chris Weedon. 1994. *Cultural Politics: Class, Gender, Race, and the Postmodern World*. Hoboken, NJ: John Wiley & Sons.

Kabeer, Naila. 2000. *The Power to Choose: Bangladeshi Women and Labour Market Decisions in London and Dhaka*. New York: Verso.

Kamat, Sangeeta. 2002. *Development Hegemony: NGOs and the State in India*. New York: Oxford University Press.

Katzenstein, Mary Fainsod. 1998. *Faithless and Fearless: Moving Feminist Protest inside the Church and Military.* Princeton, NJ: Princeton University Press.

Keck, Margaret E., and Kathryn Sikkink. 1998. *Activists beyond Borders: Advocacy Networks in International Politics.* Ithaca, NY: Cornell University Press.

Khasnabish, Alex. 2008. *Zapatismo beyond Borders: New Imaginations of Political Possibility.* Toronto: University of Toronto.

Kornhauser, William. 1959. *The Politics of Mass Society.* Glencoe, IL: The Free Press.

Landim, L. 1988a. "Catálogo de ONGs no Brasil." Pp. 53–61 in *Sem fins lucrativos: As organizações não-governamentais no Brasil.* Rio de Janeiro: ISER.

——. 1988b. "A serviço do movimento popular: As organizações não-governamentais no Brasil." Pp. 24–52 in *Sem fins lucrativos: As organizações não-governamentais no Brasil.* Rio de Janeiro: ISER.

——. 1993. "Defining the Nonprofit Sector: Brazil." In *Working Papers of Johns Hopkins Comparative Nonprofit Sector Project 9,* edited by Lester M. Salamon, and Helmut K. Anheier. Baltimore, MD: The Johns Hopkins Institute for Policy Studies.

Lang, Sabine. 1997. "The NGOization of Feminism." Pp. 101–20 in *Transitions, Environments, Translations: Feminisms in International Politics,* edited by Joan W. Scott. New York: Routledge.

Lazreg, Marnia. 2000. "The Triumphant Discourse of Global Feminism: Should Other Women Be Known?" Pp. 29–38 in *Going Global: The Transnational Reception of Third World Women Writers,* edited by Amal Amireh, and Lisa Suhair Majaj. New York: Garland.

Le Bon, Gustave. 1960. *The Crowd: A Study of the Popular Mind.* New York: Compass Books, The Viking Press.

Lebon, Nathalie. 1996. "Professionalization of Women's Health Groups in São Paulo: The Troublesome Road towards Organizational Diversity." *Organization* 3: 588–609.

——. 1998. "The Labor of Love and Bread: Professionalized and Volunteer Activism in the São Paulo Women's Health Movement." Ph.D. thesis, Department of Anthropology, University of Florida, Gainesville.

Lim, Linda Y.C. 1983. "Capitalism, Imperialism, and Patriarchy: The Dilemma of Third-World Women Workers in Multinational Companies." Pp. 70–93 in *Women, Men and the International Division of Laor,* edited by June C. Nash, and Maria P. Fernandez-Kelly. Albany, NY: State University of New York Press.

Lima, Isa Maria Meira Rocha de. 1992. "Mulheres na luta pela terra e as relações patriarcais na família camponesa." M.A. thesis, Department of Social Service, Federal University of Pernambuco, Recife.

Lind, Amy. 2000. "Negotiating the Transnational: Constructions of Poverty and Identity among Women's NGOs in Bolivia." Paper presented at the XXII International Congress of the Latin American Studies Association. Miami.

——. 2005. *Gendered Paradoxes: Women's Movements, State Restructuring, and Global Development in Ecuador.* University Park, PA: Penn State Press.

Lister, Ruth. 1993. "Tracing the Contours of Women's Citizenship." *Policy and Politics* 21: 3–16.

Little, Cynthia Jeffress. 1978. "Education, Philanthropy, and Feminism: Components of Argentine Womanhood, 1860–1926." Pp. 235–53 in *Latin American Women: Historical Perspectives,* edited by Asunción Lavrin. Westport, CT: Greenwood Press.

Lobo, Elizabeth Souza. 1987. "Mulheres, feminismo e novas práticas sociais." *Revista de Ciências Sociais* 1: 221–29.

Loker, William M., ed. 1999. *Globalization and the Rural Poor in Latin America.* Boulder, CO: Lynne Rienner.

Lowe, Lisa. 1996. *Immigrant Acts.* Durham, NC: Duke University Press.

MacDonald, Laura. 1997. *Supporting Civil Society: The Political Role of Non-Governmental Organizations in Central America.* New York: St. Martin's Press.

Mackie, Vera. 2001. "The Language of Globalization, Transnationality and Feminism." *International Feminist Journal of Politics* 3: 180–206.

Mander, Jerry, and Edward Goldsmith, eds. 1996. *The Case against the Global Economy and for a Turn toward the Local.* San Francisco: Sierra Club Books.

Mani, Lata. 1989. "Multiple Mediations: Feminist Scholarship in the Age of Multinational Reception." *Inscriptions: Traveling Theories* 5: 1–23.

Mansbridge, Jane. 1973. "Time, Emotion, and Inequality: Three Problems of Participatory Groups." *Journal of Applied Behavioral Sciences* 9: 351–68.

———. 1995. "What is the Feminist Movement?" Pp. 27–34 in *Feminist Organizations: Harvest of the New Women's Movement,* edited by Myra Marx Ferree, and Patricia Yancey Martin. Philadelphia, PA: Temple University Press.

Marchand, Marianne H., and Anne Sisson Runyan, eds. 2000. *Gender and Global Restructuring: Sightings, Sites and Resistances.* New York: Routledge.

Martin, Patricia Yancey. 2005. *Rape Work: Victims, Gender, and Emotions in Organization and Community Context.* New York: Routledge.

Marx, Karl. 1972. *Capital: A Critique of Political Economy.* London: J.M. Dent & Sons.

Massey, Doreen. 1994. "A Global Sense of Place." Pp. 146–54 in *Space, Place, and Gender,* edited by Doreen Massey. Minneapolis: University of Minnesota Press.

Matthews, Nancy. 1994. *Confronting Rape: The Feminist Anti-Rape Movement and the State.* New York: Routledge.

Maybury-Lewis, Biorn. 1994. *The Politics of the Possible: The Brazilian Rural Workers' Trade Union Movement, 1964–1985.* Philadelphia: Temple University Press.

McAdam, Doug. 1982. *Political Process and the Development of Black Insurgency, 1930– 1970.* Chicago: University of Chicago Press.

McAdam, Doug, and Dieter Rucht. 1993. "The Cross-National Diffusion of Movement Ideas." *The Annals of the American Academy of Political and Social Science* 528: 56–74.

McAdam, Doug, Sidney Tarrow, and Charles Tilly. 2001. *Dynamics of Contention.* New York: Cambridge University Press.

McCarthy, John D., and Mayer N. Zald. 1977. "Resource Mobilization and Social Movements: A Partial Theory." *American Journal of Sociology* 82: 1212–41.

Melucci, Alberto. 1985. "The Symbolic Challenge of Contemporary Movements." *Social Research* 52: 789–816.

———. 1988. "Getting Involved: Identity and Mobilization in Social Movements." Pp. 329–348 in *International Social Movement Research,* edited by Bert Klandermans, Hanspeter Kriesi, and Sidney Tarrow. Greenwich, CT: JAI Press.

———. 1989. *Nomads of the Present: Social Movements and Individual Needs in Contemporary Society.* Philadelphia: Temple University Press.

Meyer, Mary K. 1999. "Negotiating International Norms: The Inter-Agency Commission of Women and the Convention on Violence Against Women." Pp. 58–71 in *Gender Politics in Global Governance,* edited by Mary K. Meyer, and Elisabeth Prugl. Lanham, MD: Rowman & Littlefield.

Miller, Francesca. 1990. "Latin American Feminism and the Transnational Arena." Pp. 10–26 in *Women, Culture, and Politics in Latin America,* edited by Emilie Bergmann, Janet Greenberg, Gwen Kirkpatrick, Francine Masiello, Francesca Miller, Marta Morello-Frosch, Kathleen Newman, and Mary Louise Pratt. Berkeley: University of California Press.

———. 1991. *Latin American Women and the Search for Social Justice.* Hanover, NH: University Press of New England.

Miller, J. Hillis. 1996. "Border Crossings, Translating Theory: Ruth." Pp. 207–233 in *The Translatability of Cultures: Figurations of the Space Between,* edited by Sanford Burdick, and Wolfgang Iser. Stanford, CA: Stanford University Press.

MMTR. 1992. "Avaliação do Sétimo Encontro." Serra Talhada, Brazil.

———. 1994. *Uma história de mulheres: Uma história da organização do Movimento das Mulheres Trabalhadoras Rurais do Sertão Central de Pernambuco no interior do movimento sindical.* Serra Talhada, Brazil: MMTR.

Moghadam, Valentine M. 2005. *Globalizing Women: Transnational Feminist Networks*. Baltimore: Johns Hopkins University Press.

Mohanty, Chandra Talpade. 1991. "Cartographies of Struggle: Third World Women and the Politics of Feminism." Pp. 1–47 in *Third World Women and the Politics of Feminism*, edited by Chandra Talpade Mohanty, Ann Russo, and Lourdes Torres. Bloomington, IN: Indiana University Press.

——. 2003a. *Feminism without Borders: Decolonizing Theory, Practicing Solidarity*. Durham, NC: Duke University Press.

——. 2003b. "Under Western Eyes: Feminist Scholarship and Colonial Discourses." Pp. 51–80 in *Third World Women and the Politics of Feminism*, edited by Chandra Talpade Mohanty, Ann Russo, and Lourdes Torres. Bloomington, IN: Indiana University Press.

Morais, Josimar Jorge Ventura de. 1988. "A teia das articulações: Um estudo sobre estrutura de poder interno no sindicato de trabalhadores rurais de Arcoverde—PE." M.A. thesis, Department of Sociology, Federal University of Pernambuco, Recife.

Morgen, Sandra. 2002. *Into Our Own Hands: The Women's Health Movement in the United States, 1969–1990*. Piscataway, NJ: Rutgers University Press.

Morris, Aldon D., and Carol McClurg Mueller, eds. 1992. *Frontiers in Social Movement Theory*. New Haven, CT: Yale University Press.

Moser, Caroline O.N. 1993. *Gender Planning and Development: Theory, Practice, and Training*. New York: Routledge.

Mueller, Carol McClurg. 1995. "The Organizational Basis of Conflict in Contemporary Feminism." Pp. 263–75 in *Feminist Organizations: Harvest of the New Women's Movement*, edited by Myra Marx Ferree, and Patricia Yancey Martin. Philadelphia, PA: Temple University Press.

Murdock, Donna F. 2008. *When Women Have Wings: Feminism and Development in Medellín, Colombia*. Ann Arbor, MI: University of Michigan Press.

Nagar, Richa. 2002. "Footloose Researchers, 'Traveling' Theories, and the Politics of Transnational Feminist Praxis." *Gender, Place and Culture* 9: 179–86.

Naples, Nancy A. 2002. "Changing the Terms: Community Activism, Globalization, and the Dilemmas of Transnational Feminist Praxis." Pp. 3–14 in *Women's Activism and Globalization: Linking Local Struggles and Transnational Politics*, edited by Nancy A. Naples, and Manisha Desai. New York: Routledge.

Narayan, Uma. 1997. *Dislocating Cultures: Identities, Traditions, and Third World Feminism*. New York: Routledge.

Neverdon-Morton, Cynthia. 1989. *Afro-American Women of the South and the Advancement of the Race, 1895–1925*. Knoxville: The University of Tennessee Press.

Oberschall, Anthony. 1973. *Social Conflict and Social Movements*. Englewood Cliffs, NJ: Prentice-Hall.

Ong, Aiwha. 2006. *Neoliberalism as Exception: Mutations in Citizenship and Sovereignty*. Durham, NC: Duke University Press.

Orloff, Ann Shola. 1993. "Gender and the Social Rights of Citizenship: The Comparative Analysis of Gender Relations and Welfare States." *American Sociological Review* 58: 303–28.

Our Bodies Ourselves. 2009. "Information on Women's Health and Sexuality—Our Bodies Ourselves." Accessed August 27, 2008 from www.ourbodiesourselves.org.

Pacheco, Maria Emília Lisboa, and Silvia Camurça, eds. 1997. *Programa Integrado de Capacitação em Gênero: Desenvolvimento, democracia e políticas públicas*. Rio de Janeiro/Recife, Brazil: CCLF, FASE, IBASE, SOS Corpo.

Papma, Adrie, and Ellen Sprenger. 1994. "NOVIB and Gender: State of Affairs and Current Issues." Pp. 201–20 in *Engendering Development*, edited by Maruja Barrig, and Andy Wehkamp. The Hague: NOVIB.

Pateman, Carole. 1988. "The Fraternal Social Contract." Pp. 101–27 in *Civil Soviety and the State: New European Perspectives*, edited by John Keane. New York: Verso.

———. 1992. "Equality, Difference, Subordination: The Politics of Motherhood and Women's Citizenship." Pp. 17 –31 in *Beyond Equality and Difference: Citizenship, Feminist Politics and Female Subjectivity*, edited by Gisela Bock, and Susan James. New York: Routledge.

Pearce, Jenny. 1997. "Between Co-option and Irrelevance? Latin American NGOs in the 1990s." Pp. 257–274 in *NGOs, States and Donors: Too Close for Comfort?*, edited by David Hulme, and Michael Edwards. New York: St. Martins Press.

———. 2007. "Is Social Change Fundable? NGOs and Theories and Practices of Social Change." Paper presented at the XXVII International Congress of the Latin American Studies Association, Montreal.

Pereira, Anthony W. 1997. *The End of the Peasantry: The Rural Labor Movement in Northeast Brazil, 1961–1988*. Pittsburgh, TX: University of Pittsburgh Press.

Pereira, Luiz Carlos Bresser. 1996. *Economic Crisis and State Reform in Brazil: Toward a New Interpretation of Latin America*. New York: Lynne Rienner.

Pessar, Patricia R. 2004. *From Fanatics to Folk: Brazilian Millenarianism and Popular Culture*. Durham, NC: Duke University Press.

Petchesky, Rosalind P. 2000. "WSSD+5 Gains for Women." *WEDO News & Views* 13.

———. 2003. *Global Prescriptions: Gendering Health and Human Rights*. New York: Zed Books/ UNRISD.

Petchesky, Rosalind P., and Karen Judd, eds. 1998. *Negotiating Reproductive Rights: Women's Perspectives across Countries and Cultures*. New York: Zed/IRRRAG.

Peters, Julie, and Andrea Wolper, eds. 1995. *Women's Rights, Human Rights: International Feminist Perspectives*. New York: Routledge.

Petras, James. 1997. "Imperialism and NGOs in Latin America." *Monthly Review* 49(3): 10–27. Accessed April 23, 2007 from www.monthlyreview.org/1297petr.htm.

Pettman, Jan Jindy. 2004. "Global Politics and Transnational Feminisms." Pp. 49–63 in *Feminist Politics, Activism and Vision: Local and Global Challenges*, edited by Luciana Ricciutelli, Angela Miles, and Margaret H. McFadden. New York: Zed Books.

Piscitelli, Adriana. 2005. "As viagens das teorias no embate entre prácticas acadêmicas, feminismos globais e activismos locais." *Gênero nas fronteiras do Sul*: 143–62.

Poletta, Francesca. 2004. "Culture is not just in Your Head." Pp. 97–110 in *Rethinking Social Movements: Structure, Meaning, and Emotion*, edited by Jeff Goodwin, and James M. Jasper. Lanham, MD: Rowman & Littlefield.

Portella, Ana Paula. 1998. "Há gênero na adolescência?" Recife, Brazil: SOS Corpo.

Portella, Ana Paula, and Taciana Gouveia. ND. "Idéias e dinâmicas para trabalhar com gênero." SOS Corpo.

Portella, Ana Paula, Carmem Silva, and Simone Ferreira. 2004. *Mulher e trabalho na agricultura familiar*. Recife, Brazil: SOS Corpo.

Radcliffe, Sarah A., and Sallie Westwood, eds. 1993. *Viva: Women and Popular Protest in Latin America*. New York: Routledge.

Rathgeber, Eva M. 1990. "WID, WAD, GAD: Trends in Research and Practice." *The Journal of Developing Areas* 24: 489–502.

Razavi, Shahrashoub, and Carol Miller. 1995. *From WID to GAD: Conceptual Shifts in the Women and Development Discourse*. Geneva, Switzerland: UNRISD.

Ready, Kelley. 2000. "Between Local Constituencies and Transnational Funding: Situating Salvadoran Feminism." Paper presented at the XXII International Congress of the Latin American Studies Association. Miami.

Red Entre Mujeres. 1989. "Conclusiones del Seminario de Montevideo: Conclusiones de los grupos de trabajo día 3 y día 4."

———. 1993. "Cooperacíon internacional y género: Una propuesta para el debate." Lima.

———. ND. "Entre Mujeres: Un diálogo sur-norte." Lima.

Reichmann, Rebecca, ed. 1999. *Race in Contemporary Brazil: From Indifference to Inequality*. University Park, PA: The Pennsylvania State University Press.

Reinelt, Claire. 1995. "Moving onto the Terrain of the State: The Battered Women's Movement and the Politics of Engagement." Pp. 84–104 in *Feminist Organizations: Harvest of the New Women's Movement*, edited by Myra Marx Ferree, and Patricia Yancey Martin. Philadelphia, PA: Temple University Press.

Rew, Alan. 1997. "The Donor's Discourse: Official Social Development Knowledge in the 1980s." Pp. 81–106 in *Discourses of Development: Anthropological Perspectives*, edited by R. D. Grillo and R. L. Stirrat. Oxford: Berg Publishers.

Risse-Kappen, Thomas, ed. 1995. *Bringing Transnational Relations Back In: Non-State Actors, Domestic Structures, and International Institutions*. New York: Cambridge University Press.

Roelofs, Joan. 2003. *Foundations and Public Policy: The Mask of Pluralism*. Albany, NY: State University of New York Press.

Rogers, Everett M. 1995. *Diffusion of Innovations*. New York: Free Press.

Roland, Edna. "The Soda Cracker Dilemma: Reproductive Rights and Racism in Brazil." Pp. 195–205 in *Race in Contemporary Brazil*, edited by Rebecca Reichmann. University Park, PA: The Pennsylvania University State Press.

Romero C, Maria Eugenia. Oct. 26, 2007. "XI Encuentro Feminista Latinoamericano y del Caribe se realizará en 2009." Red de Salud. Accessed June 24, 2008 from www.reddesalud. org/espanol/sitio/info.asp?Ob=1&Id=428.

Roth, Silke. 2003. *Building Movement Bridges: The Coalition of Labor Union Women*. Westport, CT: Praeger.

Rubin, Gayle. 1975. "The Traffic in Women: Notes on the Political Economy of Sex." Pp. 157–210 in *Towards an Anthropology of Women*, edited by Rayna Reiter. New York: Monthly Review Press.

Rubin, Jeffrey W., and Emma Sokoloff-Rubin. Forthcoming. "Paradox and Persistence: Brazilian Women's Fight for Rights in Politics and at Home." *Journal of Peasant Studies*.

——. Forthcoming. *The Enchantment of Activism: A Father-Daughter Adventure and a Women's Movement in Southern Brazil*.

Ruiz Bravo, Patricia. 1994. "¿Imposición o autonomia? Notas sobre la relación entre ONGs y agencia's de cooperación a propósito de la perspectiva de género." *Documentos para el Debate*. Lima: Entre Mujeres.

Rupp, Leila J. 1997. *Worlds of Women: The Making of an International Women's Movement*. Princeton, NJ: Princeton University Press.

Ryan, Bryce, and Neal C. Cross. 1943. "The Diffusion of Hybrid Seed Corn in Two Iowa Communities." *Rural Sociology* 8: 15–24.

Saffioti, Heleieth I. B. 1976. *A mulher na sociedade de classes: Mito e realidade*. Petrópolis: Vozes.

——. 1992. "Rearticulando gênero e classe social." Pp. 183–251 in *Uma questão de gênero*, edited by Albertina de Oliveira Costa, and Christina Bruschini. Rio de Janeiro: Editora Rosa dos Tempos/Fundação Carlos Chagas.

Said, Edward W. 1983. "Traveling Theory." Pp. 226–47 in *The World, the Text and the Critic*, edited by Edward W. Said. Cambridge, MA: Harvard University Press.

Sangtin Writers, and Richa Nagar. 2006. *Playing with Fire: Feminist Thought and Activism through Seven Lives in India*. Minneapolis: Minnesota Press.

Santos, Maria Cecilia MacDowell. 1998. "The Battle for a Feminist State within a Context of Globalization: The Case of Women's Police Stations in São Paulo, Brazil." Paper presented at the XXI International Congress of the Latin American Studies Association. Chicago.

——. 2005. *Women's Police Stations: Gender, Violence, and Justice in São Paulo, Brazil*. New York: Palgrave Macmillan.

Sardenberg, Cecilia M. B., and Ana Alice A. Costa. 1993. "Feminismos e feministas." *Revista Baiana de Enfermagen* 6: 5–29.

Sassen, Saskia. 1998. *Globalization and Its Discontents: Essays on the New Mobility of People and Money*. New York: New Press.

——. 2002. "Counter-geographies of Globalization: Feminization of Survival." Pp. 89–104 in *Feminist Post-Development Thought: Rethinking Modernity, Post-Colonialism and Representation*, edited by Kriemild Saunders. New York: Zed Books.

Schaff, Alie van de. 2001. *Jeito de mulher rural: A busca de direitos sociais e da igualdade de gênero no Rio Grande do Sul*. Passo Fundo, RS: Universidade de Passo Fundo Editora.

Schild, Verónica. 1998. "New Subjects of Rights? Women's Movements and the Construction of Citizenship in the 'New Democracies.'" Pp. 93–117 in *Cultures of Politics, Politics of Cultures: Re-Visioning Latin American Social Movements*, edited by Sonia Alvarez, Evelina Dagnino, and Arturo Escobar. Boulder, CO: Westview Press.

Schmitt, Frederika E., and Patricia Yancey Martin. 1999. "Unobtrusive Mobilization by an Institutionalized Rape Crisis Center: 'All We Do Comes From Victims.'" *Gender & Society* 13: 364–84.

Scott, Joan W. 1991. *Gênero: Uma categoria útil para análise histórica*. Recife, Brazil: SOS Corpo.

Scott, Joan Wallach. 1988. "Gender: A Useful Category of Historical Analysis." Pp. 28–50 in *Gender and the Politics of History*. New York: Columbia University Press.

Sen, Gita, and Caren Grown. 1988. *Development, Crises and Alternative Visions: Third World Women's Perspectives*. London: Earthscan.

Shapiro, Ester R. 2005. "Because Words are not Enough: Latina Re-Visionings of Transnational Collaborations Using Health Promotion for Gender Justice and Social Change." *NWSA Journal* 17: 141–72.

Shih, Shu-mei. 2005. "Towards an Ethics of Transnational Encounters, or 'When' Does a 'Chinese' Woman Become a 'Feminist?'" Pp. 3–28 in *Dialogue and Difference: Feminisms Challenge Globalization*, edited by Marguerite Waller, and Sylvia Marcos. New York: Palgrave Macmillan.

Shiva, Vandana. 1993. "The Greening of the Global Reach." Pp. 53–60 in *Global Visions: Beyond the New World Order*, edited by Jeremy Brecher, John Brown Childs, and Jill Cutler. Boston: South End Press.

Silliman, Jael. 1999. "Expanding Civil Society: Shrinking Political Spaces—The Case of Women's Nongovernmental Organizations." *Social Politics*: 23–53.

Silva, Luciana da Luz. 2009. "Participação das mulheres no MSTS: Gênero e classe no conflito fundiário urbano." Unpublished paper, accesssed June 2, 2009 from www.mujeresdelsur.org.uy/ensayo1.pdf.

Sindicato de Trabalhadores Rurais do Sertão Central, FETAPE. 1985. *Primeiro Encontro de Mulheres Trabalhadoras Rurais do Sertão Central, dezembro 15–16, 1984*. Serra Talhada, Brazil: STR.

Skidmore, Thomas E. 1989. "Brazil's Slow Road to Democratization: 1974–1985." Pp. 5–42 in *Democratizing Brazil: Problems of Transition and Consolidation*, edited by Alfred Stepan. New York: Oxford University Press.

Slatter, Claire. 2001. "Tensions in Activism: Navigating the Global Spaces at the Intersections of State/Civil Society and Gender/Economic Justice." *Workshop on Gender & Globalization in Asia and the Pacific: Feminist Revisions of the International*. Canberra: Australia National University.

Smelser, Neil J. 1962. *Theory of Collective Behavior*. New York: The Free Press.

Smith, Dorothy E. 1987. *The Everyday World as Problematic: A Feminist Sociology*. Boston: Northeastern University Press.

Smith, Jackie, Charles Chatfield, and Ron Pagnucco, eds. 1997. *Transnational Social Movements and Global Politics*. Syracuse, NY: Syracuse University Press.

Smith, Michael Peter. 2001. *Transnational Urbanism: Locating Globalization*. Malden, MA: Blackwell.

Snow, David A., and Robert D. Benford. 1988. "Ideology, Frame Resonance, and Participant Mobilization." *International Social Movement Research* 1: 197–218.

——. 1992. "Master Frames and Cycles of Protest." Pp. 133–55 in *Frontiers in Social Movement Theory*, edited by Aldon D. Morris, and Carol McClurg Mueller. New Haven, CT: Yale University Press.

——. 1999. "Alternative Types of Cross-National Diffusion in the Social Movement Arena." Pp. 23–39 in *Social Movements in a Globalizing World*, edited by Donatella della Porta, Hanspeter Kriesi, and Dieter Rucht. New York: St. Martin's Press.

——. 2000. "Framing Processes and Social Movements: An Overview and Assessment." *Annual Review of Sociology* 26: 611–39.

Snow, David A., E. Burke Rochford, Steven K. Worden, and Robert D. Benford. 1986. "Frame Alignment Processes, Micromobilization, and Movement Participation." *American Sociological Review* 51: 464–81.

Snyder, Margaret. 2006. "Unlikely Godmother: The UN and the Global Women's Movement." Pp. 24–50 in *Global Feminism: Transnational Women's Activism, Organizing, and Human Rights*, edited by Myra Marx Ferree, and Aili Mari Tripp. New York: New York University Press.

Soares, Maria Clara Couto. 1995. "Who Benefits and Who Bears the Damage under World Bank/IMF-Led Policies?" Pp. 8–16 in *Fighting for the Soul of Brazil*, edited by Kevin Danaher, and Michael Shellenberger. New York: Monthly Review Press/Global Exchange.

SOF. 2009. "O Que é a Marcha Mundial das Mulheres?" Accessed from www.sof.org.br/marcha/?pagina=aMarcha.

SOS Corpo. 1982. *SOS: Corpo de mulher*. Recife, Brazil: SOS Corpo.

——. 1996. "Eleny falando para o mundo." *A Moriçoca*, April: 1–2.

——. ed. 1997a. *O que as mulheres de Pernambuco querem como políticas públicas municipais de 1997 ao ano 2000*. Recife, Brazil: Fórum de Mulheres de Pernambuco.

——. 1997b. "Sobre a cooperação." *A Muriçoca*, March: 9.

——. 1998. "Plano de Ação Estratégica 1999–2003." Recife.

Spalter-Roth, Roberta, and Ronnee Schreiber. 1995. "Outsider Issues and Insider Tactics: Strategic Tensions in the Women's Policy Network during the 1980s." Pp. 105–27 in *Feminist Organizations: Harvest of the New Women's Movement*, edited by Myra Marx Ferree, and Patricia Yancey Martin. Philadelphia: Temple University Press.

Speed, Shannon, R. Aida Hernández Castillo, and Lynn M. Stephen. 2006. *Dissident Women: Gender and Cultural Politics in Chiapas*. Austin: University of Texas Press.

Sperling, Valerie, Myra Marx Ferree, and Barbara Risman. 2001. "Constructing Global Feminism: Transnational Advocacy Networks and Russian Women's Activism." *Signs: Journal of Women in Culture and Society* 26: 1155–86.

Spindel, Cheywa R. 1987. "The Social Invisibility of Women's Work in Brazilian Agriculture." Pp. 51–66 in *Rural Women and State Policy: Feminist Perspectives on Latin American Agricultural Development*, edited by Carmen Diana Deere, and Magdalena León. Boulder, CO: Westview Press.

Spivak, Gayatri Chakravorty. 1988. "Can the Subaltern Speak?" Pp. 271–313 in *Marxism and the Interpretation of Culture*, edited by Cary Nelson, and Lawrence Grossberg. Urbana: University of Illinois Press.

——. 1996. "'Woman' as Theatre: United Nations Conference on Women, Beijing 1995." *Radical Philosophy*: 2–4.

Stacey, Judith. 1991. "Can There Be a Feminist Ethnography?" Pp. 111–19 in *Women's Words: The Feminist Practice of Oral History*, edited by S.B. Gluck, and Daphne Patai. New York: Routledge.

Staggenborg, Suzanne. 1986. "Coalition Work in the Pro-Choice Movement." *Social Problems* 33: 374–89.

——. 1988. "The Consequences of Professionalization and Formalization in the Pro-Choice Movement." *American Sociological Review* 53: 585–606.

——. 1995. "Can Feminist Organizations Be Effective?" Pp. 339–55 in *Feminist Organizations: Harvest of the New Women's Movement*, edited by Myra Marx Ferree, and Patricia Yancey Martin. Philadelphia, PA: Temple University Press.

Steinberg, Marc W. 1998. "Tilting the Frame: Considerations on Collective Action Framing from a Discursive Turn." *Theory and Society* 27: 845–72.

———. 1999. "The Talk and Back Talk of Collective Action: A Dialogic Analysis of Repertoires of Discourse among Nineteenth-Century English Cotton Spinners." *American Journal of Sociology* 105: 736–80.

Stepan, Alfred. 1989. "Introduction." Pp. vii-xvii in *Democratizing Brazil: Problems of Transition and Consolidation*, edited by Alfred Stepan. New York: Oxford University Press.

Stephen, Lynn. 1997. *Women and Social Movements in Latin America: Power from Below.* Austin: University of Texas Press.

Sternbach, Nancy Saporta, Marysa Navarro-Aranguren, Patricia Churchryk, and Sonia E. Alvarez. 1992. "Feminisms in Latin America: From Bogotá to San Bernardo." Pp. 207–239 in *The Making of Social Movements in Latin America: Identity, Strategy, and Democracy*, edited by Arturo Escobar, and Sonia E. Alvarez. Boulder, CO: Westview Press.

Stetson, Dorothy McBride. 1987. *Women's Rights in France.* New York: Greenwood Press.

Strang, David, and Sarah A. Soule. 1998. "Diffusion in Organizations and Social Movements: From Hybrid Corn to Poison Pills." *Annual Review of Sociology* 24: 265–90.

Tarrow, Sidney. 2005. *The New Transnational Activism.* New York: Cambridge University Press.

Taylor, Verta. 1989. "Social Movement Continuity: The Women's Movement in Abeyance." *American Sociological Review* 54: 761–75.

Taylor, Verta, and Nancy Whittier. 1992. "Collective Identity in Social Movement Communities: Lesbian Feminist Mobilization." Pp. 104–29 in *Frontiers in Social Movement Theory*, edited by Aldon D. Morris, and Carol McClurg Mueller. New Haven, CT: Yale University Press.

Teles, Maria Amélia de Almeida. 1993. *Breve história do feminismo no Brasil.* São Paulo, Brazil: Brasiliense.

Thayer, Millie. 2000. "Negotiating the Global: Rural Brazilian Women and Transnational Feminisms." Pp. 158–78 in *Rethinking Feminisms in the Americas*, edited by Debra Castillo. Ithaca, NY: Cornell University, Latin American Studies Program.

———. 2001a. "Feminismo transnacional: Relendo Joan Scott no sertão." *Revista Estudos Feministas* 9: 103–30.

———. 2001b. "Transnational Feminism: Reading Joan Scott in the Brazilian *Sertão*." *Ethnography* 2: 243–71.

———. Forthcoming. "Translations and Refusals in the Feminist Counterpublic." *Feminist Studies.*

———. Forthcoming. "Translating against the Market: Transposing and Resisting Meanings as Feminist Political Practice." In *Translocalities/Translocalidades: Feminist Politics of Translation in the Latin/a Americas*, edited by Sonia E. Alvarez, Claudia de Lima Costa, Verónica Feliú, Rebecca Hester, Norma Klahn, and Millie Thayer, with Cruz C. Bueno.

Thomas, Jan E. 1999. "'Everything about Us is Feminist': The Significance of Ideology in Organizational Change." *Gender & Society* 13: 101–19.

Tilly, Charles. 1978. *From Mobilization to Revolution.* Reading, MA: Addison-Wesley.

Tripp, Aili Mari. 2006. "The Evolution of Transnational Feminisms: Consensus, Conflict, and New Dynamics." Pp. 51–75 in *Global Feminism: Transnational Women's Activism, Organizing, and Human Rights*, edited by Myra Marx Ferree, and Aili Mari Tripp. New York: New York University Press.

Tsing, Anna Lowenhaupt. 1997. "Transitions as Translations." Pp. 253–72 in *Transitions, Environments, Translations: Feminisms in International Politics*, edited by Joan W. Scott, Cora Kaplan, and Debra Keates. New York: Routledge.

———. 2005. *Friction: An Ethnography of Global Connection.* Princeton, NJ: Princeton University Press.

Turner, Ralph H., and Lewis Killian. 1957. *Collective Behavior.* Englewood Cliffs, NJ: Prentice-Hall.

Twine, France Winddance. 1997. *Racism in a Racial Democracy: The Maintenance of White Supremacy in Brazil.* New Brunswick, NJ: Rutgers University Press.

Vargas, Virginia. 1996. "Disputando el espacio global. El movimiento de mujeres y la IV Conferencia Mundial de Beijing." *Nueva Sociedad* 141: 43–53.

——. 2003. "Feminism, Globalization and the Global Justice and Solidarity Movement." *Cultural Studies* 17: 905–20.

——. 2006. "Las nuevas dinámicas feministas en el nuevo milenio." *LASA Forum* 37: 33–36

Visweswaran, Kamala. 1994. *Fictions of Feminist Ethnography*. Minneapolis: University of Minnesota.

Vogel, Ursula. 1991. "Is Citizenship Gender-Specific?" Pp. 58–85 in *The Frontiers of Citizenship*, edited by Ursula Vogel, and Michael Moran. New York: St. Martin's Press.

Wallerstein, Immanuel. 1974. *The Modern World-System: Capitalist Agriculture and the Origins of the European World-Economy in the Sixteenth Century*. New York: Academic Press.

Wapner, Paul Kevin. 1996. *Environmental Activism and World Civic Politics*. Stony Brook, NY: SUNY Press.

Ware, Vron. 1992. *Beyond the Pale: White Women, Racism, and History*. London: Verso.

Warner, Michael, ed. 2002. *Publics and Counterpublics*. New York: Zone Books.

Waterman, Peter. 1998. *Globalization, Social Movements & the New Internationalisms*. London: Mansell.

Williams, Mary Wilhelmine. 1945. *The People and Politics of Latin America*. Boston: Ginn and Company.

Wing, Susanna D. 2002. "Women Activists in Mali: The Global Discourse on Human Rights." Pp. 172–85 in *Women's Activism and Globalization: Linking Local Struggles and Transnational Politics*, edited by Nancy A. Naples, and Manisha Desai. New York: Routledge.

Wolf, Diane. 1996. "Situating Feminist Dilemmas in Fieldwork." Pp. 1–55 in *Feminist Dilemmas in Fieldwork*, edited by Diane Wolf. Boulder, CO: Westview Press.

Yuval-Davis, Nira. 1991. "The Citizenship Debate: Women, Ethnic Processes and the State." *Feminist Review*: 58–68.

——. 2006. "Human/Women's Rights and Feminist Transversal Politics." Pp. 275–95 in *Global Feminism: Transnational Women's Activism, Organizing, and Human Rights*, edited by Myra Marx Ferree, and Aili Mari Tripp. New York: New York University Press.

INDEX